THE

AMERICAN REVOLUTION

Volume II

THE

AMERICAN REVOLUTION

BY THE RIGHT HON.

SIR GEORGE OTTO TREVELYAN, BART.

AUTHOR OF "THE LIFE AND LETTERS OF LORD MACAULAY"
AND "THE EARLY HISTORY OF CHARLES JAMES FOX"

NEW EDITION

VOLUME II

NEW IMPRESSION

LONGMANS, GREEN AND CO.
55 FIFTH AVENUE, NEW YORK
LONDON, BOMBAY, CALCUTTA, AND MADRAS
1922

CONTENTS

OF VOLUME II

CHAPTER XII

CHAPTER XIII

CHAPTER XVI

CHAPTER XVII

CHAPTER XVIII

CHAPTER XIX

CHAPTER XX

APPENDICES

At the end of the volume

Map of the Country which was the Scene of Operations of the Northern Army.

Map of the Northern Part of New Jersey, and of New York and its Environs.

THE AMERICAN REVOLUTION

CHAPTER XII

POLITICAL DISCONTENT IN ENGLAND. THE LOYAL
ADDRESSES. A LAST CHANCE FOR PEACE

THE news of Lexington took six weeks to reach England, and came by an unusual channel. Massachusetts
was eager to have the first word, but careful that that
word should be an accurate one. A committee appointed by her Provincial Congress held sittings in the
district which had been the scene of hostilities, and took
a large mass of evidence on oath. An account of the
battle, addressed to the Inhabitants of Great Britain,
was drawn up by another committee, over which Joseph
Warren himself presided. The narrative was studiously
moderate. The successes of the minute-men, and the
disasters of the British, were related briefly, and in terms
below the truth; as if the writers could not dwell with
satisfaction on the details of a conflict between fellow-
countrymen. Americans, (so it was stated,) had no
quarrel with their sovereign, whose person, family, and
crown they were as willing to defend as ever. But
they would face death rather than tamely submit to the
persecutions of a cruel ministry, and looked forward
with assured hope to the time when, in a constitutional
connection with the mother-country, Englishmen on
both sides of the Atlantic would live, always and all
together, as one free, united, and happy people.

Captain Derby of Salem was commissioned to fit out
his ship as a packet; and the document was committed

to his charge, with orders to deliver it into the hands
of the Agent for Massachusetts in England. On the
twenty-ninth of May, 1775, the leading London newspapers, which then appeared only three times a week,
published the story in a special issue; and it was repro-
duced by the provincial journals as fast as the mail bags
could be carried through the island.

The ministers, who were as yet without information,
sent up and down the City in search of Captain Derby;
but he was hard to find, and, when found, he would say
nothing. Lord Dartmouth was deeply affected by the
intelligence, and could not bear to discuss it. Governor
Hutchinson in vain insisted that the paper was inspired
by Adams; that the master of the ship belonged to
"one of the most incendiary families;" and that
General Gage, when he came to be heard, would put a
very different complexion upon the matter. Dartmouth
had seen the colonists on their best side, and knew them
for men most unlikely to invent and to set afloat an
offensive and humiliating tale which a few hours, or at
latest a few days, would prove to be unfounded.

A sloop bringing the official despatches had started
four days before Captain Derby, and arrived eleven
days behind him. The account of the affair in the
"London Gazette," when read by itself, was not of a
very alarming character. It was admitted that the
British force had retired, and that before and during
the retreat they had been annoyed by rebel sharpshooters. Several of the regulars had been killed and
wounded in one place, and some few in another. The
officers had distinguished themselves, and the men had
behaved with their customary intrepidity. Gage had
his own way of putting a case; but the traditions of
honesty which govern our War Office are sternly regardless of a commander's susceptibilities. The return
of losses, faithfully and minutely presented to the public, showed that the fighting had been very serious. As
for the general military result of the whole proceeding,
it was confessed that the Northern Colonies had risen

in arms, and that Boston was closely invested by a force
of insurgents three times the size of the royal garrison.

On the twenty-fifth of July came the story of Bunker's
Hill. This time there was a victory, and, according to
the text of Gage's despatches, a victory without a drawback. Nothing was said about the attacks which had
failed; and yet those failures, retrieved as they were,
signally enhanced the credit of our arms. In his report
of Lexington the general had coolly taken it for granted
that the loss of the Americans was much greater than
our own : a groundless assumption, which the authorities at home had the good sense to keep out of the
Gazette. But at Bunker's Hill the field remained in his
own possession, and the slain lay there for everyone to
count; and so he fell back upon the theory that during
the action the colonists had been busily employed in
carrying off their dead friends and burying them in
holes. There is no stronger proof of the military
quality of our race than the disgust which that deplorable excuse for not having killed enough of the enemy
has always excited even among our civilians. It is
the way of our people to measure the importance of
an engagement by its practical consequences, and to
regard the statistics of the adversary's loss as the
adversary's own concern.[1] Every reader of the newspapers was well aware that the circuit of the American
lines was still untouched; that the battle had resulted
in the occupation of a small peninsula which hitherto
had been no-man's land; and that the acquisition was
purchased by a great slaughter of British soldiers, and

[1] The dignified attitude of a fine soldier with regard to this question is
exemplified in Napier's account of the first battle of Sauroren. It was the
turning point of the nine terrible days in the Pyrenees, and a conflict
which Lord Wellington, fresh from the fight, with homely emphasis called
bludgeon work. "Two generals and eighteen hundred men had been
killed or wounded on the French side, following their official reports ; a
number far below the estimate made at the time by the allies, whose loss
amounted to two thousand six hundred. The numbers actually engaged
were of French twenty-five thousand, of the allies twelve thousand ; and,
if the strength of the latter's position did not save them from the greater
loss, their steadfast courage is more to be admired."

something very like a massacre of British officers. Private letters from the army showed that old campaigners did not under-rate the cost, or exaggerate the value, of the triumph which they had won. The colonel who led the Light Infantry companies against the rail-fence, and for a marvel had not been shot, informed his friends at home that the rebels had behaved beyond any idea which he could ever have formed of them, and predicted that every inch of ground still remaining to be conquered would be stiffly disputed. "We have lost," he said, "a great number of our officers; I am told, above eighty killed and wounded; a great smash by such miscreants."[1] In the interior circle of the Ministry there were no illusions. William Eden, a young politician just on the eve of being taken into office, wrote to Lord North on the third of August: "We certainly are victorious; but if we have eight more such victories there will be nobody left to bring the news of them."[2]

No intelligence more unexpected, or more visibly and inevitably fraught with coming evil, ever reached this country. The spirit in which it was accepted was honourable to our ancestors. There were few truer patriots among them than John Wesley and Horace Walpole; and they both sadly acknowledged Great Britain's responsibility for an event which they viewed as the common calamity of the entire British race. Walpole had been born and nurtured amidst the stable and quiet prosperity which the nation enjoyed under his father's rule, and he had witnessed the conquests and glories of Lord Chatham. He now, after the break of a month in his correspondence with Sir Horace Mann at Florence, took up his pen unwillingly, since he had nothing pleasant to tell. "Can the events of a civil war be welcome news? One must be deeply embarked on one side or the other, if one ever rejoices. They who wish well to the whole can have but one cheerful moment, which is that of peace, — a moment that seems at a great dis-

---

[1] *Historical Manuscripts Commission:* Eleventh Report, Appendix, Part V.   [2] *Auckland Manuscripts.*

tance. During the first part of my life all was peace and happiness. The middle was a scene of triumph. I am sorry to think the last volume so likely to resemble a considerable part of our story. Who can wish to have lived during the wars of York and Lancaster, or from 1641 to 1660?"

Walpole, even while he sate in Parliament, confined himself to the functions of an observer, and, so far as his own exertions were concerned, allowed public affairs to take their own course ; but John Wesley was one of those who could not be tranquil until he had cleared his conscience. He addressed the prime minister in a memorial, of remarkable ability, couched in the form of a private letter. It was the production of a statesman, and of a prophet likewise; for the paper is dated two days before the battle of Bunker's Hill. "I am a high churchman," (so he told Lord North,) "the son of a high churchman, bred up since my childhood in the highest notions of passive obedience and non-resistance. And yet I cannot avoid thinking, if I think at all, that an oppressed people asked for nothing more than their legal rights, in the most modest and inoffensive manner that the nature of the thing would allow. But, waiving all considerations of right and wrong, I ask, is it common sense to use force towards the Americans? These men will not be frightened. They are as strong men as you. They are as valiant as you, if not more abundantly valiant, for they are one and all enthusiasts for liberty."

Wesley gave North the benefit of his own personal knowledge of America, revived and supplemented as it was by frequent communication with the colonies, where he had a substantial and rapidly increasing body of religious adherents. He warned the prime minister to beware of those who spoke soft words, and who dwelt on the circumstance that the colonists were divided among themselves. "No, my lord," he said, "they are terribly united; not in New England only, but down as low as the Jerseys and Pennsylvania. The bulk of the people are so united, that to speak a word in favour of the present English measures would almost endanger a man's life. Those who informed me of this are no sycophants ; they say nothing to curry favour ; they have nothing to gain or lose by me." And then the famous preacher, who was such a master of condensation, shortly and frankly exposed the difficulties of a war conducted across a vast ocean, and with Europe hostile. It is impossible to read that plain and forcible statement without reflecting on the lamentable fact that the middle class of citizens, to which Wesley belonged, was to all intents and purposes excluded from the higher administration of the country.

The most important paragraph in Wesley's letter contained his description of the temper and the tone which prevailed among the great mass of the common people throughout the kingdom. His remarks were not the carpings of a political opponent. Wesley was no ordinary supporter of the Government. He was soon to give as singular a proof as man ever gave that his partisanship knew no limits when the King and the King's ministers stood in need of a defender. Still less did his conclusions about the trend of popular opinion proceed from slight or hasty observation ; for he was intimately acquainted with Ireland and Scotland, and England he knew as a benevolent and active-bodied country gentleman knows his paternal estate. He had already for five-and-thirty years been traversing the land from Berwick to Penzance, and from Tenby to Colchester ; going everywhere on horseback, and reading as he rode, in accordance with his comfortable theory that safety for an equestrian lies in a loose rein ; but keeping his eyes and ears open for anything that was worth his notice. With him one day told another, and one night, (and short nights they were,) certified another. On Monday the seventeenth of June, 1782, he preached in the morning at Rothbury in Northumberland ; rode in sultry heat twelve miles southward, over a road which still retains some of its terrors, and preached again at noon in front of a solitary cottage ;

and then, after travelling twenty miles more, he delivered his third sermon to an immense multitude, hard
by the old Priory at Hexham. That was how he spent
his seventy-ninth birthday, when he was already conscious that he was beginning to grow old. But in 1775
he was in all the vigour and energy of three score
years and twelve; and, if anyone had special opportunities of ascertaining what homely and unprivileged
people all the country over were thinking and saying
among themselves, it was John Wesley, and no other.
After commenting to Lord North on the defenceless
state of Great Britain, and the threatening attitude of
foreign powers, Wesley went on to say that the most
dangerous enemies of the Government were those of
their own household. He had conversed, (so he
claimed,) more freely, and with more persons of every
denomination, than anyone else in the three kingdoms;
he was familiar with the general disposition of the
people, — English, Scotch, and Irish, — and he knew
for certain that a large majority were bitterly angry
and profoundly disaffected.[1]

Two months afterwards Lord Dartmouth had his
turn, and received a letter which was a striking example of the truth that there is no speaking so plain
as between like and like. Great man as he was, the
Secretary of State held religious opinions which placed
him within the circle of those disciples whom Wesley,
when he saw occasion for it, was in the habit of rebuk-
ing very roundly. The Cabinet had got reports to the
effect that trade was flourishing, and that the population was well employed and well satisfied. The expression of Dartmouth's innocent gratification over the
intelligence had come round to Wesley, who wrote to
his friend as follows: "Sir, there cannot be a more
notorious falsehood than has been palmed upon the
Administration for truth. In every part of England
where I have been, (and I have been East, West, North,

[1] *The Life and Times of the Rev^d. John Wesley,* by the Rev. L. Tyerman:
Vol. III., pages 197–200.

and South within these two years,) trade is exceedingly decayed, and thousands of people are quite unemployed. I except three or four manufacturing towns, which have suffered less than others. I aver that the people in general, all over the nation, are so far from being well satisfied that they are far more deeply dissatisfied than they appear to have been even a year or two before the Great Rebellion, and far more dangerously dissatisfied. The bulk of the people in every city, town, and village where I have been do not so much aim at ministry, but at the King himself. They heartily despise his Majesty, and hate him with a perfect hatred. It is as much as ever I can do, and sometimes more than I can do, to keep this plague from infecting my own friends; and nineteen out of twenty to whom I speak in defence of the King seem never to have heard a word spoken for him before. I wonder what wretches they are who abuse the credulity of the ministry by those florid accounts." [1]

Such, according to a competent judge who disliked the conclusions to which he found himself driven, was the feeling in Great Britain when the American Revolution began. The condition of opinion that prevailed among the commonalty of England, by which Wesley was so painfully impressed, did not fill a large space in the thoughts of the political actors of the day. Cabinet Ministers, — and, during the earlier years of the war, the statesmen of the Opposition too, — made little account of the tradesmen, and yeomen, and small manufacturers who gave bed and board to an itinerant Methodist preacher; and still less of the mill-hands and colliers who, year by year, listened to his sermons with growing respect and in ever larger numbers. Those were not the sort of people who raised and upset governments. The voteless multitude which stood, row behind row, drinking in John Wesley's message in the green amphitheatre at St. Ives, outnumbered many

[1] *Historical Manuscripts Commission :* Fifteenth Report, Appendix, Part I.

times the aggregate constituencies of all those Cornish villages which between them sent forty-two members to Westminster. Even the solid business-men of the counties, freeholders as they were, each of them possessed but the three hundredth, or four hundredth, part of the political power exercised by the burgage-holder of a close borough, or the Councilman of a Corporation which negotiated parliamentary elections in the silence and privacy of their town-hall. Thoughtful and patriotic citizens of the middle and lower classes were disheartened by a sense of their own powerlessness. They were disheartened, but gravely displeased; and their displeasure was all the more ominous because it could not be favourably affected by a circumstance which in this country, ever since 1832, has mitigated, and often extinguished, political exasperation.

It may be doubted whether any Cabinet, which has once completely lost the confidence of the nation, ever recovers reputation during its tenure of office. But in the course of the last two generations few serious public evils have resulted from the unpopularity of Governments, because, when a Government has become unpopular, its fall is only a question of a session or two at the longest. In 1775, however, the discredit and dislike under which the administration suffered were of old date; but there had been no real change of ministry. For ten years past Secretaries of State, and even First Lords of the Treasury, had been installed and ejected, and thrust up-stairs and down-stairs; but, whoever might be left out or put out, the King and the King's friends had always been in. During that period electoral rights had been trodden under foot; free discussion had been treated as a crime; venality had spread fast, and in alarming volume, through every department of the state; and a singular indifference had been exhibited by rulers to the sentiments and opinions of the ruled. The reason was not far to seek. Court favour had come to be the one sure way of obtaining and holding those honours which ought to be at the disposal of the people.

Public men knew only too well that, if they opposed the faction which pulled the hidden strings of politics, they soon lost all opportunity of serving the Crown. If they submitted to that faction, they lost the respect of their country.[1] In the finest piece which ever came from under his pen Burke pronounced this circumstance, and this only, to be the cause of what as long back as 1770 he called the Present Discontents. No remedy had been applied; and in the year 1775 they were the present discontents still, with sharpness added. In the May of that year John Wesley solemnly warned Lord North that the bulk of the population were effectually cured of all love and reverence for the King and his Ministry, that they were ripe for open rebellion, and that they wanted nothing but a leader. The prediction was only partially verified; for our country had the same good fortune which has attended her at more than one great crisis of her history. A leader, hailing from a quarter whence he was least expected, successfully brought her people not into open rebellion, but into constitutional resistance to that unconstitutional influence which began by corrupting the parliament, and ended by half ruining the nation.

In the summer of 1775 Charles Fox was not yet in a position to proclaim a general crusade against that system of personal government the baleful foundation of which his own father had done so much to lay. But, with or without a leader, the mood of the people portended ill for a ministry, which was already face to face with a colonial rebellion, and was pursuing a policy almost certain to result, sooner or later, in a whole handful of foreign wars. It was a moment of peril to the Cabinet, and a day of possible salvation for the empire. On the twenty-third of August Burke wrote thus to Lord Rockingham: "The hinge between war and peace is a dangerous juncture to ministers; but a

[1] *Thoughts on the Cause of the Present Discontents.* The works of Edmund Burke ; edition of 1837, pages 142 and 149 of Vol. I.

determined state of the one or the other is a pretty safe position. When their cause, however absurdly, is made the cause of the nation, the popular cry will be with them. The style will be, that their hands must be strengthened by an universal confidence. When that cry is once raised, the puny voice of reason will not be heard." Sandwich and North knew the situation every bit as well as Burke, and a great deal better than the virtuous and diffident Whig nobleman whom Burke was in vain inciting to energetic action. The ministers exerted themselves to tide over the next few months with an appearance, at any rate, of having the country behind them. A Loyal Address, calling upon the Crown to suppress the rebels, and reflecting with severity upon their aiders and abettors in the British Parliament, was welcomed, (and, if need was, invited,) from any community which contained enough people of weight and standing who were willing to sign it.

The scheme obtained a certain measure of success; but it was not much to the taste of the monarch. A writer, who has mastered his case, remarks that the capacity of George the Third embraced the arts of obtaining power, but that our history can hardly produce a sovereign less capable of governing an empire;[1] and the description is correct in all particulars. The gaining and keeping of political influence was the King's special province; and in that department of public affairs he knew all which was worth knowing. He thoroughly understood the conditions under which he pursued the central object of his existence. He held that petitions, addresses, associations of freeholders, and open meetings in shire-towns, were the weapons of a popular opposition, which an arbitrary minister would do well to abstain from handling. He instinctively foresaw the time when the machinery of a political propaganda would be set in motion with formidable results to the cause which he had at heart. " It is impossible," he

[1] Page xiv of Sir William Anson's preface to the *Autobiography of the Third Duke of Grafton:* London, 1898.

wrote to North, "to draw up a more dutiful and affec
tionate address than the one from the town of Manchester, which really gives me pleasure, as it comes
unsolicited. As you seem desirous that this spirit should
be encouraged I certainly will not object to it; though
by fatal experience I am aware that they will occasion counter-petitions." His Majesty proceeded to indicate that, if the nobility and gentry of property, in their
respective counties, would add half a guinea to the
bounty for recruits to fill the regiments destined for
America, they would be doing at least as real a service
as by affixing their signatures to Loyal Addresses, however bravely worded.

The Manchester Address was said to have emanated
from old Jacobites whom the King had converted into
Hanoverians by his adoption of the Stuart principles
and processes. Mason, in an epigram poor enough to
have been written by the Poet Laureate, hinted that the
signatures had been paid for by the Court. But the
King asserted the contrary ; and, when George the Third
stated anything as a matter of fact, and not of opinion,
a fact it was. Other towns, and several counties, imitated the example of Manchester; but the more important communities were intractable, or silent, or spoke
with divided voice. No Address could be obtained from
Edinburgh or Glasgow. The Guild of Merchants in
Dublin thanked those Peers who had opposed the restraint of liberty in America; and their view was supported and enforced by five hundred leading citizens of
Cork, who were Protestants to a man. The King's
apprehensions of the danger involved in an appeal to
public opinion were amply justified. Wherever one
party pronounced itself, the other accepted the challenge.
The Common Council of London, sincerely anxious for
peace, waited on His Majesty with a Petition carefully
weeded of all factious and disrespectful phrases, and
implored him to grant the colonists a breathing-space,
and an opportunity for tendering proposals of accommodation. A large number of gentlemen and traders

in the City of London, — unwilling to be represented in matters political by any municipal body, however ancient and dignified, — expressed disapprobation and abhorrence of the proceedings of some among the American colonies; and thereupon a still larger number of the same class in the same city protested that they, for their part, disapproved and abhorred the measures of the Government. The Middlesex Justices petitioned decorously in favour of war, and the Middlesex freeholders noisily and somewhat confusedly against it. A Loyal Address from the Bristol Corporation was at once answered by a Loyal Remonstrance from near a thousand Bristol merchants. In one county the policy of the Cabinet was endorsed by two hundred among the inhabitants, and condemned by nineteen hundred, with the names of two Dukes at the head of the signatures. A less uncertain sound proceeded from some other quarters. The first Battalion of Devonshire militia, arguing by platoons, defended the course taken by Ministers, and denounced the manœuvres of the Opposition. The University of Oxford was not less emphatic on the same side. Burke complained in the House of Commons that a body of learned and religious people, whose vocation, (if they could be brought to recognise it,) was to instruct and train the young, should rush into an intricate political controversy, and recommend a violent policy with extreme intemperance of language. He had himself, (he said,) a son at Oxford; and he resented that son being told by grave men that his father was an abettor of rebels.

The sister University was not so amenable as Oxford to the seductions of the Ministry. Cambridge Whigs had no love for the clique of London wirepullers which had provided them with a Chancellor in the person of the Duke of Grafton, while he was still in the mire of a famous scandal; and which very nearly contrived to force the Earl of Sandwich upon them as their High Steward. While resisting the invasions directed against the honour of the University they had learned how to organise and employ their forces; and they now put their experience to use in defence of political tenets with which, as they proudly claimed, that University had long been identified. Prominent among them was Doctor Richard Watson, the Regius Professor of Divinity; who, on Restoration day in the year 1776, had courage to preach before the Heads of Colleges a sermon vindicating the principles of the Great Revolution. The courtiers of a King, who derived his title from that Revolution, condemned the sermon as treasonable; but Dunning sagely remarked that it contained just such treason as ought to be preached once a month at St. James's. Doctor Watson now stoutly refused to call upon the Government to draw the sword on what he regarded as the wrong side of a constitutional quarrel; and he did not stand alone in his refusal. Lord Rockingham, stirred at last, wrote to testify his indignation at "the Whig University of Cambridge being called upon to play the second fiddle to the Tory University of Oxford" in so lamentable a concert. One of the Cavendishes, — glad to take any amount of trouble to associate himself with the great memories of 1688, — travelled to Cambridge to vote, and brought all the help he could. But other eminent members of the Opposition hesitated as to the propriety of "going down, as it were by surprise, to prevent what may be the sense of the resident persons in the University." There were no such scruples in the opposite camp. "The Tories," Doctor Watson reported, "beat us by eight votes in the Whitehood house. They owe their victory to the ministerial troops which were poured in from the Admiralty and Treasury beyond expectation." So close a poll was no great triumph for Government at a time when the vast majority of residents at the University were in holy orders; when promotion in the Church was the recognised reward of party services; and when the clergy, as Doctor Watson significantly observed, could hardly escape having a professional bias to support the powers that were, be they what they might.[1]

[1] Doctor Watson to Lord Rockingham; Nov. 25, 1775.

The Ministry had selected their own method for elic-
iting the expression of public opinion; and they had
consulted the classes from whom they had most reason
to expect a favourable response. Even so, it was impossible to flatter themselves that the nation accepted
their policy with unanimity, or anything near it. The
responsibility which lay upon the rulers of the country
was exceptionally grave; because feeling in the country
was so nearly balanced that the executive Government,
with the enormous influence then at its command, could
easily and effectively turn the scale in the direction
either of implacable repression or of patient conciliation. Lord North himself, at every stage of the protracted business, hated war as cordially as did the leaders
of the Opposition; and he had far stronger personal
motives than any of them to incline him towards pacific
courses. His tranquillity of mind, and his fair reputation in the history of his country, were both at stake;
and seldom indeed had the chief of any Cabinet been less
in love with the task on which he was engaged. His
outward bearing was described in a letter written between the arrival in England of the tidings about Lexington and of the tidings about Bunker's Hill. "His
Lordship dined yesterday according to annual custom
with the West India merchants, upon which occasion he
generally affects to be joyous; but it was remarked that
he was unusually dull."[1] North, however, served a
master who was his own prime minister, and whose sen-
sations at any given moment were more important
than those of all his councillors together. "Nothing,"
wrote Burke, "can equal the ease, composure, and even
gaiety of the great disposer of all in this lower orb. It
is too much, if not real, for the most perfect King-
craft."[2] There was no affectation about George the
Third's high spirits. He felt the joy of a strong man
who sees his work plain before him. Profoundly displeased with the Bostonians, and with their sympa-

[1] *American Archives*, Letter from London, July 1, 1775.
[2] Burke to Rockingham; Broad Sanctuary, Aug. 4, 1775.

thisers in America, he looked upon himself as commissioned by Providence to punish them : and he was fully
persuaded that he would be favoured in the undertaking.
" I am not apt," he told Lord Dartmouth, "to be over-
sanguine; but I cannot help being of opinion that with
firmness and perseverance America will be brought to
submission.   If not, old England will, though perhaps
not appear so formidable in the eyes of Europe as at
other periods, but yet will be able to make her rebellious children rue the hour that they cast off obedience.
America must be a colony of England, or treated as
enemy." [1]   The construction of these sentences might
be awkward; but their meaning was plain enough.   The
King thought it his duty, if he could, to re-conquer
America; and at the worst he was resolved, in case she
became independent, to leave her in such a condition of
ruin and exhaustion that she would, for many years to
come, be no great loss or menace to the British Empire.

Anger, from first to last, had played a prominent part
in determining the action of Great Britain.   The policy
adopted by the Court, the Ministry, and the Parliamentary Majority was so indefensible on the side of prudence and expediency that its authors were driven to
assume high moral ground, and to represent themselves
to the world as the instruments of justice, bound by an
obligation to inflict merited correction upon an erring
colony.   A curious tribute to their point of view has
been paid of late years by ingenious writers in the
United States, who have raised a protest against the
spirit and the style in which the story of their Revolution has too often been told.   Under the impulse of a
wholesome reaction against the inflated panegyric, and
overloaded denunciation, which in past days have formed
the stock in trade of too many American chroniclers,
they especially insist on bringing to a test the estimation
in which the heroes of that Revolution have been popu-
larly held.   The biographies of those heroes, it is contended, were to a large degree legends; the best of them

[1] The King to Lord Dartmouth; Kew, June 10, 1775.

were human, and the worst very bad indeed; and from these premises the conclusion has been deduced that George the Third and his Cabinet could not have been so greatly in the wrong. Samuel Adams, we are told, showed himself unscrupulous as to the means which he employed in the pursuit of public ends; John Adams was vain and sensitive; Arthur Lee, when an envoy from Congress in Paris, insinuated that his colleague Silas Deane was a rascal, and Deane openly said the same of Lee, while Franklin distrusted and disliked them both; the merchants of Boston were smugglers, the mob was ruffianly, and throughout New England no serious efforts were made by the more respectable citizens to exact retribution for violence and cruelty committed against partisans of the Crown. All this may be valuable history. It may all be worth telling. It is quite in place as an explanation of the sentiments excited in the British Parliament by the transactions in America; but as an argument for or against the wisdom of the British policy it is of no account at all. The same argument had been used to defend the course pursued by Parliament in the matter of Wilkes and his constituency. The Ministerial case, (as Burke wrote in 1770,) was that the English had a very good government, but were a very bad people; that with a malignant insanity they opposed wise measures expressly designed to promote their peace and prosperity; and that the disorders which convulsed the State had been manufactured by a few sorry libellers and designing politicians, without virtue, parts, or character. Very perverse indeed, (so Burke admitted with melancholy irony,) must be the disposition of that people among whom such a disturbance could be excited by such means. "We seem," he said, "to be driven to absolute despair; for we have no other materials to work upon but those out of which God has been pleased to form the inhabitants of this island." [1]

[1] This line of reasoning is developed in the opening paragraph of *Thoughts on the Cause of the Present Discontents.*

C

The inherent wickedness of the governed has been in all ages a plea for misgovernment; and the statement of that plea by such a pen as Burke's is its refutation. The inhabitants of New England and of Old England were made out of much the same materials; and, the colonists being what they were, if certain known steps were taken, certain inevitable results were bound to follow. The question to be determined at successive points of the American controversy was in every case a clear and simple issue. Whether Boston should be subjected to a military occupation; whether the tea-duty was to be retained or removed; whether the Port Bill was to be passed, and the Charter of Massachusetts broken; whether the petitions and remonstrances from the first Congress were to be respectfully considered or contemptuously thrown aside; — were problems demanding nothing beyond good sense and good feeling for their right solution. There would indeed have been some shadow of palliation for the action of the Ministry and of their followers if, at the time, they had been insufficiently forewarned what the consequences of that action were sure to be. But, as it was, sagacious statesmen in both houses of Parliament, — Lord Chatham and Lord Camden, the Duke of Richmond and Lord Shelburne, Burke, Conway, and Dunning, — with pertinacity and sincerity, and from the fullness of knowledge, never wearied of pleading in favour of reason and moderation. The same lesson was every second morning repeated to the town by vigorous well-informed journalists whose writings had a wide circulation. But the Ministerialists could not be forced to read newspapers; and in the Commons they took care to hear as little as possible of that which did not meet their own views. The device of shouting down discussion, perfected by practice during the heats of the Middlesex Election, was applied unsparingly throughout the earlier American debates to speakers who opposed the Government. It may well be doubted whether it is the function of history to find apologies for men who over and over again, at a

very great crisis, adopted a wrong course in defiance
of the opinion strongly held, and fearlessly urged, by
many among the best and most far-seeing of their own
contemporaries.

One more chance for a peaceful solution of the dispute between England and America now presented itself. The action of Congress in July 1775 was directed
by a man the sincerity of whose desire to maintain the
connection with the mother-country has never been
questioned. John Dickinson of Pennsylvania, the author of the "Farmer's Letters," was a devoted subject
of the Crown, proud to enthusiasm of his British citizen-
ship. Already he had a difficult task in harmonising
loyalty to his sovereign with loyalty to the Colonial
cause. Samuel Adams, — acute, indefatigable, and
strong-willed to a fault, — had convinced himself that
the independence of America should be declared forthwith, and was working by pen and voice, in public
debate and private conversation, to impress that conviction upon his colleagues at Philadelphia. The news of
Bunker's Hill accentuated the opposition between the
two statesmen. Adams saw in that event a final indication that the controversy had been transferred to the
battle-field; and he was firmly persuaded that war could
not be waged to a successful result by people who believed, or even tried or pretended to believe, that they
still owed allegiance to the titular chief of their adversaries. Dickinson, on the other hand, regarded the
slaughter of the seventeenth of June as a foretaste of
the horrors which would signalise a protracted contest
between two sections of a brave and obstinate race. He
was ready to make great exertions, and large concessions, in order to prevent that dire calamity; and his
love and admiration for the rulers of Great Britain inspired him with a confident anticipation that they would
not be so wanting in prudence and humanity as to reject
unconditionally the advances of the colonists. He urged
that the King should be approached with all those forms

of respectful submission which in his own case were not lip-worship; and his advice prevailed. He drafted a petition beseeching that the royal authority might graciously be interposed to assuage mutual fears and jealousies; requesting His Majesty himself, from his own wisdom, to direct the mode by which the applications of his faithful colonists might be improved into a happy and permanent reconciliation ; and assuring him that they, on their part, retained too tender a regard for the kingdom from which they derived their origin to ask for such a settlement as might in any manner be inconsistent with her dignity and welfare. George the Third, as was well known, would not take official cognisance of any document issued on the authority of a body professing to represent the united provinces of America. It was accordingly stated in a preamble that the petition emanated from certain of His Majesty's subjects in various colonies, (each of which was separately named,) who had taken advantage of having met together as deputies to a Congress in order to address His Majesty on behalf of themselves and their fellow-countrymen.

The petition, adopted and signed on the eighth of July, was entrusted for presentation to Richard Penn, a grandson of William Penn by the second marriage. That celebrated man had died in England; old, poor, hardly used, and as unhappy as his equable and courageous temperament, and his serene religious faith, would allow him to be. The distresses and embarrassments, which beset his later years, arose for the most part from the peculiarities of his immense but undefined position as the founder and proprietor of a state not inferior in extent and resources to more than one modern European kingdom. But after his death, in the course of two generations, the influence of his family in Pennsylvania became consolidated, and their worldly fortunes revived. One or another of them, when so minded, held the governorship of the province; and at all times they had to the full such power and dignity as would be enjoyed by the members of a royal house in a country the whole of which was, or lately had been, Crown-land. Episcopalians of a mild type, they very generally retained the confidence and esteem of the Quakers, whose repugnance to war and rebellion they personally had the best of reasons for sharing. Their wealth was enormous; and, — consisting, as it did, of quit-rents, mining royalties, ferry-rights, reserved lands, and all the other appurtenances of territorial monopoly, — it was certain not to survive a revolution. The placing a petition in such hands was in itself an announcement that the petitioners had the success of their prayer most earnestly at heart.

Penn discharged his mission with alacrity. He sailed at once; the winds were favourable; he arrived at Bristol on the thirteenth of August, and was the next day in London. But no minister would see him. A week elapsed before the Secretary for the Colonies consented to look at even a copy of the paper; and it was not until September had begun that Dartmouth submitted it to the King. Three days afterwards Penn was told that, as the address had not been received on the throne, no answer would be given. But, in truth, a very sufficient answer had already been made public. On the twenty-third of August there appeared a Royal Proclamation inviting all subjects of the realm to give information against all persons in any manner or degree aiding or abetting those who now were in open arms and rebellion against the Government within any of the Colonies of North America, in order to bring to condign punishment the authors, perpetrators, and abettors of such traitorous designs.[1]

[1] An American historian implies that the Proclamation of the twenty-third of August was prepared in answer to the petition, a copy of which had for forty-eight hours been in the hands of Ministers. But, writing on August 18, the King mentions the Proclamation as already drawn up. The world, however, which did not see behind the scenes, naturally supposed that the Proclamation was expressly issued to preclude the hope of a favourable reply to the petition, and thought that in any case the Government might at least have waited until they were in official possession of what the Americans had to say.

In accordance with custom the Proclamation was read at the Royal Exchange, at high noon. The Corporation did not withhold the services of the officer on whom the duty of reading fell. But he was sent forth on foot, without the Mace, and alone; so that, by way of providing himself with at least one attendant, he came accompanied by the common crier. The touch of John Wilkes, then Lord Mayor, was easily recognised in the arrangement of the ceremony. Its shabbiness was much to the taste of the Londoners, who greeted the last sentence of the manifesto with a hiss. When such was the reception of the Proclamation in Cornhill and Threadneedle Street, it was not likely to be welcomed in the State House of Philadelphia. The consternation of Dickinson and his followers on hearing themselves denounced as traitors was deep and lasting. Sorely disappointed, Dickinson himself was not converted, or even shaken, in his view of the relations which should subsist between the Colonies and the Crown. He struggled manfully to retain in their allegiance both his native state, and the general body of the Provinces. His efforts proved fruitless; and during the progress of the controversy his popularity among his countrymen, which had been very precious to him, entirely disappeared. But, though America rejected his advice, he still believed that she had justice on her side in her original quarrel with the British Parliament; and he took service as a private soldier in the ranks of the Continental army. Dickinson had risked and lost much for the privilege of remaining a subject; but the royal master, for whom the sacrifice was made, would not allow him to be anything but a rebel.

Lord Stanhope,—a fair and exact historian, and a Tory who was proud of the name,—comments with grave severity on the treatment accorded to the American petition. Its courteous reception, he observes, might have averted the further growth of civil strife, and once more united together the two great branches of the British race. Its rejection, on the contrary, though little considered at the time in England, was never forgotten in America; and was repeatedly and successfully employed to confirm waverers in their resistance to the Crown, by reminding them that all the blood and all the guilt of the war must be charged to British and not to American counsels.[1]

George the Third clearly perceived that in the summer of 1775 the critical period had come. He saw that whatever policy was then adopted could not afterwards be retraced, or even seriously modified; and he laid down in no ignoble language what in his view that policy should be. "I am certain," (so he had written in July,) "any other conduct but compelling obedience would be ruinous and culpable; therefore no consideration could bring me to swerve from the present faith I think myself in duty bound to follow." The King did not attempt to deceive himself about the gravity of the enterprise which he had undertaken. Foreseeing that the struggle must be arduous, and might be long, he resolved that preparations for the forthcoming campaign should be taken strongly in hand from the first moment. Side by side with military business, he effected an important change in the composition of his Ministry. He was dissatisfied with some of his principal servants; and one of those servants was gravely dissatisfied with him. The Duke of Grafton had long been uneasy. He continued to hold the Privy Seal because his sovereign urged him; but he had never re-entered the Cabinet after he quitted it in January 1770 in consequence of having been over-ruled on the question of the tea-duty. George the Third, with genuine delicacy, expressed a wish that the ex-prime-minister should still be kept informed on all secret Government business; and Grafton exchanged news freely with Lord Dartmouth, "the only one," he said, "among the King's confidential servants who had

[1] Lord Stanhope's *History of England*, chapter liii. John Jay, the first Chief Justice of the United States, used to say that, until the second petition of Congress in 1775 had been presented and ignored, he never heard any American, of any class or any description, express a wish for the independence of the Colonies.

a true desire to see lenient means adopted towards the Colonies." The Duke now learned that Mr. Penn had come over from Philadelphia with a petition, and that no notice was to be taken of it by the Ministry. The effect produced on Grafton's mind is told at length in his Autobiography. It was evident, (he said,) to all considerate men that the connection of the two countries hung on the reversal of that unfortunate decision. The day before the Petition was handed in he wrote to Lord North a letter suggesting that, when the Session opened, the Government should procure the intervention of Parliament in favour of an attempt at pacification. An Address might be moved in both Houses, praying His Majesty to order his generals to inform the rebel army that, in case the Colonies would depute persons to state to Parliament their wishes and expectations, no hostile steps would be taken on his part until the issue of the negotiation should be known. So gracious an offer, if accepted by Congress, might still be in time to restore a good understanding. If it was declined, the colonists would be obliged to confess that Great Britain was reluctant, though not afraid, to fight; and our own people would respond to the demands of war with an assured conscience, and an enthusiasm which at present was not in existence.[1]

Grafton's letter remained unanswered for seven weeks; and the reply, when at last it arrived, was unfavourable. He obtained an audience, and told George the Third in so many words that the Ministers, deluded themselves, were deluding His Majesty. "The King," the Duke said, "vouchsafed to debate the business much at large; and appeared to be astonished when I answered earnestly, to his information that a large body of German troops was to join our forces, that His Majesty would find too late that twice that number would only increase the disgrace, and never effect his purpose." Having made his protest in the Closet, he repeated it in the House of Lords with quiet and solemn emphasis. "If my brother,

[1] Grafton's *Autobiography*, chapter viii.

or my dearest friend," he said, "were to be affected by the vote I mean to give this evening, I could not possibly resist the faithful discharge of my conscience and my duty." The next day the Duke was summoned to the Palace. On this occasion he was bidden to bring the Privy Seal with him; and, when the interview was over, it remained on the King's table. George the Third thanked North, (who held Grafton's views about America, but was not man enough to act on them,) for his handsome conduct when compared with the "shameful desertion" of others. The Crown had much to give; but shame and self-respect were matters outside the range of its disposal. In early life, when Grafton himself was at the head of the Government, he had learned by very cruel experience that there is no royal road to honour.

Two out of three Secretaries of State were, in the King's judgement, unequal to the requirements of the situation. Lord Dartmouth was too weak, as certainly he was too good, for the post which he held; and Lord Rochford, in troubled times, was unfit for any post whatever. Dartmouth was unwilling to be shifted. He made difficulties,—not greater indeed than are ordinarily made on such occasions by the members of a Cabinet which is not very much afraid of its prime minister,—but sufficient to distress his sovereign, who could not bear to hurt him. At last he consented to accept the Privy Seal, in an hour propitious to his reputation and his happiness. Henceforward he had abundant leisure for those religious and benevolent undertakings which constituted his real vocation. His official duties were much what he pleased to make them. The Cabinet gladly turned over to him all the business for which he had an inclination, and especially such matters as brought the minister in charge of them into contact with a bishop. When local opinion in Birmingham was divided on the question of equipping the town with a licensed theatre, Dartmouth sate in judgement on the case. After hearing all that was to be said for and against the proposal,

— and the arguments, though not perhaps in his eyes, were as comical as any farce that was likely to be represented on the boards, — he decided to throw the weight of the Government into the scale opposed to the concession. That was the sternest act of coercion for which he was thenceforward responsible. It was a very different thing from making arrangements to invade, burn, and devastate a land inhabited by people with whom he was in as close sympathy as with his countrymen at home. During the last five years of the war, (as far as the Parliamentary History records,) he never opened his lips on the subject of America. His popularity in that country revived. Even those colonists, who hated the rest of the Cabinet, trusted and liked him; and he, in return, felt a pained and placid concern for their welfare, regretting only that they could not view their own interests in the same light as himself and his royal master. That master he now saw only on his best side; while George the Third had always valued what was good in Dartmouth, if indeed there was anything except good about him. When in the course of time the Government fell, and the separation between monarch and minister could no longer be averted, the King broke the news in a letter honourable to them both. " I have ever esteemed Lord Dartmouth, since I have thoroughly known him, in another light than any of his companions in Ministry. What days has it pleased the Almighty to place me in, when Lord Dartmouth can be a man to be removed but at his own request! But I cannot complain. I adore the will of Providence, and will ever resign myself obediently to his will. My heart is too full to add more." [1]

From Lord Rochford the King parted at once and finally. The retiring minister did not go empty-handed. His claim upon the Treasury, in George the Third's estimation, was quite irrespective of the actual condition, or the future prospects, of the national balances. Royal gratitude was never sparing towards a public servant who, at a pinch, had done his duty to the mind of his

[1] The King to the Earl of Dartmouth; March 27, 1782.

sovereign ; and that, in a marked degree, was the case with Rochford. In January 1770 he had voted in the Cabinet against Grafton, and in favour of maintaining the tax on tea. Grafton now surrendered his place with no compensation except a quiet conscience, which he never again lost; but Rochford insisted on something much more substantial being settled upon him for life. "Though my finances," so George the Third wrote to Lord North, "are in a very disgraceful situation, yet, with the desire I have to make the situation you are in happy, I cannot require one minute's time for consideration, but most willingly consent to give Lord Rochford a pension of 2500*l.* per annum." Rochford was grateful. "This morning," he wrote on the tenth of November to the Lord Lieutenant of Ireland, " I resigned the Seals : not with my own choice, but with my hearty concordance, as it contributes to an arrangement thought necessary for the King's affairs. I have, however, obtained a most honourable retreat; a very considerable pension for my life, and a promise from the King that he will confer the Garter upon me the first Chapter His Majesty holds. I venture so far to trespass upon your friendship as to beg your Lordship will give me a little sinecure place of about fifty or sixty pounds a year for an old servant that has lived with me thirty years. I have now no way of providing for him but by keeping him myself, which will be a great charge to me." "It is," (so he explained to the Irish Secretary,) " for our old friend my butler, who has poured you out many a glass of good Burgundy." And thus Rochford fell soft, and his butler likewise, who had so often helped his master's guests to fall soft before.[1]

One of the vacant offices was given to Lord Weymouth, who had resigned a Secretaryship of State five years before, for reasons which are still obscure. He left office in December 1770 during the difficulty which had arisen with Spain about the Falkland Islands ; and it was remarked at the time that he did not know how

[1] *Harcourt Papers*, in the British Museum.

to make a peace, and did not wish to make a war. But in 1775 the American war was already made; and the King had no intention whatever of allowing his Secre-taries of State to see whether they could make a peace. The Bedfords, now dominant in the Cabinet, could not be easy until they had Weymouth back among them. He was a Bedford, endowed largely with the personal and political attributes of the clan. When Weymouth was quite young, George the Second had said of him that he could not be a good kind of man, as he never kept company with any woman, and loved nothing but play and strong beer. He so far mended his ways as to take to wine; and he could converse over it brilliantly and agreeably until that hour of the morning when the ban-quet had lost all resemblance to a feast of reason. Ut-terly ruined early in life, he was ill thought of even in circles whose rule of conduct was easy beyond the verge of laxity. To save him from his creditors, he was appointed Lord Lieutenant of Ireland, and received the money for his outfit; but Ireland would not have him. The first, and perhaps the most important, of Weymouth's public services was to enable an English prime minister to ascertain the low-water mark of character which would qualify a nobleman for the occupation of Dublin Castle. He was now forty-one years old, and not likely to grow any worse. The King could endure Sandwich, and might reasonably be expected to put up with Weymouth, who at all events had one vice the less. In the House of Lords he generally spoke well, and always shortly. Those were his antecedents, and those were his titles to public employment. Weymouth was a wonderful personage to be added to a Government which professed to entertain the hope of winning back into loyalty all that was honest and respectable among the population of New England.

The other in-coming minister was Lord George Ger-maine. As a rising soldier, while he still was called Lord George Sackville, he had seen hard service. His military qualities had obtained high praise from two such judges

of valour as General Wolfe and the Duke of Cumberland.
He was shot in the breast at Fontenoy, having led his
regiment so far within the enemy's position that his
wound was dressed in Louis the Fifteenth's own tent.
In much later days a noted Whig duellist warmly acknowledged that, in all the affairs in which he had been
engaged, he had never met anybody who behaved better
than Germaine. A man whose courage was conspicuous
at thirty, and at five-and-fifty, could never have been
anything but brave. It was under the influence, not of
personal fear, but of other unworthy motives, that he
made the mistake of his career at Minden.[1] When in
command of the cavalry during that battle he disobeyed
an order which, to Ligonier or Granby, would have been
more welcome than an offer of the Garter and ten thousand a year for life. He kept the British dragoons
standing idle beside their horses while one after another
of Prince Ferdinand's aides-de-camp in vain urged him
to charge home and complete the victory which the
British infantry had won. His punishment was exemplary. He was dismissed the service. He was struck
off the Privy Council. He lost his numerous employments and rich endowments. At his own earnest request
he was granted a court-martial, but was informed that,
if sentenced to die, he would certainly be shot. He was
found guilty of disobedience in presence of the enemy,
and adjudged to be unfit to serve His Majesty in any
military capacity whatever. George the Second confirmed the sentence, and had it recorded in the order-
book of every regiment in the army, accompanied by a
warning that high birth, and great place, would not

---

[1] "It is difficult to believe that a Sackville wanted common courage.
This Sackville fought duels with propriety ; in private life he was a surly,
domineering kind of fellow, and had no appearance of wanting spirit. It
is known, he did not love Duke Ferdinand ; far from it ! May not he have
been of peculiarly sour humour that morning, the luckless fool; sulky
against Ferdinand, and his 'saddling at one o'clock; ' sulky against
himself, against the world and mankind ; and flabbily disinclined to heroic
practices for the moment?" Carlyle's *Frederick the Great :* Book XIX.
chapter iii.

shelter an offender from censures worse than death to a man who had any sense of honour.   So vast was the scandal, and so durable the memory of it, that it has ever since been a sort of sinister protection to Germaine's reputation.   His connection with all those misfortunes which befel our arms during the war of the American Revolution is well nigh forgotten; and he is remembered in military history principally, and almost exclusively, as the man who made "the great refusal" on the plains at Minden.[1]

[1] Neither friend nor ill-wisher ever thought of Lord George Germaine apart from the central event of his career.   In August 1775 Gibbon was writing to Holroyd on electioneering matters.   Both of them knew Lord George intimately in society, and acted with him in politics; and yet, twice in the same letter, Gibbon referred to him under the nickname of " Minden."

The identity of the Secretary of State with the commander of Prince Ferdinand's cavalry was sometimes mercifully concealed from people who had not kept themselves abreast of recent changes in the peerage.   A Crown living in the neighbourhood of some Government powder-mills had chanced to fall vacant.   It was said that a sprightly young divine, who had been selected to fill it, waited upon Lord George Germaine, and told him that he was much obliged for the offer, but that he liked powder as little as Lord George Sackville.   The story may be found in the corner of contemporary magazines; but it bears the mark of having been manufactured at Brooks's.

CHAPTER XIII

THE HESSIANS. PROCEEDINGS IN PARLIAMENT

THE effect which these appointments produced upon
public opinion may be estimated by the judgement
passed upon them by George Selwyn, who was an
easy man of the world, and in this particular case
the least harsh of critics. For he was a silent, obedient,
and, (so far as he had convictions,) a convinced supporter
of the Government, on whose continuance in office his
own sinecures depended. "This new acquisition in each
House," he wrote, "will have so many gross things said
to them that I do not know what may follow from it.
The talent of public speaking bears certainly a great
price in this country; and the strongest proof of it is
that Ministers will move heaven and earth to get one
of these glib orators on their side, in spite of the most
odious or despicable character whatever." [1] When the
posts were allotted, George the Third did not forget the
past history of his most recent ministerial recruit. "Lord
George Germaine," he wrote to North, "cannot treat with
the Continent." Germaine, accordingly, had the colonies;
Lord Weymouth was replaced in the Southern Department, and entrusted with the diplomatic relations between
Great Britain, and France and Spain; while Lord Suffolk
was retained in the Northern Department, where business was done with Germany.

That business was now of a very delicate and special

[1] Letter from Selwyn to Lord Carlisle: *Historical Manuscripts Commission;* Fifteenth Report, Appendix, Part VI. The date suggested in the
volume is February 1776: but internal evidence clearly indicates that the
letter was written on the second of November, 1775.

nature, and could not be entrusted to a personage whose name, when that name was Lord George Sackville, had been a byword in German military circles. A civil war had already broken out; foreign wars were only too sure to supervene; and our armaments had been allowed to dwindle until the means of offence and defence were almost entirely wanting. The bare facts and dates, without epithet or comment, sufficiently characterise the improvidence of the Ministry. When the Army and Navy Estimates were moved in December 1774, the seamen were reduced by four thousand, and the land forces were fixed at a number below eighteen thousand effective men. So it came to pass that in August 1775, before active operations had continued for a quarter of a year, the kingdom at home had been denuded of all but a few weak and scattered regiments; and our only considerable organised body of troops was shut up in Boston. It was not the King's fault. His Majesty had long contended that the Peace establishment, in both the services, was far too low. Early in the summer of 1775 he had urged, and at last had insisted, that exceptional efforts should be made to obtain a supply of men, and that recourse should be had to unusual sources. The example of Chatham in the Seven Years' War was remembered and imitated; and the clansmen of the Scottish Highlands were enlisted to fight in a cause that certainly was not Chatham's.

The North of Scotland was a more promising recruiting-ground than ever; for the full effect was now being felt of the process by which Highland chiefs, when their military power had been broken, converted themselves from feudal superiors into rack-renting landlords. After the rebellion of 1745 had been suppressed the British Government neglected a unique opportunity. Wise and humane statesmen, of our famous Anglo-Indian type, would have seized the occasion for framing a just and comprehensive land-settlement, under which all classes should receive their due. But, as it was, the Highlands were abandoned to the mercy of the Court of Session at Edinburgh,

which recognised the Chief as sole and absolute proprietor of the entire territory occupied by the clan. In
1773, when Doctor Johnson was travelling through the
Hebrides, he had watched with grave disapproval the
consequences entailed upon the inhabitants of those
regions by that fatal and one-sided policy. The chieftains, (so Johnson learned,) had flattered themselves
with golden dreams of much higher rents than could
reasonably be paid.[1] Those clansmen who were reck-
less and improvident bid against each other in order to
secure farms; while the industrious and the enterprising,
who likewise were the most prudent, surrendered their
old homes, and sought a career beyond the seas. The
tacksmen, the flower of the tribe for the purposes both
of peace and war, had been the hardest hit by the new
system. Great numbers of them had emigrated to the
colonies; many others were on the eve of going; and
they were accompanied on their voyage by the most
stout-hearted of their humbler neighbours, whose fathers
their fathers had so often led into battle. Johnson in-
dignantly exclaimed that a nobleman of France would
never be permitted to force the French King's subjects
out of the country. If these rapacious chieftains, (he
declared,) resided in Normandy or Brittany, they would
be admonished by a letter of the sort which, while the
Bastille stood, their monarch was in the habit of sending to those who incurred his displeasure.[2] And so it
came about that when, in the autumn and winter of
1775, troops were needed to suppress rebellion in the
colonies, the best fighting men of Argyllshire and In-

[1] Conversation between Doctor Johnson and Donald M'Queen on the
thirteenth of September, 1773.

[2] A hundred and thirteen years were still to elapse before the British
Government, by methods more constitutional than a *lettre de cachet*, took
effective measures for restoring security and contentment to the agricultural
population of the Highlands. The Act of 1886, which gave the Crofter
an assured tenure upon payment of an equitable rent, was not seriously
opposed either in the House of Commons or the House of Lords. This
unanimity of Parliament, — always soft-hearted where the Highlander is
in question,— conferred singular force and authority upon a healing measure
which undid all that it still was practicable to undo of the wrongs of ages.

verness-shire eagerly hailed the chance of winning by
their swords a settlement in America more secure than
that which their progenitors had held, by the tenure of
the sword, in the valleys of their native Scotland.

King George's call for soldiers met with a less lively
response in other parts of his dominions. "Beating
orders," as the phrase then ran, were sent to Ireland;
and the poorer Catholics of Connaught and Munster
were invited into the ranks. But it was a bad time for
tempting Irish farmers away from their cabins, which
were overflowing with unwonted plenty. The Dublin
Government reported in October that agriculturists had
never experienced so prosperous a year. "Corn of all
kinds," wrote Lord Harcourt, "and potatoes, the chief
food of the people, are a drug. They are now sold in
the North for fourpence a hundred-weight. They were
never known at so cheap a rate before."[1] Recruiting
moved slowly in Ireland, and almost imperceptibly in
England, where hardly any enthusiasm for the war
existed among the classes from which soldiers were
drawn. That enthusiasm was fainter in no one than
in the man who stood at the summit of military administration. Lord Barrington disliked the measures adopted
to procure recruits, and disbelieved in their efficacy.
The King attributed the slackness and despondency
which prevailed at the War Office to the right cause.
That department, left to itself, was not likely to produce shining results when there was a minister at the
head of the Army who disapproved of having a war at
all, and thought that, if hostilities could not be avoided,
they should be carried on exclusively by sea.[2] But the
master's vigour and high courage reinforced the deficiencies of the servant. George the Third had all the family
love of military details; he never spared himself or his
carriage-horses; he was always on the spot, or within
a few miles of it; and, if not actually in St. James's,
he was ready at an hour's notice to come up from Kew,

Harcourt Papers.
[2] The King to North; Kew, August 26, 1775.

or, at furthest, from Windsor. Week after week, and
year by year, Lord Barrington was complaining; pleading weak health and a sore conscience; and reminding
the King that his resignation had been sent in months
before, and that no notice had been taken of it. But
all his protests were unheeded by his inexorable sovereign, who kept him in office against his will, and did
very much the most important part of his work for
him.

A pressing concern of the Ministry was to make
arrangements by which England's wealth might be
used to hire foreigners for the purpose of fighting
battles which Englishmen were not keen to fight themselves. Sir Robert Gunning, our Envoy Extraordinary
to Russia, was personally a favourite with the Empress;
and Catherine had conveyed to him an expression of
her regret for the difficulties in which his Government
was plunged. Gunning followed up what he assumed
to be his advantage, and persuaded himself and his
employers that twenty thousand disciplined Russian
infantry, fully equipped, would sail for Canada as soon
as the Baltic was open in the spring of the coming
year. They were to serve, not as auxiliaries, but as a
component part of the British army under the command of a British general. Burke, who had long contemplated American freedom and prosperity with a
sense of personal satisfaction, was shocked by the gro-
tesque proposal. "I am on thorns": he wrote. "I
cannot, at my ease, see Russian barbarism let loose to
waste the most beautiful object that ever appeared upon
this globe." Gibbon, a cheerful cynic, familiarised by
his studies of the Roman decadence with the idea of
paying outlandish tribes to defend a civilised empire,
took the matter more lightly. "When the Russians
arrive," so he asked his friend Mr. Holroyd, "if they
refresh themselves in England or Ireland, will you go
to see their camp? We have great hopes of getting
a body of these barbarians. In consequence of some
very plain advances, George with his own hand wrote

D 2

a very polite epistle to sister Kitty, requesting her friendly assistance." But other potentates besides George the Third were getting letters written, and advice whispered, to the same august quarter. The story of the communications which were passing between England and Russia soon became the common property of every Chancery in Europe; and still less was it a secret that the British Government had run short of soldiers. Lord Barrington with his own mouth had informed Monsieur de Guines, the French Ambassador at St. James's, that England must take the field with three separate armies, marching respectively from New York, Boston, and Canada; that those armies would between them demand not less than forty to fifty thousand men; and that the country itself, at the very outside, could not produce an active force of more than eighteen thousand rank and file.[1]

The Russian court was besieged by warnings and expostulations from the capital of every country which feared, or hated, or envied Britain. France was earnest and active, and Spain also: but the most effective and dexterous opposition came from Potsdam. Harris, our minister at Berlin, informed Lord Suffolk that the Empress of Russia, from the very first moment of the negotiations, had taken the King of Prussia into her confidence. Those negotiations, (it was added,) had been wrecked, not by official diplomacy, but through very influential agents indeed, — of the sort, it may be presumed, who during Catherine's widowhood were seldom wanting at St. Petersburg, — whom Frederic the Great had found means to secure to his own interests.[2] In September 1775 Catherine, speaking, whether she was so or not, like a true friend of England, adjured Gunning to see that his royal master settled the dispute with America by peaceful methods. "You know," she

---

[1] *Histoire de la Participation de la France à l'établissement des États Unis de l'Amérique;* par Henri Doniol. Tome Premier; Annexes du chapitre vi.

[2] Decipher of Letter from Harris to Lord Suffolk, of December 1775.

said, "that my situation has been full as embarrassing; and, believe me, I did not rest my assurance of success upon one mode of action. There are moments when we must not be too rigorous." It was curious that such doctrines should be preached to a constitutional King of England by the autocrat of Russia. The wise counsel was neglected; and some weeks afterwards Catherine gave her final answer in a letter flavoured by a sublime impertinence which might have been inspired by Frederic himself. There was, the Empress contended, an impropriety in employing her troops in another hemisphere, at the disposal of a foreign Government, and at a distance removed from all correspondence with their own sovereign. Besides, (so she assured the King of England,) she had not only her own dignity to consider, but that of His Majesty also. It would be an ill compliment from her to him that she should consent to a course of action implying that he was one of those monarchs who could not put down their own rebellions. The King took the affront calmly, like the gentleman that he was. " The letter of the Empress," he wrote to his prime minister, " is a clear refusal, and not in so genteel a manner as I should have thought might have been expected from her. She has not had the civility to answer in her own hand, and has thrown out some expressions that may be civil to a Russian ear, but certainly not to more civilised ones."

Germany remained; — the fruitful parent of strong men who had not yet been taught to reserve themselves for occasions when they would be wanted to fight in defence of Germany's native interests. It required the terrible experiences of nearly forty more years before the Fatherland learned that lesson; and in 1775 the smaller states were still recruiting-grounds for every ambitious ruler who had a design on the territory of his neighbour, and for every royal martinet who liked to see tall and sturdy Protestants in the front line of his show regiments. George the Third had a claim of loyalty over one section of the German people. As Elector of Hanover he made to the King of England what he himself described as a loan of five battalions, who were sent to garrison Gibraltar and Minorca, and release an equivalent number of British troops for service in America. Our country, as always, did things handsomely; and Hanover was no loser by the transaction. The whole force received British pay, which was on a much more generous scale than was fingered by the inmates of any barrack in Germany. The opportunity was taken of getting the British taxpayer to provide all ranks with a complete outfit, of which the officers in particular stood woefully in need; and a British Colonel, who knew something of the life on board a transport, was told off for the duty of fortifying their minds against the terrors of the voyage; because, as the King remarked, though brave on shore, Continental forces feared the sea.[1]

Over and above the assistance which he drew from the regular military establishment of his hereditary dominions, George the Third took measures for collecting by voluntary enlistment a body of foreign troops for the service of the British Crown. Such a force, in the eighteenth century, was composed of very different materials from that King's Foreign Legion which took its share in the labours and glories of the Peninsula and of Waterloo. The soldiers of Baron Ompteda, who fought with intelligence and devotion for the common cause of Germany and of England, rivalled in courage the soldiers of Hill and Picton, and maintained before the eyes of their British comrades a valuable example of discipline and personal conduct. But it was otherwise at the period of the American rebellion. The Continental system of enlistment, which passed finally away during the wars of the French Revolution, had spread misery and corruption far and wide throughout the humbler classes during the two generations which preceded its extinction. The baleful results of its influence on army morals was analogous to the deterioration

[1] The King to North; Kew, August 1 and 4, 1775.

of civil society by the institution of slave labour. In most cases the agents of the system were debauched and fraudulent, and not seldom infamous. The *racoleurs*, which was the name by which those agents were called and loathed, pervaded Northern Europe in various disguises, scraping acquaintance with likely lads; entrapping them across the frontier on false pretences; stupefying them with drugged liquor, or securing their persons by methods of hateful violence. Sometimes these worthies appeared in their proper dress and their true character, strutting in front of a tent at fair or market, with hat cocked and sword trailing, and the general air of a bully with whom the world was going well. They would harangue the peasants and apprentices on the charms of colonial service, in regions where oranges and bananas and pomegranates might be had for the picking, and gold or diamonds for the stooping; and they warned their hearers to beware of the prejudices which parents and relatives entertained against the only career in which a young fellow of spirit was sure to acquire a fortune.

Among the dupes whom they enticed and captured there were decent quiet men who made the best of their wretched lot, though they never became reconciled to it; and in war-time the more wayward and turbulent natures found congenial excitement in the hazards of a campaign, and the hopes of plunder and promotion. But the greater number sank into moral ruin, and became worthless citizens, and dishonest and disreputable soldiers. Always, and especially during a long peace, Europe swarmed with a nomad population of mercenaries. The tramps and vagrants of military life, they would serve one month in Turin, and another at Munich, and the next at Stuttgart; taking to the fields at the first opportunity which offered itself as soon as they had secured a bounty. They played this game in France, in Austria, in Holland, and, (much more cautiously, and only as a desperate resource,) in Prussia.[1]

[1] Some German princes had a wonderful eye for an old soldier. Duke

Whatever garrison town might be their temporary domicile, they were everywhere watched like convicts, and punished with frightful severity. Each in his time had ridden the wooden horse, with a couple of muskets strapped to either foot; or had lain in a mouldy dungeon, or dragged a cannon-ball at his ankle on the ramparts, for years together; or had run the gauntlet of a battalion armed with switches as far down the line as he could stagger before he fainted. Without honour, without patriotism, they were thieves and drunkards; seducers in time of peace, and something much worse when during an invasion they had a village or farmhouse at their mercy. Hardly able, some of them, to name a country where they could ever make a home, and settle down to a trade, without the almost certain prospect of being shot as deserters, they lived for the passing moment, intent only on misusing it in some manner agreeable to themselves.

George the Third was German enough thoroughly to understand the system, and Englishman enough to be somewhat ashamed of being directly mixed up with it. His necessities obliged him to have recourse to Continental enlistments; but the worst abuses which were connected with it he was sincerely desirous to avoid. He sent orders to Hanover to raise four thousand men, and named two garrisons where the recruits should be closely kept. But he absolutely and repeatedly declined to bribe and stimulate any professional recruiter by the offer of a Commission under his own hand and in his own army. "The only idea these Germans ought to adopt," he wrote, "is the being contractors for raising recruits, and fixing the price they will deliver them at Hamburgh, Rotterdam, and any other port they may propose." Farther, and lower, than this he would not go. "The giving commissions

---

Charles of Wurtemberg, who flourished during the American war, made it a standing rule that any traveller, with the look of a deserter, should be brought into his presence and offered the choice between enlistment or imprisonment for life.

to officers, or any other of the proposals that have been made, I can by no means consent to, for they in plain English are turning me into a kidnapper, which I cannot think a very honourable occupation." [1]

The laws of Germany, as the King admitted, did not allow him to extend his operations outside the confines of Hanover. The bishop who was Prince of Liège, and the archbishop who was Elector of Cologne, allowed him to establish recruiting centres within their respective territories; but the lay statesmen of the Court at Vienna took another view of German honour and German obligations. They wrote to the Free Cities that Great Britain had no more connection with the empire than Russia or Spain, neither of which powers was permitted to recruit within its limits. Hampered by that Constitutional difficulty, as well as by his own scruples, George the Third fell back upon a project of hiring ready-made battalions wholesale from needy, or, (if such could be discovered,) friendly and sympathetic foreign powers. The army of Holland contained a fine brigade whose officers were Scotch by descent, although the rank and file were no longer drawn from Scotland, as had been the case until the middle of the century. Our ambassador was instructed to request that this body of troops should be transferred from the service of the Netherlands to the service of Great Britain. But in Holland such an application could not be granted before it had been openly examined and discussed. When the matter came on for debate it was opposed on the practical ground that a commercial state should never, except from necessity, become involved in any quarrel; and by the historical argument that the Dutch, who owed their national existence to what in its day had been termed a rebellion, should be chary of helping to subdue a people who possibly were as brave, and as ardent for liberty, as their own forefathers. The States General agreed to send the Scotch brigade across to England on condition that it should not be employed

[1] King to North; Kew, August 26, and November 14, 1775.

outside Europe.   That reply, courteous in form, was
intended as a refusal by the Hague ; and as such it was
construed at Whitehall.

The British Government thenceforward directed its
efforts to more promising quarters.   Charles, Duke of
Brunswick, in the course of a long reign had spent,
sometimes on objects of very dubious morality, all that
he could extract from his own people, and all that he
could induce capitalists in other countries to lend him.
His family already knew the feel of English money.
The Hereditary Prince, who had recently been asso-
ciated with his father in the administration of the
Duchy, had married Augusta, a sister of George the
Third ; had received with her an enormous dowry ;
and had given her very little happiness indeed in return
for it.   The reigning house of Brunswick now, for the
second time, struck a hard bargain with the King of
England.   They engaged to provide him four thousand
infantry and three hundred dismounted dragoons.   As
long as the force received our pay, the Duke of Brunswick was to get, for his own share, fifteen thousand
pounds a year from the English Treasury; and that
subsidy was not only to be continued, but was actually to
be doubled, during the two years succeeding the return
of the said troops into His Serene Highness's dominions.
General Riedesel, who commanded the contingent, was
a man of honour and prowess.   The dragoons, and two
of · the battalions, belonged to the regular Ducal army,
which the Hereditary Prince kept in a state of high
efficiency.   But these choice articles were only, so to
speak, the upper layer in the consignment of the goods
which ultimately were delivered.   In order to make up
the full tale of men, the Brunswick authorities put in
force the utmost rigours of conscription.   The product
of their industry was not admirable to a good military
eye.   Colonel Harcourt was an excellent officer, who
subsequently rose to great commands ; and who, as an
inmate of George the Third's household, was destined
for many years together to enjoy and deserve the inti-

mate confidence of his sovereign. "The Brunswickers," so Harcourt reported, "arrived at Portsmouth a few days before, a sad sample of what is to be expected; no intermediate age between grandfathers and grand-children; with coaches and every other impediment for their officers, and without a necessary for their men. The generals marched, or rather reeled, off the parade."[1] This account was afterwards confirmed by an observer who, for his misfortune, had a longer and closer acquaintance than Harcourt with the worse elements among our German auxiliaries. An English officer, one of the captives of Saratoga, complained that several of the Brunswick regiments in Burgoyne's army were utterly unfit for warfare. The reigning Duke had forced into the ranks all his subjects who at any time had been soldiers; and had obliged old officers to leave their retirement, and take service once more, on pain, if they refused, of forfeiting their half-pay. "Only pic-ture to your imagination," this gentleman exclaimed, "ensigns of forty and fifty commanding troops not much younger, and judge how proper they are for an active and vigorous campaign in the thick woods of America."[2]

The hope of gain disturbed the equanimity of all Serene Highnesses, between the Elbe, the Danube, and the Rhine, who owned a guard-room and a drill-yard. To use Burke's unsavoury, but most expressive, meta-phor, they snuffed the cadaverous taint of lucrative war; and the sky above the British Treasury was soon alive with royal vultures. The Prince of the little state of Waldeck wrote off at once to offer six hundred men who, like their ruler, demanded nothing better than to sacrifice themselves for His British Majesty. The sacri-fice made by the Prince himself was to receive five thousand pounds sterling for every year that the wood-cutters and charcoal-burners of Waldeck were shooting,

---

[1] *Harcourt Papers:* Letter of the Hon. Colonel William Harcourt, of April 3, 1776.
[2] *Travels through the Interior Parts of America,* in a Series of Letters by an Officer. London, 1791.

and being shot by, the lumberers of Maine and Con-necticut. The spontaneous advances of one potentate were rejected on the ground that his troops were among the worst in Germany. Another, who had just wits enough to keep up sixteen recruiting stations on the territory of his neighbours, pressed a battalion on the acceptance of George the Third in a letter so crazy that it could not be translated into rational English. London society correctly analysed the motive which prompted such an outburst of warlike zeal among the princes of the Empire. "The civil discord between the parent country and its enraged colonies boils over with inex-pressible violence; whilst the administration, too late, are now preparing to send out a most formidable force. Environed with incendiaries, and accounting all helps as scarce sufficient to quench the conflagration,

> To Hesse, Brunswick, Hanover they run.
> 'Oh ! cross the Atlantic every mother's son;
> Or that milch cow, Britannia, is undone.' " [1]

So one man of fashion wrote to another in London; and the proud and fiery aristocracy, which held high debate in the Dublin parliament, was more outspoken still. Four thousand British troops had been shipped for America from Ireland; and Lord North designed to fill their place with an equal number of foreign Protestants. But Ireland was the very last country in the world which needed to import fighting Protestants; and so the prime minister learned to his cost before the war had ended. The Lord Lieutenant at once declared that such a proposition would not bear discussion in either Chamber. "I say it," Lord Harcourt wrote, "with concern and shame, that I know no one of those who have been called the ancient and confidential ser-vants of the Crown whom I should dare to trust in such an exigency without a risk of having the measure defeated." [2]

[1] Sir Charles Wintringham to Captain Monk; Dover Street, March 25, 1776.
[2] Lord Harcourt to Lord North; October 17, 1775.

There was one German ruler whose willingness to lend his troops was more important than that of any, or indeed of all, of the others. The Hessian army, which, when engaged in Continental war, exceeded in strength the British army on a peace footing, was strictly disciplined and exceedingly formidable. It was raised by conscription from a people docile to authority, strong in body, with hardy habits, and of a courageous nature. The Landgrave of Hesse now held the call of the military market. He had a large stock of wares, of undeniable quality, manufactured and in store; and he used his advantage shrewdly. He agreed to place at the disposal of George the Third twelve thousand foot soldiers, and thirty-two pieces of cannon. The details of the treaty were minutely contested; and, at every stage of the discussions, Cassel never failed to get the better of London. Point after point, each of them involving a difference of hundreds of thousands, or even millions, of crowns, was settled in favour of Hesse; but the master-stroke was the arrangement of the sum which was contributed over and above the pay and expenses of the troops. The German negotiators insisted that Great Britain should promise a double subsidy of a hundred and ten thousand pounds a year, which went into the coffers of the Hessian Government as so much clear profit. That subsidy was to run for a complete twelve-month after His Britannic Majesty had given notice to the Landgrave that payment was to cease; which notice was not to be given until the contingent had returned from America, "and had actually arrived in the dominions of the said prince, namely in Hesse, properly so called." [1]

The magnitude of the transaction, and the one-sided character of the bargain, impressed public imagination to the exclusion of all besides; and so it came to pass that German mercenaries in the American war, then, and

[1] Translation of the Treaty between His Majesty and the Landgrave of Hesse Cassel: signed at Cassel, the thirteenth of January, 1776. *Parliamentary History*, Vol. XVIII., page 1160.

ever since, were familiarly known as Hessians. The whole force did not consist of made and trained soldiers. The Landgrave could not afford to draw upon his regular army for so large a detachment; and the unhappy country was bled to the quick by an unsparing and special conscription. To escape impressment many Hessians fled to Hanover; and King George was requested to turn back the fugitives from his frontier, and to assist the Landgrave to fulfil his engagements with Great Britain. One in every four of the able-bodied men in Hesse was sooner or later shipped off to fight, at a distance of a thousand leagues from his home, in a quarrel about which he knew very little, and cared even less. It has been calculated that a compulsory levy, enforced upon England and Wales with the like severity, would have produced an army of four hundred thousand men.[1] Even so, the ranks were not filled up; and the Landgrave had recourse to voluntary enlistment, as it then was practised in Germany. Side by side with Hessian peasants and artisans, there] marched adventurers from every country in Europe. Some regiments, which were well manned and perfectly drilled, wanted nothing except a belief in their cause to make them as good as the best; but others were below mediocrity, and almost all of them contained a proportion of bad materials. In the license of a foraging party, and in the stress of battle, there was greater variety of behaviour among the auxiliaries than between one English regiment and another. Certain German battalions were the weakest links in the chain which was to bind America; as was proved at Trenton and at Bennington, on two occasions when the British expectations of a successful issue to the war appeared to be on the very eve of fulfilment.

Everything comes to a reputation which waits; and the Landgrave of Hesse has had his turn of being whitewashed by history. He has of recent years been made the subject of an elaborate and ingenious apology

[1] Bancroft's *History:* Part III., chapter 57.

from the point of view of Hessian, as opposed to Prussian and German, patriotism.[1] It is argued that he took part in the American war in order to assert the title of his State to rank among the military powers of the world; and his conduct has been compared to that of Count Cavour, when Sardinians were despatched to the Crimea as the allies of France and England. The same statesmanlike wisdom, it is asserted, was shown at Cassel in 1775 and at Turin in 1855. But the Crimean policy of the great Italian was adopted as a first step towards the liberation and consolidation of Italy; whereas the Landgrave of Hesse cannot be credited with any aspiration to promote either the freedom or the unity of Germany. We are told, in a passage not destitute of pathos, how the Elector "never ceased to mourn over the long absence of his army, his dear subjects;" and how anxiety, and years of quiet grief, weighed on his noble heart, so that, a few months after the return of the last of his soldiers, he died suddenly, and all too soon for the love of the people whom he governed. The lapse of time places bounds to the retrospective operation of human sympathy; and our generation has no tears to spare for the circumstance that Frederic the Second of Hesse expired before receiving from London the last instalment of his consolation-money.

A more solid argument in favour of the Elector of Hesse was the effect of British munificence upon the finances of the Electorate, and upon the private budgets of the officers and soldiers of the Contingent. The advocate and panegyrist of the Landgrave assures us that the men were better paid, and their commanders much better paid, than the corresponding ranks of the English establishment. There never, (he says,) was an army so well off as the Hessians who served in America. A married subaltern could support his family in Ger-

[1] Summary and statement of a pamphlet published in Cassel in 1879, communicated by Joseph G. Rosengarten to the *Pennsylvania Magazine of History and Biography:* July 1899.

many, while he himself lived well in the colonies : and
the captains, and those above them, laid by money fast.
It was a common thing for colonels to have from six
thousand, to thirteen thousand, dollars standing to their
credit.   The subjects of the Elector, who remained at
home, had their share in this unparalleled prosperity.
The Landgrave raised his country from poverty and
squalor by the improvement of his capital and of the
neighbouring palace ; by roads, parks, museums, semi-
naries, hospitals, universities, libraries, opera house, and
chapel.   When he came to the throne, the Hessian
Treasury owed two and a half millions of dollars.
When he died, it was twelve and a half millions to the
good.   The source of all this beneficent expenditure,
and of all these savings, "was of course the English
subsidy ; " — and, (it might have been added,) an indefi-
nite prolongation of the misery and suffering which
was inflicted upon America.   Whatever the argument
is worth, it is a poor defence when addressed to an
Englishman whose income-tax, on account of those old
subsidies, is to this day higher by a perceptible fraction
of a penny.   Nor is it an argument of much value in
the estimation of a German patriot.   Men do not ap-
prove conduct which they would scorn to imitate ; and,
since the days of Blucher, and Stein, and Körner, no
true German would so much as entertain the idea of
trafficking in German valour.   The best of the rulers
who shared in the profits of that unworthy commerce
had reason, in the course of events, bitterly to repent it.
The Hereditary Prince of Brunswick was a valiant warrior ; but he died the most unhappy of generals.   Foiled
at Valmy by the enthusiasm of the young French republic, — and utterly ruined, with all that he held dear,
on the fatal day of Auerstädt and Jena, — he was
heavily punished for having helped to pervert and en-
feeble the national spirit of Germany by selling her
sons into the armies of the foreigner.

Information soon reached the colonists that a scheme
was on foot for effecting their subjugation by means of

a body of troops who did not speak their language, and who came from countries where the idea of liberty, as Anglo-Saxons understood it, was totally unknown. The tidings were everywhere received with surprise, indignation, and cruel anxiety. Those feelings were strongest in the quiet, well-ordered homesteads of the settled districts which, ever since the red man had retreated westwards, had been exempt from the terror of rapine, and conflagration, and outrage. It was indeed a grievous prospect for farmers who lived along the Hudson River, or to the east of the Delaware. The German officers, and a great majority of their men, might be respectable and law-abiding, in so far as military law was any protection to the inhabitants of a rural district which had been proclaimed rebellious; but a considerable percentage of the rank and file in some of the regiments was composed of refuse from all the barrack-rooms in Europe. The near future proved only too well that the apprehensions entertained by dwellers in the sea-board provinces were not exaggerated. A threatened invasion by alien mercenaries affected Americans not only as householders who trembled for their roof-trees, their orchards, and for the welfare and honour of their families. As citizens, also, and as politicians, they warmly resented the interference of foreigners in a national quarrel. Both in America and Great Britain, the struggle was regarded as a civil war; and such a war, odious under many aspects, has at any rate one thing in its favour. If honestly fought out, it affords a rough, but not inadequate, test of the proportions in which the public opinion of the nation concerned is divided on one side of a question or the other. It was already manifest that England was lukewarm; native Englishmen came but slowly forward to support in arms the cause of the Ministers; and for those Ministers to tempt Germany into the ring by preposterously lavish offers of English treasure was to play the game unfairly. Such was the view held by the colonists in 1775; and that view has ever since been taken by our own his-

torians. "The conduct of England," (so Mr. Lecky
writes,) "in hiring German mercenaries to subdue the
essentially English population beyond the Atlantic,
made reconciliation hopeless, and the Declaration of
Independence inevitable. It was idle for the Americans to have any further scruple about calling in foreigners to assist them when England had herself set
the example." [1]

So speaks the voice of posterity; but even then Lord
North and his colleagues had a foretaste of the condemnation which was ultimately in store for them. In February 1776 the treaties with Brunswick and Hesse were
communicated to Parliament. On the fifth of March
the House of Peers debated a proposal to countermand
the German troops, and suspend hostilities in America.
The question was moved by the Duke of Richmond, a
fiery and haughty nobleman, and a gallant soldier who
had distinguished himself at Minden; though indeed
that circumstance was not now a passport to the favour
of the Court. The Duke, setting scornfully aside the
charge that he was giving information to a probable
enemy, spoke openly about the undefended condition of
the kingdom, which he affirmed to be so notorious that
nothing remained to be concealed. He computed our
home force at seven thousand men; and when the
metropolis, and the three great arsenals of Plymouth,
Portsmouth, and Chatham, had been provided with the
ridiculously insufficient garrison of a thousand apiece,
only two very weak brigades would be left to meet an
invader in the field. Those were the circumstances
under which three out of every four of our regiments
were despatched across the Atlantic to conquer America;
with the prospect, if ever the conquest was effected, of
remaining there as an army of occupation and repression
until the end of time. But, even so, all the troops who
could be scraped together from every corner of Great
Britain and Ireland proved not enough for the task; and

[1] *A History of England in the Eighteenth Century:* chapter 12.

their efforts were to be seconded by a host of mercenaries, hired on terms so profuse as to humiliate our
nation in the eyes of Europe, and to excite the jealousy
of our own less favoured military people. It was all
very well, (Richmond argued,) for the ministers to assert
that they had the constituencies with them. The chief
support of their policy was not public opinion but private interest. The two most powerful men in the House
of Commons, whether they spoke much or little, were
Mr. Rigby and Sir Gilbert Elliot, the Paymaster of the
Forces and the Treasurer of the Navy. Their gains,
(so the Duke declared,) rose and fell with the amount
of money expended upon our fighting services; and the
measures pursued by the Cabinet would be the means of
procuring to both of them princely fortunes.[1] Those
gentlemen and their connections, with the whole race of
money-jobbers and contractors, formed no small part of
the so-called independent majorities which, within and
without the doors of Parliament, had precipitated the
country into a cruel, a costly, and an unnatural civil
war.

Richmond discoursed well, and he was ably and
stoutly backed. The Duke of Grafton besought the
peers to seize upon an opportunity for peace and reconciliation which, once lost, could never be recovered. He
assured the House, as he had every right to do, that he
had always been opposed to the coercion of America.
"I perceive in it," he declared, "nothing but inevitable
ruin. I contemplate it with the most pungent anxiety.
I turn my face from it with horror. These have been
my sentiments from the very beginning, and I have
uniformly acted conformably thereto. I have argued,
prayed, and implored that the wild and destructive project might be laid aside." The Earl of Shelburne drew

---

[1] Richmond probably exaggerated, to himself and his audience, the
gains of the Treasurer of the Navy. But Rigby would certainly have
raised up a princely fortune from the American war, had not his current
receipts, and indeed his stealings as well, gone mostly into the pockets of
his creditors.

a striking comparison between war which was unnecessary and unpopular, and war in which the nation had its
heart.   He reminded his hearers how, when Lord
Chatham was defying and discomfiting France and
Spain, Great Britain sent, first and last, more than four
hundred thousand of her own citizens into the camp and
the fleet.   And yet, so far from our trade standing still
for want of hands, the exports and imports increased at
a rate unknown during any former period.   But now,
when we were opposed to a million or so of our own
colonists, whom the Ministry described as cowards, it
was contended that, without ruining our manufactures,
we could not raise one-fifth part of the native force
which flocked to our standards half a generation ago;
and therefore we were reduced to run for succour to two
paltry German principalities as the only means of securing our political salvation.

Lord Camden, who had been Chatham's Attorney
General and afterwards his Lord Chancellor, contemptuously tore in pieces the theory that the treaties with
Germany were honourable international compacts,
founded upon considerations of reciprocal support and
common interests.   " To give this bargain," he said, " the
appearance of what it really is not, the whole is stuffed
up with pompous expressions of alliance, as if these
petty states were really concerned in the event of the
present contest between this country and America.
The transaction is a compound of the most solemn
mockery and gross imposition that was ever attempted
to be put on a house of parliament.   Is there one of
your lordships who does not perceive most clearly that
it is a mere bargain for the hire of troops on one side,
and the sale of human blood on the other; and that the
devoted wretches thus purchased for slaughter are mercenaries in the worst sense of the word?"   Lord Suffolk,
the candid man of the Ministry, who always addressed
the House of Lords in that downright conversational
style which the House of Lords prefers, did not concern
himself with the dignity either of the Landgrave of

Hesse or the Duke of Brunswick. "The Treaties," so he admitted, "are filled with high-sounding phrases of alliance; but I will be so ingenuous as to confess that the true object of these treaties is not so much to create an alliance, as to hire a body of troops which the present rebellion in America has rendered necessary." Those were the words in which an English Secretary of State, talking plain common-sense to his brother peers, shattered by anticipation the defence which in our own time a German writer has set up for those German rulers who traded in the lives of their people.

The oratory in the Commons was pitched in a lower key; but it was a discussion even more damaging to the reputation of the Government. The spokesmen of the representative Chamber were business-like and minute over a question into which finance so largely entered; and they would otherwise have been wanting to themselves and to their special function in the State. Lord John Cavendish ruthlessly scrutinised the details of the German contracts; and his criticisms went home to veteran Parliamentarians, who well remembered how thriftily, in the Seven Years' War, Frederic the Great had husbanded the modest contribution which was doled out to him from our Treasury for the promotion of high objects common to England and to Prussia. More good fighting, (so a famous authority has reckoned,) was got out of that poor six hundred thousand a year than out of any of the millions "which we have funded in that peculiar line of enterprise."[1] Lord Irnham warned the House of Commons that the old warrior of Potsdam had a tenacious memory; and that the very last thing he would be likely to forget was the manner in which, without due notice or decent apology, his British subsidy had been snatched from him at the moment when he was contending, almost without hope and against frightful odds, for his life and Crown. He would not fail to contrast that display of niggardly ill-will, which had so nearly been his destruction, with the prodigal terms that

[1] Carlyle's *Frederick the Great:* Book XVIII., chapter xi.

now were pressed upon the royal slave-drivers of Hesse and Brunswick.   In reference to those potentates, Lord Irnham, who had read "Don Quixote" to some purpose, quoted Sancho's wish that, if he were a prince, "all his subjects should be black-a-moors, as he could then by the sale of them easily turn them into ready money." Burke told the country gentlemen that it was not so long since the prime minister was beguiling them with a promise of obtaining from America a revenue which would relieve them from the land-tax. But now all pretence that the enforcement of the tea-duty was a profitable speculation for British tax-payers had been abandoned; and for every thousand foreigners whom we had taken into our service we were to spend as much as for fifteen hundred natives.   Colonel Barré commented on the circumstance that English manufacturers, in the dearth of orders, had looked forward to supplying uniforms for the Hessian Contingent as a set-off against the losses in which the war had involved them.   But that market, like others, was closed to them; inasmuch as the Landgrave had stipulated that every article of clothing and equipment should be made in Germany. The colonel went on to ask whether, if the auxiliary force was reduced to half its number by battle, pestilence, or shipwreck, the payments to the Hessian and Brunswick treasuries would be proportionately diminished; and the Secretary at War helplessly acknowledged that, until he had taken time to consider, he was not in a position to answer the question.

That reply gave some indication of the amount of forethought which had guided North and his Cabinet when they opened the flood-gates of expenditure. The division-list in both houses was affected by the wretched figure which the occupants of the Treasury benches had cut in the debate, and by the national jealousy which the German treaties aroused in the minds of a proud people, never very partial to a foreigner even when he is not feeding at their cost. Of peers actually present, three out of eleven went against the Government; and the Opposition, curiously enough, did exactly as well in the Commons.[1] But with that flicker of resentment the independence of Parliament, as applied to the question of national expenditure, for the present ended. Throughout the Session Ministers got their own way, and on most occasions got it very easily. Twelve thousand additional seamen were voted for the fleet, and the land force was raised to a strength of fifty-five thousand men. On paper, at any rate, the army was trebled by a single operation; the estimates for the fighting services were nearly doubled; and the price of Consols fell five points during the five opening months of the year 1776.[2] Such were the first fruits of those economies which were confidently promised when the methods, by which Chatham had induced America spontaneously to assist in the defence of the empire, were exchanged for the policy of compulsory taxation as propounded by George Grenville and Charles Townshend.

It was exactly what Burke had foretold. Months before the Session opened, he addressed to Lord Rockingham, and through Lord Rockingham to the Whig party, a letter of exhortation so eloquent that it might well have roused to arms even the garrison of that Castle of Indolence. "As sure as we have now an existence," he wrote, "if the meeting of Parliament should catch your Lordship and your friends in an unprepared state, nothing but disgrace and ruin can attend the cause you are at the head of. I protest to God that your reputation, your duty, and the duty and honour of us all who profess your sentiments, from the highest to the lowest of us, demand at this time one honest hearty effort, in order to keep our hands from blood, and if possible keep the poor, giddy, thoughtless people from plunging headlong into this impious war."

[1] Richmond's motion for an Address was supported by 29 peers, and opposed by 79, exclusive of Proxies. The Treaties were approved in the House of Commons by 242 to 88.

[2] The estimates for Army, Navy, and Ordnance were 3,879,264*l.* in 1775, and 7,541,049*l.* in 1776. The Funds were at 88 on the first of January 1776, and at 83 on the twenty-fourth of May.

That was no time, Burke urged, for taking public business as part of a comfortable, leisurely, scheme of life, mixed in with private occupations and amusements. The occasion was one which called for the whole of the best among them; and, above all, for Rockingham. America was his. He had saved her once, and now by taking action betimes, might very possibly save her again. If the honourable memories connected with the repeal of the Stamp Act did not move him, at any rate let him bethink himself how, only two years back, he had come up to Grosvenor Square, without waiting for the commencement of the London season, and had summoned his colleagues round him to lay their plans for defeating the proposal of an Irish Absentee Tax.

Human nature is not always at its highest level; and heroic sacrifices arise only from heartfelt motives. When their incomes were threatened by the Irish parliament, the Rockinghams did not shrink even from the hardship of living for the inside of a week in a town-house with the carpets up, and covers on the furniture. But when nothing worse was to be feared than a civil war, and two or three foreign wars to follow, they considered that the Newmarket meeting in October was a reasonable date for breaking up their establishments in the country, and coming South in order to learn what Burke wanted of them at Westminster.[1] Their lethargy was exasperating to clear-sighted patriots, and especially to such as had been in Parliament themselves, but were there no longer. " The Opposition," Horace Walpole wrote, "seemed to have lost all spirit. What little life there was, existed in the Duke of Richmond and Charles Fox." [2]

---

[1] " It may be worth your Lordship's consideration whether you ought not, as soon as possible, to draw your principal friends together. It may then be examined whether a larger meeting might not be expedient, to see whether some plan could not be thought of for doing something in the counties and the towns. The October meeting at Newmarket will be too late in the year ; and then the business of the meeting would take up too much time from the other." Burke to Rockingham ; August 23, 1775.

[2] *The Last Journals of Horace Walpole :* January 1776.

Vitality enough, of one sort or another, most certainly abounded in the last-named of that pair of kinsmen. The most industrious, in his own way, of political apprentices, he did not shape his existence after the precepts of the copy-books. He was seldom in bed before five in the morning, nor out of it until two in the afternoon; but into his fifteen waking hours he crowded a mass of great and almost continuous effort on behalf of the cause to which his life was now devoted. For that cause he was always at work, with a somewhat droll disregard of what others would consider to be the fitness of time and place. Though he was attentive, respectful, and nearly silent in company with Reynolds and Johnson over the classic suppers at the Club, he insisted that the companions of his lighter moments should take him on his own terms. Most of them had seats in one house of Parliament or the other; they were all worth convincing; and few among them in the end resisted the spell of the enchanter. Charles Fox had no notion of allowing his contemporaries, and, (where he could find such in politics,) his juniors, to have a will, or very many words, of their own about the American controversy. Haranguing and bantering, dominating and persuading, but never boring them, — since that was an effect which an otherwise bountiful Providence had made him constitutionally incapable of producing, — he soon formed around him a band of admiring comrades and declared adherents. In the Commons, meanwhile, he made himself more felt week by week, and session by session; even though he laboured under what to him was the unique disadvantage of dealing with an assembly which still professed to meet for the despatch of business at ten o'clock in the morning.

Tradition has handed down the wonderful impression caused by a single sentence which Charles Fox uttered in the debate on the Address in October 1775. Wedderburn, passing lightly over the circumstance that Boston was the only spot in the thirteen colonies where the

British flag still floated, had attempted to defend North as a war minister by drawing a parallel between him and Chatham. Speaking late in the discussion, as was usual with him for the most imperative of reasons, Fox accepted the comparison, and carried it further still. Not Lord Chatham, (he cried,) not Alexander the Great, nor Cæsar, had ever conquered so much territory in the course of all their wars as Lord North had lost in one campaign. A month afterwards Burke laid upon the table his bill for composing the differences between England and America. In view of so important an occasion, Fox appealed to Lord Ossory in a lofty and impassioned letter which is still extant, and brought over from the ministerial ranks that nobleman, and Richard Fitzpatrick with him. It was a notable testimony to their own disinterestedness, and to their young kinsman's powers of persuasion. For the two brothers were, indeed, connected by marriage with the Holland family; but they were nephews to Lord Gower, then President of the Council; — a relationship which held out to them a prospect of material advantages much superior to any that for many years to come could be expected from Charles Fox. Encouraged by that signal tribute to the effect of his personal influence, and with two voices more to cheer his oratory, Fox spoke, (according to the quaint version of the official reporter,) with infinite wit and readiness; carrying his finger along the whole row of ministers, and "happily marking the characters of each of them with a single epithet, with fine satire, and without the least breach of decorum."[1] And then, naming himself and Ossory as tellers for the Yeas, he collected in support of Burke a body of members larger by twenty-five per cent. than that which eight months previously the same statesman had been able to muster in the same parliament over the same question. And, on a Tuesday morning of the following February, Fox got himself roused and dressed in time to attend as soon as the House met, in order to move

[1] *Parliamentary History*, pages 991 and 992.

for a Committee to enquire into the Causes of the ill Success of His Majesty's Arms in North America. Ossory seconded the motion; Fitzpatrick supported it; and the three young fellows among them secured a division which showed that there was plenty of right sense and public spirit among the representatives of the nation, if only they were properly handled.[1]

But the tide of reaction was still running strong, in spite of all that individual effort could do to stem the flow. On the twentieth of November, 1775, Lord North brought in a bill to prohibit trade and intercourse with the thirteen colonies. The machinery of prohibition was drastic and simple; for it consisted in declaring that the property of Americans, whether of ships or goods, on the high seas or in harbour, was forfeited to the captors, being the officers and crews of His Majesty's vessels of war. The bill was combated in the House of Commons by a series of prophecies, every one of which in the end received exact fulfilment. Thomas Walpole, cousin to Horace, and nearly as infrequent and unwilling a speaker, belonged to a family whose members, whether they call themselves Whigs or Tories, have seldom remained for long together in antagonism to the dictates of reason and humanity. Walpole now admitted that he had begun by approving the policy of ministers: but his mind had been altered by the bad consequences of their earlier measures, and the results of this last proposal would be more calamitous still. The Americans would retaliate by admitting into their ports ships of other maritime powers, and would invite the foreigner to supply their wants; a proceeding, (he continued,) which would undoubtedly compel the British Government to seize property belonging to the subjects of other states, and so eventually involve the country in a disastrous European war. Lord George Cavendish, — who knew Lancashire well, and Yorkshire and the Midlands better still, — warned Parliament that manufactures

[1] The opposition voted 105 for Burke's bill, and 104 for Fox's Committee.

were already declining in almost every part of the king-dom, and that this bill, after it had become law, would throw above forty thousand hands out of employ-ment.

Towards the close of the debate a gentleman stood up who apparently had something which he was very much in earnest to say, and who accordingly was treated as an unauthorised intruder upon the attention of the House. But he was a West Indian merchant with so much at stake that he held his ground bravely amid a storm of jeers and exclamations. He bade those vociferous members, who were in such a hurry to have the ques-tion put, to bear with him until he had appealed to the Noble Lord on behalf of his estate which was going to be taken from him by this bill. If all trade, (he as-serted,) were stopped between our loyal and disloyal colonies, the West Indies would at once be ruined. For himself, he had in vain gone up and down the City of London, ever since it had become known that this scheme was in the air, offering a thousand guineas as insurance for his cargoes now at sea, until he could instruct his managers in Jamaica to ship no more of his produce on American vessels. And yet his own case, (so he explained,) was less desperate than that of his brother planters who were in residence on their estates. Many of them had the greater part of what they were worth in the world on board American ships, now on their passage to this kingdom. Long before informa-tion had reached them that it was expedient to insure their property against war-risks, the whole of that prop-erty would be captured and confiscated ; so that, as far as the interests of these poor people were concerned, " war might as well have been declared between Great Britain and Jamaica." When the nature of the bill had been made evident, several Honourable Gentlemen en-treated Lord North to postpone its further progress until the West Indian merchants then in town could lay before the House any information which they might judge to be necessary. The request was curtly and emphatically refused; and the Government was sustained in its inflexible attitude by overwhelming majorities.

The bill passed victoriously through all the stages; but, whether Ministers wished it or not, Charles Fox had to be heard; and heard he was. The most bigoted of his opponents were glad to listen, and the most impertinent would have been unable successfully to interrupt, while he spoke with the unpremeditated ease of private conversation, and all the charm and force of oratory. "I have always said," (such was the outline of his argument,) "that the war is unjust, and the object of it unattainable. But, admitting it to be a just and practicable war, I now say that the means employed are not such as will secure the desired ends. In order to induce the Americans to submit, you pass laws against them, tyrannical and cruel in the extreme. When they complain of one law, your answer is to pass another more rigorous than the former. You tell us that you have no choice in the matter, because they are in rebellion. Then treat them as rebels are wont to be treated. Send out your fleets and armies, and subdue them; but show them that your laws are mild, just, and equitable, and that they therefore are in the wrong, and deserve the punishment they meet with. The very contrary of this has been your wretched policy. I have ever understood it, as a first principle, that in rebellion you punish the individuals, but spare the country. In a war against a foreign enemy you spare individuals, and do your utmost to injure and impoverish the country. Your conduct has in all respects been the reverse of this. When the Boston Port Bill was under debate, I advised you to arrest and punish the offending persons. But you preferred to lay under a terrible interdict the whole population of Boston, innocent and guilty alike. And now, by the bill before us, you not only do your utmost to ruin those innocent men who are unfortunately mixed up with the guilty on the main-land of North America, but you starve whole islands of unoffending people who are separated from the rebellion by loyalty, and unconnected

with it by their political action and their political
sympathies."

It was common-sense, red-hot; and Ministers did not
venture to touch it except with the very tips of their
fingers.   In the speech which did duty for a reply to
Fox, Lord North disclaimed all intention of distressing
our sugar colonies.   If any provisions of the Bill should
injuriously affect the West India planters, he was sorry
for it; but as things were now circumstanced that danger could not be avoided.   In civil convulsions, it was
plain that many must suffer.   If this measure was a good
one, Parliament must take it with all the consequences.
It was absurd to object that it would inflict temporary
inconvenience and loss upon this body of men or that
island, on this interest or that industry.   Those were the
common-places with which the prime minister of Great
Britain excused himself for destroying the prosperity
of what were now the most valuable colonies which his
blundering policy had left to us.   Times had changed
since Sir Robert Walpole, standing on the same spot
of the floor, had expounded and vindicated the system
by which, during twenty years of peace, he fostered the
ever-growing commerce of the empire.

North's phrases did nothing to comfort those unhappy
West Indians who saw the produce of their estates trans-
formed by statute into prize money, to enrich Lord Sandwich's favourite post-captains.   The older and more
timid among the owners of plantations, who were victims
of this pitiless legislation, gave up the battle of life for
lost, and waited patiently and submissively for the day
when it should please their mortgagees to foreclose.
The bolder spirits diverted what remained of their capital into a line of business, the operators in which were
altogether independent of Acts of Parliament.   They
gratified their anger, and at the same time turned many
a dishonest dollar, by carrying on a contraband traffic
with the revolted provinces.   So far from the evil being
temporary, as North had assured the House of Commons, there were parts of the West Indies which all

through the war were at least as disloyal as Philadelphia, and much more deeply disaffected than Charleston or Savannah. As early as the spring of 1776 the Chief Justice of the Bahamas reported that the town of Nassau, in the island of New Providence, treated the royal Governor with contempt, and that things could not be worse if the place had been sold to the rebels. And in 1779 the Governor himself wrote to Lord Dartmouth as follows : " I lament exceedingly, my Lord, the necessity I am under in declaring to your Lordship that, since my arrival at the Government, I have been in a second Hell. The servants of the Crown, who are all engaged in carrying on an extensive and lucrative trade with the rebellious colonies, are now become the principal abettors." [1]

The course of the Prohibitory Bill through the Lords was rapid, and at first promised to be untroubled. Even the Duke of Richmond had informed his leader that, since British merchants had been so backward to support the Opposition in the country, he would not be at any pains to defend their interests in Parliament.[2] But he had not taken count of his own fervid temperament. A discussion was raised on the Second Reading by the Duke of Manchester, — a Montagu who did not, like Sandwich, forget on which side their common ancestors had stood when English liberties were in question at Westminster and at Marston Moor. Manchester moved the rejection of the Bill, and was cleverly answered by the nobleman who, as long as the memory of him lasted, continued to be known by the appellation of the wicked Lord Lyttelton. He belonged to a family in which such a pre-eminence is very easily earned. Though much less good than other Lytteltons, in his own generation he seems to have been no worse, and as regarded pecuniary matters considerably more prudent, than plenty of other lords. He saved all the money that he gained at cards ; a proceeding which, in the opinion of his contemporaries,

[1] *Historical Manuscripts Commission :* Fourteenth Report, Appendix, Part X., page 503.
[2] Richmond to Rockingham; Goodwood, Dec. 11, 1775.

was apparently almost as reprehensible as if he had won that money unfairly. His private morals were not blameless; but neither were they exceptionally scandalous when judged by the ideas of his time and class, and by the standard of the government to which he belonged. Lyttelton, at thirty years of age, and well outside the Cabinet, might plead the example of a Minister more advanced in life, and much more exalted and influential than himself; for the Earl of Sandwich, — who was far on in the fifties, and had no intention whatever of reforming when he got past sixty, — consorted openly with a mistress who, to the disgust of Lord Chatham's old admirals, did the honours, or dishonours, of the official residence at Whitehall. Nor, for the eighteenth century, was there anything particularly abnormal in Lyttelton's political record. When the Session commenced, as an independent peer, he had strongly condemned the Government measures; and now, as Chief Justice in Eyre of the Counties north of Trent, he defended those measures with the audacity of a recent convert. It was idle, he affirmed, to talk as if the trade of the West Indies was seriously threatened. Men of business held the opposite opinion. The borough of Bewdley in Worcestershire had expressed no uneasiness in view of the operation of the Bill; and Bewdley, according to his generous computation, produced a full twelfth part of our annual exports.

Lyttelton, as a Worcestershire land-owner, was influenced by the respect which a squire feels towards the chief commercial town in his own neighbourhood; but that circumstance did not excuse him in Richmond's eyes. Forgetting all about his grudge against the lukewarmness of the mercantile classes, the Duke sprang to his feet, and fell upon Lyttelton, and his market-town, and his political antecedents, and his recently adopted ministerial propensities, with an ardour which well became Charles Fox's uncle. "My Lords," he exclaimed, "I pronounce this bill to be fraught with all possible injustice. I do not think the people of America in rebellion. They are resisting acts of unexampled cruelty and oppression." There arose a frightful commotion. The peers, who supported ministers, shouted as if they were so many contractors and loan-mongers representing rotten boroughs in the Commons. The Earl of Denbigh stigmatised Richmond's words as treasonable, and their speaker as a traitor. Lyttelton rose once more, and eagerly assured the House that Cicero would have severely reprobated such licentious language. The Cabinet did not contain a Cicero, but they had always Sandwich with them; and Sandwich was ever ready with a Second, — or, if needed, a second-hundredth, — Philippic against the iniquities of the Colonists. The Bill, he confessed, might appear harsh; but it did nothing more than encounter cruelty with cruelty. For the Americans were a barbarous, as well as dastardly, people; and he could assure their Lordships that among other crimes they had put to death a negro of the name of Jerry, who was worth several hundred pounds.

The assembly was by this time in a state of wrath and excitement which few orators would have cared to face; but Richmond was not the man to be put down so long as he had a tongue in his head, or a rapier at his side. He spoke three times. He said straight out that he would not be intimidated, or deterred from his duty, by loud shouts or big words. He pretty plainly told Denbigh, who formerly passed for something of a Jacobite, that he, and such as he, were mighty poor authorities on a question of treason. The Duke had borne himself gallantly; but the aspect of Parliament was less reassuring than ever to the advocates of a peaceful settlement. A careful observer, not long afterwards, noted that the tone of the Government in the Lords had become much more aggressive than in the Commons; and that even in the Commons the language used by Ministers towards America grew more arbitrary, and menacing, as the Session proceeded. The friends of the Administration had changed their style; all notions of temporising were laid aside; and it was openly proclaimed that force was the remedy, and that any attempt at concession or compromise would only add to the difficulties of the situation.[1]

The most commanding preacher of this high doctrine was a public man of a very different stamp from Sandwich or Lyttelton. Lord Mansfield had now attained the culminating point of a career, splendid in personal success, and productive of vast benefits not only to his country but to mankind. That career, which was still far from ending, had begun so long ago that the earlier associations connected with his name belonged to what was already a classical period of English literature. Nearly forty years had passed since Alexander Pope had anticipated for William Murray a fame unsurpassed by the most admired orators of ancient or modern history; and twelve more years were still to run before Lord Mansfield, amidst unusual marks of affection and respect, vacated the Chair of the Lord Chief Justice of England. In that Chair, for a generation and more, he set an example not only to Judges, but to all servants of the State. There had been hardly a day when he was absent from his duties. He swept away the artificial system of procrastination, and consequent expense, which had broken the hearts of countless suitors. Whenever an important judgement was delivered, people flocked to his Court as eagerly as to the Strangers' Gallery in the House of Commons when a Chancellor of the Exchequer explains the Budget. Their expectation was seldom disappointed. The silvery tones, the dignified manner, the sparing but impressive gestures, which had so long charmed Parliament, were admirably suited to a judicial allocution. And the substance of Lord Mansfield's disquisitions was worthy of the vehicle. Before he retired into private life, he had completed the task of enlarging and defining the scope of the Common Law, and applying it to the infinite, and ever new, requirements of a rich and highly civilised community. Nor was his action confined to the more material and

[1] *Annual Register* for 1776; "History of Europe," chapter vii.

prosaic needs of his own and of coming ages. There are few notable principles of liberty, of humanity, of natural justice, and of supreme public utility, which were not aptly illustrated and immovably established in one or another of those celebrated decisions.

Lord Mansfield, who could not help being pre-eminent whether he was doing right or wrong, is the most conspicuous instance of the value of the maxim that a judge should not be a partisan. In his wise hour, no one was more profoundly convinced of that truth than himself. He three times statedly refused the Chancellorship; and that great office, (it is hardly too much to assert,) was always open to his acceptance from 1756, when Lord Hardwicke resigned the Seals, until Lord Thurlow assumed them in 1778. But, though he would not desert the King's Bench, Lord Mansfield long retained a hankering for political work and political influence. He sat in Cabinets; he presided over the deliberations of the Lords in the character, and with the salary, of their Speaker; for three months he was nominally, at any rate, Chancellor of the Exchequer; and, when party fighting grew hot, he frequently descended into the *mêlée*. But his heart was all the while set upon the due performance of his judicial functions. He could not give the requisite time and thought to affairs of State; and, if he had consulted his reputation and his self-respect, he would have abstained altogether from public controversy. Parliament after Parliament, while he still was in the House of Commons, he had held his own with William Pitt. But in the Lords his lifelong antagonist outmatched and overcame him; and on more than one occasion he was buffeted and flouted by adversaries, not despicable indeed, but far less formidable than Lord Chatham.

Mansfield, to please the Court, adopted quarrels so far from just that he came to them, not thrice-armed, but equipped with an altogether incomplete and ineffective legal panoply. And, (what was even more unfortunate,) his senatorial action was of a nature to impair his authority, and cast suspicion on his fairness, as a Judge. Through all the miserable business of the Middlesex election, the Ministry were continually endeavouring to punish in the law-courts those opponents by whom they had been out-argued in the newspapers. Oppressive prosecutions of publishers and printers in the King's Bench alternated with angry, and sometimes undignified, debates in the House of Lords; and Mansfield too often had to pick his way back out of the tumult with his composure ruffled and his ermine soiled. His fame suffered, and his comfort was sorely disturbed, by attacks compounded in deadly proportions out of truth and calumny by the infernal skill of Junius. Before 1775 that storm had been finally laid, and the Lord Chief Justice was again in calm water. But the American question then became acute; and ministers felt themselves so weak in the House of Lords that they could not dispense with the assistance of their doughty ally. That assistance was given by Lord Mansfield without stint, and with no thought for the consequences to his own reputation and popularity. His advice to his countrymen, — as the mature fruit of his wisdom and experience, — was that they should decline the friendly advances of Congress, and rely, for the recovery of their American colonies, upon force, and upon force alone. On the third reading of the Prohibitory Bill he bore the main burden of debate. He summed up his argument in an anecdote which soon ran the round of England and America; and able opponents of the Government in both countries took care to extract, out of what was at best a most unlucky utterance, the utmost amount of horror which it was capable of yielding. The relations of the mother-country and the revolted colonies, (so Lord Mansfield declared,) recalled to his mind an address made by a general of Gustavus Adolphus to his soldiers on the eve of battle. "Pointing to the enemy, who were marching down to engage them, he said: 'My lads, you see those men. If you do not kill them, they will kill us.'"

CHAPTER XIV

SIR GUY CARLETON IN CANADA. HOWE'S ARMY

THOSE were the terms on which, in the view of Lord Mansfield, the armies of Great Britain went forth to reconquer her thirteen provinces; for nothing short of a reconquest the undertaking would have to be. In King's Speeches His Majesty was still made to talk about "my colonies," and "my subjects in America." He might just as well, (so an Opposition journalist remarked,) have spoken of "my kingdom of France." Whatever words his advisers put into his mouth, George the Third understood, more fully and much sooner than any of them, the reality which he and they had to face. He discountenanced their tattle about American cowardice. He awakened them sharply out of their Fool's Paradise, and forced them to follow him into a course of vigilant and unsparing toil. In a surprisingly short space of time his energy had created the means of grappling with a task the dimensions of which his insight had promptly recognised. His fleets conveyed to the scene of action a host more than twice as large as that which Philip the Second of Spain placed on board the Great Armada. In 1775 the Secretary at War had informed the French Ambassador that three columns of attack, amounting· in all to between forty and fifty thousand men, would converge upon the centre of the rebellion from Boston, New York, and Canada. Boston, now in the hands of the enemy, could no longer be reckoned upon as a base of operations. The invading force which marched in the summer of 1776 was, indeed, not less strong by a single soldier than Lord Barrington had anticipated; but it was in two divisions, instead of in three; and the Southern portion, on which the brunt of the work fell, was more readily handled, and far more formidable, when acting as an undivided army under the personal superintendence of one and the same general.

The Northern expedition was commanded by General Guy Carleton, the Governor of Canada. His record as an officer was better than fair. He had been placed to the front at the capture of Quebec, of the Havannah, and of Belleisle on the coast of Brittany; and he was wounded on each of those three notable occasions. Carleton had learned to fight in Pitt's war; and he was taught something even more important than the art of soldiering by a close observation of Pitt's policy. In that age of slow travel, and precarious communications, it was a distinct public advantage that, at critical times and in distant regions, the civil and military authority should be in the same hands; if only those hands had the right sort of head and heart to direct them. Carleton was a sagacious, and a very good, man; and his goodness and wisdom together, when all else was lost, preserved Canada to the empire.

If anything could by any possibility be accurately foretold in war and politics, it would have seemed most unlikely that England should succeed in retaining the district north of the St. Lawrence at a time when the English-speaking provinces, for whose sake and by whose aid we had wrested that district from France, were in open and hot insurrection. So far were the Canadians from speaking English that not four people in a thousand talked anything except the old seventeenth century French which had been brought across the ocean in the days of Frontenac and La Salle; — the French which may be heard in Canada still. [1] The

---

[1] "*Lord North.* Does the General know the proportion of old subjects to those of new ones in Canada ?

General Carleton. The Protestants in Canada are under 400; about 360; but the French inhabitants, who are all Catholics, amount to 150,000."

Examination of General Carleton before the House of Commons in Committee : June 2, 1774.

country was intensely Catholic. Very few books were read; and those few had certainly not been written by Voltaire. The priests were respected and powerful, as their character and conduct merited; and by far the most important factor in Canadian politics was the goodwill of the Bishop. A land system on lines of strict feudality was everywhere in force. The seignior held his estates from the Crown, and granted them to his vassals on condition of a fixed and moderate annual payment. The vassals were bound to grind their corn in the seignior's mill, to bake their loaves in his oven, and to hand over to him every tenth salmon which they caught in his waters. This population, with nothing Anglo-Saxon in its composition, and which even the peasants of rural La Vendée would have regarded as behind the times, was ceded to Great Britain by the Treaty of Paris in 1763, and soon found itself in strange conditions. The British governed Canada with equity and benevolence, but after a fashion sadly wanting in imagination, and altogether incomprehensible to their new subjects. A constitution was granted, in principle more liberal and democratic than that enjoyed by England and Wales then; or, indeed, in one respect than that enjoyed now; for the payment of tithe to the clergy was no longer enforced by the State. French Civil Law was superseded by the Common Law of England, enriched with all Lord Mansfield's most recent improvements. A Court of King's Bench was set up, and a Court of Common Pleas, in both of which the proceedings were in the English form. The people were emancipated from the liability of being imprisoned under *lettres de cachet*, — a danger that had never greatly disturbed them; and they obtained trial by jury, which they heartily abominated.[1] Above all, Canada received the inestimable boon of self-government, in the shape of

---

[1] "*Mr. Mackworth*. Did they disapprove the trial by jury?

General Carleton. Very much. They have often said to me that they thought it very extraordinary that English gentlemen should think their property safer in the determination of taylors and shoemakers than in that of the Judges."

a parliament from which no one was excluded who had taken the oaths of Allegiance and Supremacy, together with the declaration against Transubstantiation. As may well be believed, it was a parliament that never met; and the administration was carried on by the Governor, with the co-operation of an executive Council, the members of which the Governor himself selected and nominated.

The outward semblance of British institutions was accompanied by the substance of British public spirit and financial probity. Canada, as a dependency of France, had been the prey of corrupt officials. It was a country, as Montcalm bitterly acknowledged, where all the knaves grew rich, and true men were ruined. But administrative honesty came in with English rule; and the effects of that salutary change were all the more visible because Canada, almost for the first time in her history, enjoyed real and stable peace. The French Government had treated the province as a military outpost, and its people as the garrison. In seed-time or in harvest, — when the creeks were swarming with fish, and choice fur was selling at Albany or Boston almost for its weight in silver,[1] — the farmers and trappers who lived within the French border were torn from their occupations, and marched off to fight along the Alleghany and the Susquehanna, or to spend winter after winter huddled into forts and blockhouses in regions even more remote from their homes. There was no respite from their involuntary toils and perils. Even during those rare intervals when war was not declared between the mother-countries, French and English settlers were constructing earthworks, and planning

---

[1] An English officer wrote from Montreal in 1777: " Caprice and novelty has made these furs more or less in fashion. That they are so with a witness, the enormous price your sister gave for a muff and tippet is a convincing proof. Here they are very dear: the commonest fur cap standing you in two guineas." Beaver skins ruled high ; and sables ranged between four and twelve guineas. Even with regard to the more common sorts a Boston merchant reported in 1774, " Red Fox are at thirty-five shillings ; Minks at thirty-three shillings and ninepence." The letter is among the papers of Mr. Russell Sturgis, privately printed at Oxford.

ambushes, and getting each other scalped and toma-
hawked, in the valley of the Ohio. The Canadians had
been military colonists every whit as much as the Cos-
sacks of the Don, with a far less acute enjoyment of the
situation; but, as soon as they became British subjects,
that period of storm and stress was over. Thenceforward
on the Continent of America there was no one for them
to fight, unless they themselves thought fit to get up a
rebellion.

Not the least important contribution to the security of
the province was the firm and temperate attitude which
the British Government maintained in dealing with the
primæval inhabitants of the American wilderness. The
history of Canada, for the first two centuries, was red and
lurid with the periodical outbreaks of that ill-used and,
(whenever it found an excuse for misconduct,) most ill-
conditioned family of mankind. French villages were
laid in ashes, and French Missions delivered over to torture and murder under circumstances which, in the estimation of their Church, qualified the victims for the
honours of martyrdom. But the English authorities,
while they did not neglect military precautions, endeavoured to acquire the confidence of the Indians, and inspire them with an interest in the preservation of order.
The red man was placed in safe possession of his hunt-
ing-grounds; and private adventurers were effectually
restrained from practising on the fatal facility for divest-
ing himself of his property which beset him when within
scent of a whisky-cask. So commenced, (as a local historian truly remarks,) that just and honest policy towards
the Indians which has ever since been followed by the
government of Canada.[1] The signs of improved administration soon became apparent on the surface of society.
Trade and agriculture revived, and by the end of ten

[1] This observation is made by Mr. J. Bourinot, Honorary Secretary of
the Royal Society of Canada. "Lands," Mr. Bourinot writes, "could be
alienated by the Indians only at some public meeting or assembly called
for that special purpose by the Governor or Commander-in-Chief where
such lands were situated."

years had reached an amazing development. **Nothing** was wanting except some reasonable concession to that national sentiment the due recognition of which conduces, even more than commercial prosperity, to the establishment of national happiness and tranquillity.

When Carleton had resided long enough in Canada to have thoroughly mastered the needs of the province, he returned to England, and applied himself to the task of indoctrinating the Ministry with his own broad and sound views. That process demanded a much more protracted leave of absence than he had originally contemplated; but he comforted himself by reflecting that he was better employed when furthering the interests of his colony in London than if, (like Governor Bernard and Governor Hutchinson,) he was undermining those interests in despatches written on the spot, and filled with abuse of the people over whom he had been appointed to rule. In the spring of 1774 Carleton's opportunity came. Ministers were then engaged on the penal laws directed against the town of Boston and the colony of Massachusetts; and Carleton persuaded them to insert into that batch of vindictive and provocative measures a bill framed with the object of conciliating Canada. His advice was all the more readily adopted by the Court party because the proposed enactment was intensely offensive to the prejudices of New England. The bill "for making more Effectual Provision for the Government of the Province of Quebec" relieved Roman Catholics from all tests whatsoever, save and except the oath of Allegiance. The clergy of the old religion were permitted to conduct their worship in freedom, and to claim "their accustomed dues" from such persons as professed their creed. Questions of property, and of civil rights, were to be decided according to French legal procedure; while criminal cases were reserved for the English law. It was a rational distinction. The Criminal law of England, severe as it then was according to our modern notions, at all events excluded the use of physical torture, — or of that moral torture, almost more perilous to the innocent, which has not yet disappeared from investigations conducted by French tribunals.[1]

Other provisions of the bill were more open to damaging criticism. The Canadian parliament was abolished; if that can be said of an assembly which never had a corporate existence. Law-making was entrusted to a Legislative Council appointed by the Crown; and the boundaries of the Province were extended to the Ohio and the Mississippi. The whole area covered by what are now the States of Michigan, Indiana, Ohio, Wisconsin, and Illinois was converted into a Crown Colony arbitrarily ruled from Downing Street. Such was the condition to which it was the intention of North and Sandwich to reduce a vast region, which had before it an unlimited future of progress and civilisation. But this part of the scheme existed only on paper ; and, in order to turn it into a concrete fact, many thousand reams of that commodity would have to be burned in cartridges.

The Quebec bill had faults; but the main plan was strongly conceived and boldly filled in. From among the truculently impolitic laws, by which it is surrounded in the Statute-book, it stands out as the work of states-

---

[1] In 1834 Macaulay went to India, for the purpose of drawing up that Penal Code which has met with acceptance and approbation from our leading jurists. In his cabin, on the way out, he studied and annotated with minute care Baron Locré's treatise on the Civil, Commercial, and Criminal Legislation of France. "I believe," Macaulay wrote on the margin of the seventh chapter, "that the commercial law of France, like that of England, was in a very good state before the Revolution. It required not to be amended, but to be consolidated and digested."

It was, however, very different when he came to the portion of the book relating to the Criminal procedure of old France ; — to the secret inquisition ; the refusal of legal assistance to the accused ; the power, in many cases, given to judges of arbitrarily allotting to the criminal any punishment which they chose ; and, above all, the horrible nature of the punishments, (as Locré describes them,) "the pincers, the melted lead poured into the wounds, the wheel, and the furnace." Those paragraphs are freely scored with such pencil notes as "Odious!" "A most absurd practice." "Altogether detestable!" Locré introduced into his text a rather misty anecdote about a compliment paid to the French Criminal law, at the expense of England, by a personage entitled Le Grand-Juge d'Angleterre. "What Grand-Juge?" Macaulay wrote. "Our penal code is bad enough; but Monsieur le Baron Locré is an ass."

men, and not of policemen. The speakers of the Opposition, naturally but most unfortunately, were not in a mood to discriminate between what was good, and what was bad, in the ministerial recommendations. They threw in their lot with the three or four hundred English people scattered throughout the province, who assumed to themselves the invidious title of "old subjects," and who clamorously insisted that the civil and ecclesiastical vestments of Canada should be cut according to English pattern. In order to enlist the sympathy of Nonconformists against the bill, the Whigs raised, feebly and unsuccessfully, a cry of No Popery; — that ill-omened watchword which, in after days, was often employed for their discomfiture by opponents who understood, better than they, the art of turning national passion to political account. So high did party spirit run that the most respected adherents of Rockingham and Chatham resorted to this unworthy device. Before the debates on the Quebec Act finally closed, the Peers were treated to the astonishing spectacle of Lord Camden being impressively and most properly rebuked by Lord Lyttelton. The principles of the bill, (that eminent moralist contended,) emanated from the Gospels, and breathed the spirit of early and unadulterated Christianity. They were principles not, as Camden had averred, of Popery and servitude, but of toleration unfettered by odious restrictions. It was a great and judicious measure; calculated, by the beneficence of its aspect, to remove those rooted prejudices which were carefully instilled into the minds of all, who had at any time been the subjects of France, against the laws and the institutions of England.

Having secured the Quebec Act, General Carleton hastened back to his province, and made his preparations for meeting the storm which was soon to break. He had only a handful of troops; but that want was more than counterbalanced now that he possessed the means of assuring the fidelity of the civil population. He at once proceeded to place eight Roman Catholics upon the Legislative Council. He arranged that the members should be at liberty to debate either in French or English, and that the ordinances which they framed should be published in both languages. He had acquired the warm co-operation of the Bishop, and the confidence and support of the seigniors; greatly to the annoyance of the nobility in France, who favoured the American Revolution, and thought it a very fine thing that all men should be born free and equal so long as it was not in their own hemisphere. The merchants and large shop-keepers of Quebec, who alone among the British inhabitants of the province had much to lose, dreaded an invasion, and were quite prepared to fight for the protection of their property whenever Carleton should give the signal. American patriots had great hopes of the French farmers; and, if those hopes had been well founded, it would have mattered very little how the rest of the Canadian population had felt and acted. The Congress at Philadelphia issued a spirited address, calling upon the tillers of the soil to assert themselves against the aristocracy, and appealing to the immortal doctrines taught by Montesquieu and Beccaria. But in a community where there was only one printing house, and that an English one, those great names had no meaning for anybody except the priests; and the priests feared and suspected the French political philosopher less indeed, but not very much less, than they detested the Italian philanthropist. The mass of the rural people adored their clergy, and had no quarrel with their seigniors. The most obtuse and inobservant peasants had already learned that a feudal superior, under British rule, would have to be exceedingly careful lest any well-founded complaint should be made of the manner in which he exercised his privileges.[1]

[1] The very able author of the "History of Europe," in the *Annual Register* of 1776, acknowledges the anti-American attitude of Canadians, both French and English, frankly but rather reluctantly. The event completely stultified many predictions made during the discussions in Parliament by that political party to which the writer belonged.

Armed with his new Constitution, and as yet with little besides, Carleton made head, as best he could, against the American invasion. The earlier exploits of the colonists were conducted with energy, and crowned with almost uniform success. In the May of 1775 Ticonderoga, the key which locked the chain of lakes running north and south between the Hudson and the St. Lawrence, had fallen before them as easily as Jericho fell to Joshua; and, in the early autumn of the same year, a column of two thousand militia marched to the attack of Canada.[1] The expedition was led by Richard Montgomery, who was of good Irish birth, and whose excellent abilities, and singularly loveable nature, had been refined by a liberal education. He served under Wolfe with credit, while still a lad; and he had but lately attained the good military age of five-and-thirty, — no small advantage for a general whose enemy had to be sought, at the cost of infinite toil and hardship, on the further side of an almost pathless wilderness.

Montgomery made his way through marsh and thicket, against violent headwinds on Lake Champlain, and amid treacherous rapids as he descended the Sorel river. At length he arrived before the fort of St. John's, which blocked the water highway at a point some twenty miles to the southeast of Montreal. The English general attempted to raise the siege, but was badly beaten; and on the third of November the place and the garrison were surrendered to Montgomery. Carleton, by one stroke, was deprived of more than half the regular troops whom he had at his disposal. The gateway of his province was beaten in. Eleven British vessels, with crews and stores on board, fell into the hands of the Americans. Montreal was occupied without resistance; the approaches to Quebec were beset by the enemy; and the royal Governor with difficulty contrived to enter his own capital in the darkest hour of the night, and dressed as a peasant.

---

[1] At the end of this volume will be found a map of the country between Quebec and Albany, adapted from Marshall's *Life of Washington*, published at Philadelphia in 1807.

One solitary reverse befell the invaders; and even that was something of a blessing in disguise to their cause. Among Montgomery's colonels was Ethan Allen, who had captured Ticonderoga in the name of the Great Jehovah. On the strength of that achievement he obtained a detached command, and took the earliest opportunity of falling upon the British in true Old Testament style. His projected operation, in the outline of the plan, and the numbers and distribution of the assaulting force, bore a curious resemblance to the enterprise of Gideon; but the event was different. The larger of Allen's two bands did not appear at the appointed time and place; and he, together with his own small following, was made a prisoner. His part in the Revolution, memorable and serviceable as it had been, was played out. The tidings of his misadventure affected his military superiors with something very like a sense of relief. It would have been far from easy for Washington to find Ethan Allen employment which would both suit and satisfy him, now that the war had got to a stage altogether beyond the tactics of the Book of Judges.[1]

Meanwhile danger was advancing upon Canada from another quarter. Washington had despatched from the camp before Boston a detachment of picked soldiers under the guidance of Benedict Arnold. Arnold was a New Englander, well born, and most certainly well seasoned. During the course of a wandering life, he shot in a duel a British captain who had sworn at him for a Yankee. The unfortunate officer was in the right, if only he had expressed his opinion in more becoming language; for Arnold was abundantly endowed with the restless vigour, and variety of resource, which marked

[1] Mr. Bancroft, who seldom bears hardly on a celebrity of the Revolution, admitted that Allen was dazzled by vanity and rash ambition. Washington made known his opinion in very plain words. "Colonel Allen's misfortune," he wrote to General Schuyler, "will, I hope, teach a lesson of prudence and subordination to others who may be too ambitious to outshine their general officers, and, regardless of order and duty, rush into enterprises which have unfavourable effects on the public, and are destructive to themselves."

the race of men bred between the Hudson and the sea.
When fifteen years old he ran away from home to fight
the French on the northern frontier.   Disgusted with
military service, — for some unknown motive, which may
have been anything except dislike of the smell of
powder, — he returned to New England, having traversed the intervening forest without a companion.   He
made his living as clerk in a store, then as a shop-keeper,
and afterwards as a foreign merchant who sailed as his
own supercargo.   After the Revolutionary war had
broken out, Arnold never missed an occasion for show-
ing the stuff of which he was made.   He was as impetuous a forward fighter as Marshal Ney; and he was
destined to an even more terrible fate.

With a courage proof against all the trials and labours
of war he started on an expedition compared with which
Montgomery's advance upon St. John's was a holiday
parade.   His route lay up the Kennebec, down the
Chaudière, and across the rugged and savage uplands
which separated the sources of the two rivers.   The
fallen timber of centuries had choked the channels; and
the water-shed was deep in snow.   Provisions failed.
The travellers soon became barefoot, and their clothes
were torn off their backs by thorns.   They towed their
little boats up to the waists in water.   They retraced
some sections of their march three or four times over in
order to bring up the baggage of the party, and their
sick and dying comrades.   After the first six weeks
they subsisted on roots and berries, and the game which
they could make shift to snare or shoot.   They had
hauled the barges by sheer strength of arm up a hundred and eighty miles of current, and had carried them
across forty miles of broken ground.   They started
eleven hundred in number on the nineteenth of September.   On the nineteenth of November Arnold, with
six hundred and seventy-five men who had come through
the journey alive, selected a position on the St. Lawrence, eight leagues above Quebec, and there awaited
the arrival of Montgomery.

On the third of December Montgomery came to the rendezvous, bringing with him a force which the exigencies and losses of the campaign had reduced even below what Arnold could muster. But heroism is independent of numbers; and the siege of Quebec at once began. There was a hero on both sides of the wall. Carleton, though brave as a lion, passes among writers for an indifferent strategist. He was, however, a justly popular ruler and a most capable organiser; and the state of affairs was such that his special qualities and aptitudes now came splendidly into play. He had with him a poor three hundred red-coats; if that name can be applied to soldiers who had worn their uniforms in those latitudes, and at that season, through months of frightful weather and almost continuous disaster; but his humane and dexterous policy had united the whole population of the city and the neighbourhood in ardent support of the British cause.[1] He landed five or six hundred seamen and marines, and allotted them their posts in the circle of the defence; and he enrolled about as many French Canadians, together with every English burgess who was not too young, or very much too old, to carry a musket. The Americans assaulted Quebec on the night which divided the years 1775 and 1776; but they found the English awake and expecting them. Montgomery was killed; Arnold fell severely wounded; and three or four hundred of the assailants remained as prisoners in the hands of the garrison.

Arnold, with a leg disabled, was worth more than an average general who had every limb whole. With a remnant of dejected American minute-men, and a few hundred Canadian allies who had begun to perceive that they had thrown in their lot with the losing party, he maintained a front such that he imposed respect on Carleton, and kept up the appearance of an effective

---

[1] "With respect to the better sort of people, both French and English, seven eighths are Tories, who would wish to see our throats cut, and perhaps would readily assist in doing it." Colonel Hazen to Major-General Schuyler, from Montreal, April 1, 1776.

investment of the city. He was joined erelong by several detachments of militia, who marched to his support in considerable numbers from New England, from the Jerseys, and from Pennsylvania. They were bent on avenging Montgomery and eradicating the last vestige of British rule from the soil of their Continent; but they paid a heavy toll, in life and health, along the road to Canada; and, on reaching their destination, they found themselves in a scene of disease, destitution, and misery. The American army was wasted by small-pox; the French inhabitants would bring in no supplies that were not paid for in ready money, and of ready money there was none left; while in the magazines there remained something over one hundred-weight of gun-powder, and provisions for a very few days. General Thomas, — marked out for preferment on account of his having superintended the occupation of Dorchester Heights which decided the event at Boston, — had been appointed by Congress to the command in Canada. On the first of May, 1776, he arrived at the camp before Quebec, and ascertained that, of the forces which Arnold and Montgomery had brought, and of the militia who had come northward since, there remained less than two thousand men, of whom half were in hospital, and all on the brink of starvation.

Before another week was out three English ships of war, the first swallows of the military summer, forced their way through the ice on the St. Lawrence, carrying reinforcements which enabled Carleton to take the offensive. He sallied from the gates with six field-pieces, and two strong columns of infantry; whereas three hundred men were the utmost that General Thomas could succeed in concentrating from his ex-tended and denuded lines. The Americans fled, leav-ing behind them all their artillery, and a large number of their sick. These poor people were sadly anxious about the treatment in store for them, and crept from bed to search for a hiding-place. But Carleton, who had his own ideas of the spirit in which policy demanded that a civil war should be conducted, issued a proclamation inviting them to come and be nursed in the city, and promising that they should have liberty to return home as soon as they were sufficiently recovered to undertake the journey.[1] General Thomas, closely pursued for many miles, continued to retreat until he reached the town of Sorel, where the river bearing that name discharges itself into the St. Lawrence. The fortune of war had turned decisively; and those denizens of the country who were not stable and convinced politicians, but who liked fighting both for its own sake and for what they could get by it, now chose their side in grim earnest. A force composed of Indian warriors and French hunters and trappers, with a small nucleus of British regulars, beat up the American quarters to the west of Montreal, and captured nearly five hundred prisoners.

A transient gleam of hope brightened the darkness which had begun to settle down upon the prospects of the invaders. Washington, sorely grudging, had sent to Canada three thousand of his best infantry under the orders of General John Sullivan. A countryman of Montgomery, Sullivan was the best of good fellows, and a partisan true and tough as blackthorn; but in some respects he was not the most valuable sort of Irishman. While fighting under Washington's personal supervision he was an effective, and, indeed, a splendid officer; but it was otherwise when he acted on his own account at a distance from his chief. One of those fatal generals with whom America has been cursed in every war which she has ever waged, he was too loyal, too bustling, and too popular to be passed over where it was a ques-

---

[1] Carleton's Order, dated Chamblé, August 7, 1776, ran thus: "All prisoners from the rebellious provinces, who chuse to return home, are to hold themselves in readiness to embark on a short notice. The Commissary, Mr. Murray, shall visit the transport destined to them, to see that wholesome provisions, necessary cloathing, with all conveniences for their carriage, be prepared for these unfortunate men. They are to look upon their respective provinces as their prison, and remain there until further enlarged."

tion of a separate and independent command; although
the operations for which, in that capacity, he was responsible never went quite right, and sometimes resulted in
egregious failure. The troops whom Washington had
despatched reached Sorel on the fifth of June, 1776.
Three days previously General Thomas had died of the
small-pox; and Sullivan assumed the command with a
sense of exuberant enjoyment. The right man for the
place, if ink won battles, he at once proceeded to relieve
the heart of his overburdened chief by imparting to him
his own cheerful reading of the military and political
situation. "I have no doubt," he wrote, "of the general attachment of the Canadians, though I suppose
some unprincipled wretches among them will appear
against us. I find by their present behaviour that the
only reason of their disaffection was because our exertions were so feeble that they doubted of our success.
But the face of affairs seems to be changed. They
begin to complain of their priests, and wish them to be
secured. I shall, however, touch this string with great
tenderness, as I know their sacerdotal influence."

It was an epistle of the kind which poor Washington was fated often to receive from certain of his lieutenants. Himself the most modest and matter-of-fact
of very great men, he became the unwilling confidant of
as enormous an amount of extravagant and bombastic
writing as ever found its way into official correspondence. He endured the infliction always with imperturb-
ability, and, (where he knew the writer to be honest,)
almost angelic indulgence. On this occasion, as in
duty bound, he forwarded Sullivan's despatch to Congress, with a covering letter which placed in the most
favourable light that general's qualifications for the
command of the American army in Canada. But the
army was in Canada no longer. Sullivan had been in a
hurry to impress upon the French inhabitants that, (as
his letter put it,) the day of feeble exertions was over.
But he studied his ground badly. Carleton was already
very strong, and became stronger week by week, as

reinforcements successively arrived from England, Ireland, and Germany. The British front had been advanced to the village of Three Rivers, only five-and-twenty miles from Sorel; although the St. Lawrence, widened into the lake of St. Peter, lay between the two places. Sullivan sent an expedition to surprise the post; but General Fraser, who was in charge of Three Rivers, had been warned of what was coming, and was in very much larger force than his adversary knew. The surprise went the inverse way from what had been intended. The Americans were completely routed ; and, as under those circumstances people will, they tried to make up in words for what they had come short in deeds. A letter written by one of them, some days after the engagement, speaks of it as an agreeable piece of news. Only a score of the colonists had fallen, while vast havoc had been made in the British ranks. A chaplain, who claimed to have stood by and viewed the whole scene, said that the slaughter was as great as at Bunker's Hill.[1] But according to Carleton, who was a very unlikely man to falsify a return, only about a dozen of Fraser's people were dead or disabled. The American brigadier, and two hundred of his troops, remained in British custody; the rest of them made a very undignified withdrawal; and, if the colonists had as few killed and wounded as they said, it was far from a matter for boasting.

Sullivan took the repulse very seriously. " I now," he wrote, " think only of a glorious death, or a victory obtained against superior numbers." But on the fourteenth of June the English fleet, with Carleton's army on board, moved up the river under full sail ; and the American commander had the good sense to see that yet a third alternative was open to him. He broke up his camp, and retreated homewards, never reposing until he was behind the lines of Crown Point, at the further extremity of Lake Champlain, some ten or twelve miles to the north of Ticonderoga. The pursuit was languid ;

---

[1] *American Archives ;* letter of June 12 from St. John's.

but the sufferings of the colonial militia from disease, and want of food, and utter destitution of everything which makes fatigue and exposure tolerable, were appalling.   During the remainder of that summer Crown Point was a charnel-house.   Thirty new graves were dug daily ; and it was reckoned that, in little over two months, the American army of the North had lost by desertion and death more than five thousand men.[1]

That army, had the British been able to push their success home, would not have escaped defeat, or rather dissolution ; for power of resistance it had none.   Carleton was amply provided with troops, if only he could have conveyed them without let or hindrance direct to the point where victory awaited him.   The ardour and industry of George the Third had placed in the hands of his general material means, plentiful enough to have satisfied even a monarch who was going to command his army himself.   Brigadier Riedesel,[2] with the contingents from Brunswick and Waldeck, landed at Quebec on the first of June ; in time to present himself, attended by the whole body of his officers, at the levée which the Governor held on the King's birthday.   The ranks of the British regiments were full, and the soldiers in high health and buoyant humour.   The train of artillery was thought to be the finest that ever had been sent from England.   It was commanded by General Phillips, a shrewd veteran who, according to mess-room tradition, split fifteen canes on the flanks of his

[1] The British, as they urged the pursuit of the retreating army, were acquainted with the plight of their enemy.   A soldier in the advance-guard, who later in life turned historian, wrote thus : " They were encumbered with great numbers labouring under that dreadful disease, small-pox, which is so fatal in America.   It was said that two regiments had not a single man in health : another had only six, and a fourth only forty; and two more were nearly in the same condition."   *An Original and Authentic Journal of Occurrences during the late American War*, by R. Lamb, Late Sergeant of the Royal Welsh Fuziliers ; Dublin, 1809.

[2] It is on record, — as indicating the British soldier's small acquaintance with the language of his allies, and the difficulty he must have found in profiting by their conversation, — that our rank and file habitually pronounced the Brunswicker's name as " Red Hazel."

draught-horses when he was bringing up the guns at Minden. The best of the Canadian militia flocked to the standards of a chief who had inspired them with a sincere loyalty, and a sense of civic dignity and self-respect not altogether to the taste of our subalterns.[1] The Governor had been forced by peremptory orders from London to arm and employ Indians : but he steadily refused to commit his own and our national honour to their more than questionable keeping. He maintained control over each tribe through a trusty agent of his own selection ; and an American writer, who does not love the English, has adjured history to preserve the fact that, though often urged to let savages loose upon the rebel provinces, in his detestation of cruelty General Carleton would not suffer a single one of them to go on a raiding expedition across the frontier.[2]

Carleton increased his power on land by drawing freely on the complements of the ships which lay in the St. Lawrence. A strong detachment of the Royal Marines served in his army, under the command of their own officers, as was the custom throughout that war. A major of the corps had ordered the first shot to be fired at Lexington ; and many thousand cartridges were bitten by the men before the struggle ended. For George the Third, at such a crisis, was not inclined to leave as good an infantry as any in Europe pipe-claying belts, and eating rations, in their barracks at home. Moreover his admirals in America knew better than to strip the fleet of its scientific naval officers and trained mariners, and send them up country for the purpose of fighting as musketeers. And so it came to pass that the

[1] "The women are extremely lively, goodnatured, and obliging, and very neat in their persons, but have not the least pretentions to beauty. The men are far from agreeable ; for, since they have enjoyed the blessings of an English Government, they are become insolent and over-bearing. When they fancy themselves offended their cry is, ' Je vais le dire au Général Carleton.' " Those are the observations of a newly arrived British officer, whose remark on the looks of Canadian women shows that he was in a hurry to generalise from insufficient data.

[2] Bancroft's *History of the United States*, Epoch III., chapter 52.

Royal Marines were allowed a chance of proving what they could do, and had the full credit for it after it was done, just as much as if one of their generals had been sitting at the Board of Admiralty to see that they got fair play in whatever part of the world guns were firing.

The British sailors, however, were not excluded from the joys and dangers of the campaign. Carleton gave them plenty of the work for which they were professionally adapted. The real cause of the delay in his forward movement was that the forest presented an impenetrable barrier to invaders who had not the command of Lake Champlain; — an inland sea, extending seventy miles from north to south. It was impossible to take craft of any considerable burden up the turbid and broken stream of the river Sorel; and a small gang of ship-wrights was accordingly collected at St. John's, which was situated well above the Rapids. Sheds and slip-ways were extemporised; carpenters from the men-of-war were told off to assist; and the little dockyard was soon as busy as Sheerness. An eighteen-gun vessel had been brought in separate pieces from England, and was put together then and there. Five brigs and schooners mounting between them forty-four cannon, a score of gun-boats, and two hundred and fifty armed or unarmed barges for the transport of troops, were constructed on the spot, or hauled up the cataracts by dint of almost incredible exertions. Those prodigies of labour were executed by men and officers of the Royal Navy, in a spirit of contagious jollity which extended its influence beyond their own service, and, (as it has often done before and since,) contributed largely to assure the success of the conjoint expedition. Nor was that all. "Two hundred prime seamen from the transports," (so an English post-captain testifies,) "impelled by a due sense of their country's wrong, did most generously engage themselves to serve in our armed vessels during the expedition. Nor has any man of this profession uttered a single word of discontent amid all the hardships they have undergone; so truly patriotic are the motives by which they are actuated." [1]

The patriotism which takes the form of content and self-suppression cannot be said to have been universal in a camp that contained the prime grumbler of the British army; for Burgoyne was second in command. When the time came, as before long it did, for everyone to have a fling at him, his enemies disseminated a report that he had treated Carleton with the same disloyalty as he had exhibited towards Gage. The charge was probable, but has not been proved. It came mainly from Lord George Germaine, who himself hated Carleton, and habitually did his utmost to injure him in the estimation of their Sovereign. But no whisper from a minister, — or no extract, culled and copied from the letter of a disappointed general beyond the seas, if such indeed reached the royal eye, — could affect the King's approval of his wise and faithful servant. Grateful to Carleton for his recent services, George the Third made adequate and intelligent allowance for his present difficulties. He assured Lord North of his satisfaction with the reasons given for postponing the commencement of an aggressive campaign. Disregarding Lord George Germaine's attempts at dissuasion, he made the Governor of Canada a Commander of the Bath, (a much rarer honour in those days than in ours,) and pleased himself by sending out the red ribbon in charge of the new Knight's own wife, together with a special warrant authorising him to bear the title, and wear the ensigns, even though the King's sword had not as yet touched his shoulder. By the end of September 1776, all was ready to Sir Guy Carleton's mind; and he commenced his stately and leisurely progress towards the south at the head of twelve thousand effective soldiers, perfectly disciplined, carefully exercised to fight in the woods and row their flotilla along the lakes, and abundantly provided with all the appliances of war.

[1] Letter from Captain Douglas of the *Isis:* October 1776, *American Archives.*

Meanwhile our principal army, and the larger portion of our transatlantic fleet, had been despatched to the middle colonies in order to strike at the heart of the rebellion. General William Howe continued to command the land force; while the naval operations were entrusted to his elder brother, Richard, Lord Howe, whose past had been as honourable as his future was glorious. Over and over again, for the best part of two generations, Richard Howe was found exactly where his country most wanted him. In June 1754, — a young post-captain, who already knew how a gun-shot felt, — he captured a French battleship in the Gulf of St. Lawrence, after saluting her with the first broadside that was fired in the Seven Years' War. At Quiberon Bay, in a battle which ranks with the victory of the Nile, he was named by Hawke to lead the British squadron into action; and, though his ship was out-sailed by some of her consorts, when once she got among the enemy she was out-fought by none. In October 1782 he relieved Gibraltar, almost under the guns of a great fleet exceeding his own by thirteen sail of the line, and gained a triumph which, all the more because it was bloodless, maintained the reputation of British seamanship at the level to which, after a period of depression, it had been raised by Rodney in the preceding April. And as his crowning service, on the first of June 1794, Howe broke the sea power of the French Republic. Those were some of the achievements which secured to him a fame and a popularity lasting over an extraordinarily protracted period of our history. In 1740 he had been taken from Eton to accompany Lord Anson on his celebrated voyage; and, well into the nineteenth century, young Englishmen of unusual manliness and dash were still known in the Navy, and in India, by the appellation of "Howe's Boys." [1]

Such was the man who, on the twelfth of May 1776, sailed from St. Helen's to conduct the naval campaign

[1] Kaye's *Life and Correspondence of Charles Lord Metcalfe;* Vol. I., chapter 5; letter of January 18, 1805.

against the insurgent colonists. He was now a Viscount, having succeeded to the title when his elder brother, as fine an officer as himself, was killed at Ticonderoga in 1758. Lord Howe thought ill of the Ministry, and especially of Lord George Germaine, with whom he had been on bad terms ever since they took part together in a calamitous expedition against the coast of France. He regarded the conflict between Great Britain and her colonies as a civil war, in which Britain was in the wrong. In conjunction with Franklin he had endeavoured to arrange conditions on which harmony might be restored; and perhaps he would have attained his object if Lord Dartmouth, who favoured that meritorious attempt, had been as bold and outspoken as Lord Sandwich, who was bent on wrecking it. Howe took up his command with a sore heart and an uneasy conscience. He was profoundly affected by the circumstance that a junior officer, whose courage he had proved, and whose judgement and character he highly valued, respectfully pleaded political convictions as a reason for declining an invitation from his old chief to serve on board the flag-ship. Howe allowed it to be known that he would not have gone out as an Admiral unless he had otherwise been invested with the functions of a negotiator. He, and General Howe, were nominated as special Commissioners "to treat with the revolted Americans, and to take measures for the restoration of peace with the Colonies." But the powers conferred upon the brothers were limited to the point of nullity, and almost of absurdity. Lord Howe, who had deceived himself into a hopeful frame of mind, was not many weeks in American waters before he had been driven to recognise that the pacific side of his mission was little better than a farce.

The younger of the two brothers came to the scene of action furnished with much more potent arguments for bringing the colonists to terms than any which the Letters Patent appointing him a Peace Commissioner permitted him to use. Simultaneously with General

Howe's embarkation at Halifax, large armaments con-
verged upon New York from various quarters of the
compass. He brought in his train the former garrison
of Boston, which in itself was an army. These troops
were not, like Carleton's, flushed with victory; but they
were angrily and proudly conscious that, though forced
to abandon the post which had been committed to them,
they had never been defeated in battle. In the same
temper, very dangerous to an opponent, the seven regiments, which had been foiled at Charleston, came from
the Carolinas under the leadership of Clinton and Lord
Cornwallis. Three thousand Highlanders had been
shipped at Glasgow; a fourth part of whom were
captured at sea by the American privateers.[1] Some
battalions came direct from English ports, and some
from Ireland. They were closely followed by two
divisions of Hessians, nine thousand strong, which,
though not of uniform quality throughout, comprised
the flower of the foreign contingent. During the
voyage the Germans complained of parsimonious diet
and bad accommodation, and especially of the light and
scanty blankets which were in painful contrast to the
feather-beds they had left behind them in the Fatherland. But they were in excellent health. The food
supplied by contractors was no worse, and more plentiful, than what they had been accustomed to in the
Cassel barracks. Their pay continued to mount up
whether they were well or sea-sick; and the discomforts
of ocean travel only increased the satisfaction which
they felt in the near prospect of placing their feet upon
solid soil.

Taken as a whole, it was a most efficient army.
The weak point in the British military system was the
impossibility of ensuring that the best man, or even
a fairly good man, should command a battalion. How

---

[1] The crews of our transports, when the enemy appeared, had refused
to defend, or even to handle, their ships; and, after the sailors had gone
below, the Scottish soldiers had made a gallant but, from the nature of
the case, a hopeless resistance.

great and wide-spread was the evil may be gathered from the condition of two regiments belonging to the comparatively small portion of Howe's army which was drawn from Ireland. "I am extremely concerned," (so the Commander-in-Chief at Dublin wrote to the Lord Lieutenant,) "that no purchaser can be found for Lieutenant Colonel B——'s commission; for, besides his infirmities, I have his own word, added to the testimony of other people, that he is mad. Since I began this, the Colonel of the seventeenth regiment has been with me, humbly requesting your Excellency's permission to dispose of his Lieutenant Colonelcy. I never saw the gentleman before; but he is in a most wretched state of health, overcome with the gout, and barely able to walk. He protests that he has been about to sell these three years, and that he shall only be put on board ship to die." [1] Such instances constantly occurred at every succeeding outbreak of hostilities; and the authorities at the Horseguards, who were not devoid of human feeling, found it no easy matter to deal with them. Duty came in a cruel shape upon a Commander-in-Chief when he was forced to compel an old brother officer with a large family, who had invested in his Commission all his property and a good deal of borrowed money besides, to make a forced sale in a market which had gone entirely to pieces, as the Commission market always did in time of war.

Even when a colonelcy was vacant, it did not necessarily fall to an officer whom the regiment knew, and who had served with it in the field. The Guards bore numerically a much larger proportion to the rest of the army than at present; their lieutenants ranked as captains, and their captains as lieutenant-colonels; and the social position and private means of those gentlemen enabled them at every successive opportunity to make the most of their advantages. During the early months of 1776 this grievance of the unprivileged sought expression in the newspapers. "The rise in the

[1] General Irwin to Earl Harcourt, September 1, 1775.

Guards," (one letter runs,) " is so rapid, from the suppression of the ranks of Lieutenant and Major, that
officers of the Line have always the mortification to
find, after long and painful service, a body of men who
supersede them in their profession, and claim most of
the elevated posts in the army. When the road seems
smooth to a regiment, an inundation of captains in the
Guards, by dint of Court rank and etiquette of pre-
cedency, defeat all the prospects of the actual soldier,
and trample on a life of dangers and fatigues." Junius,
who knew our War Office from the inside, computed
that the number of commissioned officers in the Guards
were to those of marching regiments as one to eleven;
but that the number of regiments given to the Guards,
compared with those given to the Line, were as one to
three.[1]

England, perhaps, never entered upon a great
military enterprise with so large a supply of men
qualified by standing and experience to lead her battalions. "The two last wars," wrote General Burgoyne,
" have filled the army with excellent officers from the
year 1743. The military science, which in the course
of the long peace had degenerated into the tricks of
parade and the froth of discipline, has been attentively
considered both in theory and practice; and to the
honour of the cloth be it said that there are few sets of
officers now to be met with where an ignorant man
could converse upon his profession without exposing
himself." That passage referred to a period so far back
as 1761; and the intervening fifteen years had made
havoc with the veterans of Dettingen and Fontenoy.
But, when fighting began in 1775, there were many
officers above the rank of lieutenant, (and, where a man
was poor, too often still in that rank,) who had served
under Ferdinand of Brunswick and Lord Granby in the
Seven Years' War; and in that war British valour was
guided by the minute and well-considered precepts of

[1] *London Evening Post* for February 1776. Author's note to the
Letter of Junius of December 19, 1769.

Prussian discipline. The strategy of our generals in the American campaigns is instructive to military students by warning rather than example; but, when it came to tactics, it is abundantly evident that the officers of our regiments, and our brigades, were at home in all the details of warfare. Arrangements for the march and the bivouac, for out-posts and scouting, and for the supply of food, forage, and ammunition, worked smoothly and, to all appearance, automatically. Our light dragoons gave close attention to their less showy, but not least important, duties. They were always to the front, and on the flanks, in an advance ; and, whenever general operations were suspended, they shot forth on excursions, searching the country far and near, and harrying and bewildering the Americans who, north of the Potomac at least, were no great horsemen. The essential routine of battle was admirably understood in our army. Cavalry charged at the right moment, and halted before rashness had converted a success into a disaster. Infantry were taken into action over ground reconnoitred with as much care as time permitted, and in a formation promptly and almost instinctively selected out of several which had been made familiar beforehand by frequent practice; and, when the task was beyond their strength, the coolness and method of the retreat was seldom, if ever, allowed to degenerate into a rout.

Our line regiments were officered from the less wealthy, and more hardy, section of a rural aristocracy. The sudden and recent influx of opulence, which had done so much to foster corruption in politics, and luxury in fashionable society, had not as yet penetrated to our smaller land-owners. A cadet of good family, whether the younger son of a squire, or the eldest son of a parson, (who in the nature of things was seldom an eldest son himself,) very generally lacked the means of buying his way into the upper grades of the army. Hopeless of arriving even at the threshold of high military advancement, men of this class loved their profession all the more because they loved it for itself.

Renouncing, in many cases, all hope of marriage, they looked upon the regiment as their home, and grew old in uniform. Coming of a strong-natured and whimsical race, in a century when men were never ashamed of being themselves, they not unfrequently, as years increased upon them, acquired a marked, and somewhat quaint, individuality. Great readers, many of them, during the break between one war and the next, their favourite authors were those in vogue at a time when a scholar was a man who understood Greek and Latin. If one of them took up his pen in a military controversy,—and very sensible letters they often wrote,—he would sign himself in the newspapers as "Valerius," or "Postumius"; or as "Cincinnatus," in case he had retired on half-pay. When discussing professional topics, they drew most of their illustrations from the same classical sources as those to which Fluellen resorted; but in them, as in that Welshman, there was much care and valour. The object of their life was the efficiency and the reputation of their regiment. They were sincerely respected by the subalterns, from whom they did not exact undue and unwilling deference. "Any restraint upon conversation, off parade, unless when an offence against religion, morals, or good breeding is in question, is grating; and it ought to be the characteristic of every gentleman neither to impose, nor to submit to, any distinction but such as propriety of conduct, or superiority of talent, naturally create." Those were the formal and punctilious phrases in which Burgoyne, himself the model of a field-officer, described the tone of a good English mess room containing a major and half a dozen captains who had served in Germany.

Nothing was allowed to interfere with good fellowship, and with a theory of the social equality that ought to exist between one gentleman and another; and yet the authority of a military superior, when he judged fit to exert it, was not to be trifled with. A lecture from a colonel or general was a rare occurrence, and was couched in language suited to a state of society when offence was easily taken and quickly resented; but those who listened to it knew that it meant business. [1] Kindly and tolerant towards their younger comrades, these old officers did not confine their friendliness to the commissioned ranks. They looked after the wants of the men, and were mindful of their feelings. They treated the sergeants and corporals, who frequently had been as long in the regiment as themselves, as their elder brothers at home would behave to old and trusted family servants. That was their course of life until, — with such limbs as the French cannon, and the uncompromising surgery of an heroic epoch, had left to them, — they settled down, on an income counted by tens of pounds, under a very humble roof beneath the elms of their native village.

Howe's army contained a noble specimen of this class of officer. To Colonel Enoch Markham, as the brother of an archbishop, promotion came in less stinted measure than to some; but he earned all the gifts which fortune bestowed upon him. He was forty-nine years old at the opening of the campaign, throughout which

[1] General Phillips of the Artillery had the character of understanding to perfection how a thorny matter should be handled. Some subalterns of his corps, stationed at Montreal, had been dining with a Canadian gentleman, whose daughters were pretty, and whose wine was only too good. Before the entertainment had been concluded, the guests became so impertinent that the host next morning made a complaint to the General, and threatened, unless redress was granted, to set off to Quebec, and lay the case before Governor Carleton. Phillips, at his next levee, desired the officers of the artillery to remain after the rest of the company had departed. "I do not," he said to them, "know who has been guilty of such conduct. I am sure it could not have been any of the young gentlemen; for certainly their persons and address, when they solicit the fair, would have ensured them success. I neither know who the officers were, nor do I wish to be informed; but let me advise them, when they next approach the ladies, to pursue different means, as they may rest assured that those which they have adopted will never succeed. I only desire that I may never hear more of such complaints; nor need I suggest to those gentlemen, who are conscious of being concerned, that it is compatible with their characters to make an apology to the father of the young ladies." The General's advice was taken; and the affair ended without either a duel or a court-martial, and apparently to the satisfaction of everybody concerned.

he was sedulously attentive to the comfort of the troops, and neglectful of his own. "There being," he wrote in January 1777, "a plentiful scarcity of everything here, it is with difficulty that I continue to live. If it was not for my faithful old soldier-servant, I should starve. He answers the character of Sterne's Corporal Trim. He is a charming figure for a porter at a great man's gate, or for a Yeoman of the Guard." Colonel Enoch continued to serve in America until the end of the war, with the highest character for personal courage and patriotic disinterestedness. At different times he was entrusted with a brigade, and occasionally had a separate command. He was supposed to have given offence to those above him by refusing to accept Secret Service money, "with an understanding, then too prevalent, that it was fair perquisite, and never to be accounted for to the public." We are told that "some singularities appeared in his character; but all tending to his honour. When at the head of his regiment on a march, he always made some tired soldier ride his horse, and marched through every kind of bad ground, and partook of every awkwardness of situation that his men were exposed to. His cool courage, and contempt of personal danger, were almost proverbial in the army. On one occasion, when under a heavy fire, he heard talking in the ranks. He turned his back upon the fire, commanded silence, and harangued the men upon the discipline of the Lacedæmonians." Upon another occasion his regiment, while advancing amid a shower of bullets, was brought up short by a wooden fence. Colonel Markham coolly and deliberately went up to the palings, pulled at them, and found that they might be forced. After the action, some of his officers represented to him the imminent danger to which he had exposed himself unnecessarily, as he might have sent a private upon the same service. He answered with warmth: "Good God! do you suppose I would send any man on a service of danger where I would not go myself?" Having at last been badly wounded, (and no wonder,) he was sent, by way of a health-resort, to the island of St. Lucia between Martinique and Barbadoes, where the heat of the climate brought on a dangerous illness which necessitated his retirement from the army. " He passed the rest of his life at a lodging in Lambeth, seeing very much of the Archbishop ; " — a good sample of the sterling material which made the strength of our country in the eighteenth century.[1]

The war was not popular among the rank and file of our army. There was the certainty of one voyage across the Atlantic, and the remote prospect of another for those of them who were strong enough, or lucky enough, to see the business through. It may confidently be asserted that no one has profited more by the great discoveries of modern science than the British soldier. An ambitious military man, who followed his opportunities of distinction in sailing-ships all the world over, spent more of his time on deep water, and was much more likely to terminate his career beneath it, than an officer of the Royal Navy in an age of steam. The army officer, indeed, had the worst of both professions ; for the merchantmen, which were provided to carry him from one scene of duty to another, were the very refuse of our trading fleet. The toils and perils of a campaign were to him less formidable than the hardships, the delays, and the disappointments of the voyage, — the preliminary weeks spent in the Channel, waiting for a wind inside the Solent, and sighting the Lizard on the day that he had hoped to find himself off New York ; the horrors of a gale between the decks of a crowded unseaworthy bark, with no employment or responsibility which would take his mind off the imminent danger and the ineffable discomfort ; and, in an interval of calm, the tedious round of an everyday existence which combined all that was most odious on both elements. Idleness and disgust

---

[1] The particulars relating to Colonel Markham are drawn from an unpublished history of his family ; which was kindly, and indeed generously, lent to me by Sir Clements R. Markham, K.C.B., F.R.S.

gave rise to scandals and court-martials, and to quarrels about precedence, where precedence meant the title to a cabin not quite so wretched as others, and the power of shifting quarters on board a less ill-found vessel. An officer actually fought a duel on his way out to America, was severely wounded, and had time to be cured before he arrived in port. A good commander would keep his people occupied, by setting the soldiers to shoot at a mark for prizes, and encouraging the subalterns to make up the leeway of a scamped and, (in the best of cases,) an unfinished education. But the most resourceful and unselfish of colonels or majors could do little for the health and happiness of the privates. Fetid water, kept in wine casks that never had been properly cleansed; poisonous beer; biscuits alive with maggots; beef that had been left over from the voyage before last; and, what was worse than all, (kind-hearted as they were,) the sight of their suffering and dying horses, and of their comrades swallowing the rust of the anchor-stock in brandy as a specific against the miseries of dysentery; — those were the circumstances which gained for a transport the name of a floating Hell.

Nor, in the anticipation of soldiers who left England in the spring of 1776, was it a Paradise towards which they were journeying. Letters from the garrison of Boston had been read aloud in the barrack-rooms, which depicted in very dark colours the hardships awaiting them on the further shore. They were going to a land of plenty; but the plenty was not for them. The ration of a British private, they were told, was less than half a pound of salt bony pork, and no vegetables whatever. He had to pay twenty pence for cheese, and fourteen pence for old rancid Irish butter, at a time when the rebels, outside the town, were buying large pigeons at fourpence a dozen, and the best butcher's meat at three half-pence a pound; while turkeys and roasting pigs were thrown into the scale together, and sold at the same price. This story was sent to England by a grenadier of Marines, who had been recalled to the regiment from his employment as porter in a warehouse. He had cried, (he said,) ready to break his heart for going on that damned service, instead of against the French and Spaniards.[1] But there was, in most cases, no hanging back from the call of duty. The Guards set a good example. A battalion of a thousand had been formed for service in America, by picking fifteen men from each of their sixty-four companies. The officers left at home their spontoons, and the sergeants their halberts. All ranks carried firelocks, and knew how to use them. For some time past they had been "practising with a rifle-gun in Hyde Park, against a small target three hundred yards off," — at an hour in the morning, it is to be supposed, when the citizens and their families had not yet come out to take the air. Towards the end of March they were reviewed by the King at Wimbledon, and moved off the Common in the direction of Portsmouth, taking with them a score of field-pieces, and the whole of their baggage succinctly packed into thirty waggons.

Our forefathers were accustomed to see expeditions go forth without those manifestations of enthusiasm which a French military writer has described, and deprecated, as "les ardeurs du départ."[2] The troops were allowed to leave the country very quietly; but they fought none the worse on that account. They were hard fellows, bred for the most part in rural districts; at home among horses, and better shots than the gentry of their neighbourhood either desired or approved. Many of them were in the habit of stalking game and wild-fowl over the unenclosed and undrained tracts which still covered so wide a surface of our island. Not a few had been poachers, — a circumstance to which, (as afterwards in the Peninsula and at Waterloo,) captains acquainted with the personal history of their companies attributed, in some considerable degree, the

[1] Letter in the *Evening Post*, January 1776.
[2] General Trochu's *L'Armée Française en 1867*, chapter xix.

deadly effect of the British fire.[1] Subsequently to their
arrival in America the troops were carefully instructed
to shoot, not only at a target, but in skirmishing order
among the ravines and thickets.   The next five years
tested and ascertained the warlike capabilities of our
race. For the colonists, after one twelvemonth of disorder and of very frequent defeat, were drilled and
organised up to such a point that they ever afterwards
met the regulars on an equality in the open field ; while
the British, from the very first, plunged vigorously into
a course of forest warfare against a community of hunters and backwoodsmen.   Our people, wherever and
whenever they met the enemy, often secured, and always
were bent on obtaining, victory ; and they never ac-
quiesced in a repulse, or even in a drawn battle, until
their list of killed and wounded bore impressive testimony to the efforts which they had made to avert discomfiture.

Howe's army, if the different sections could have been
united at the beginning of the campaign, would have
amounted to about thirty-five thousand men. " This
force," (so wrote a contemporary historian of high
merit,) " was truly formidable, and such as no part of the
New World had ever seen before.   Nor was it, perhaps,
exceeded by any army in Europe of an equal number,
whether considered with respect to the excellency of the
troops, the abundant military stores and warlike materials, or the goodness and number of artillery of all sorts
with which it was provided.   It was, besides, supported
by a very numerous fleet, particularly well adapted to
the nature of the service." [2]   Both fleet and army were
due to the recent exertions of the King, rather than to

[1] A similar cause largely contributed to the early victories gained by
the French in the wars of their Revolution. In the first armies of the
Republic the skirmish-lines swarmed with gamekeepers whom the aboli-
tion of feudalism had deprived of their employment, and with poachers
who,(ever since the fall of the Bastille emboldened them to work by day-
light,) had killed down all the game, and whose occupation was gone.

[2] The *Annual Register* for 1776 ; chapter v. of the "History of
Europe."

the pair of improvident ministers in charge of the War Office and the Admiralty. If things went well, the credit would accrue, not to Sandwich and Barrington, but to their royal master, and to the Secretary of State for the Colonies. Lord George Germaine, according to Selwyn, seemed in very great spirits, and quite persuaded that the first campaign would end the war, and establish, or, (if people liked that expression better,) re-establish his own reputation. For the present he had something to endure; because, when he took part in a parliamentary debate, "the Ghost of Minden was for ever brought in neck and shoulders to frighten him." [1] But Germaine, in his duel with Governor Johnstone, had stood opposite the most redoubted pistol in the House of Commons; and he did not feel himself bound to fight twice, and still less a dozen times over, in exactly the same quarrel; just as Daniel O'Connell reserved to himself the liberty of accepting or declining a challenge, when once, to his lifelong regret, he had killed his man.[2] Jack Wilkes and Alderman Sawbridge might talk about Minden till they were hoarse, for all that Germaine cared. He looked for his reward to higher quarters. George the Third did not bear his minister any grudge on account of an incident which was ancient history; and about which, in the royal opinion, more than enough had been said already. The King took no interest in the reminiscences of the Seven Years' War. The glory derived from that celebrated struggle belonged to Frederic the Great, whom he neither understood nor liked, and to Lord Chatham, whom he cordially detested. But this war was all his

[1] George Selwyn to Lord Carlisle: December 8, and 12, 1775.

[2] London opinion upon Lord George's conduct in his quarrel with Governor Johnstone is expressed in a letter from William Whitehead to Lord Nuneham of the twenty-second of December 1770. The Poet Laureate was somewhat more at home in prose than in verse. "The Minden affair, at so many years distance, has been got the better of by the drawing of a trigger. The Grecians and Romans, whom your Lordship has been reading of so much of late, did not deal in duels. They murdered and assassinated heroically; but they thought exposing themselves to any danger in defence of their country a sober, serious, honourable thing."

own. He was in sympathy with the policy which led
to it. He, and none else, had provided the means for
carrying it forward; and he now, with quiet and dignified confidence, waited for tidings of victories which
would place America at his feet.

CHAPTER XV

CONGRESS.   THE REVEREND WILLIAM GORDON.
THE PROVINCIAL GOVERNMENTS

THE statesmen of the Revolution, assembled in Congress at Philadelphia, looked forward to coming events less complacently than did the resolute and self-reliant prince who, even according to their own admission, was still their sovereign.   Within a few months, at the latest, they would have upon them a hostile army, strong in numbers and discipline, and backed by the entire resources of a stable and well-ordered empire. It was true that in Great Britain opinion was very far from unanimous; but opposition to the government policy went no further than speeches in the two Chambers, and epistles signed by one or another ancient Roman in the newspapers.   Valens, and Curio, and Decius and Marcus Brutus, might threaten North with the fate of Strafford, and might solemnly remind a shuddering public that there was such a date in the calendar as the Thirtieth of January.   But George the Third knew perfectly well that his parliamentary majority was good for several sessions; and that, if ever the Rockinghams came into office, the very last thing about which they would trouble themselves would be the impeachment of their predecessors, or the punishment of their monarch.   He and his ministers might continue to levy men and money with assured impunity so long as they kept within the letter of the constitution, however little they might respect its spirit.   Even in a shire where three freeholders out of five were against the war, the land-tax was paid to the last farthing; the militia-ballot was peaceably conducted in the

Moot Hall of the county-town; and the press-gang
gathered in the maritime population of the sea-ports at
the cost of a few more broken heads than usual. The
best of England's own citizens arraigned in words the
justice of her cause; but, when it came to deeds, she
presented to the contemplation of her rebellious children the same unbroken front which had been so often,
and so impressively, displayed before a foreign enemy.[1]

The case was different across the ocean. Political
power, so much as there was of it, rested in a collection
of individuals who called themselves a Congress; as
they might have called themselves a House of Commons, or an Assembly of Notables, or, (if they were so
minded,) a Witenagemote. With less inherent authority
than a parish vestry, — for legal standing they had
none, — they issued recommendations to those of their
countrymen who were ready to accept their advice;
they lectured the British Cabinet with every circumstance of publicity; and they treated secretly with
foreign Courts which were rejoiced to see that Cabinet
in a scrape, and were willing to do much in order to
keep it embarrassed and enfeebled. Congress then,
and for many years after, was described by John
Adams as "not a legislative assembly, nor a representative assembly, but only a diplomatic assembly."[2] No
central authority existed in America. The local governments of the separate provinces were responsible for
the ordinary course of civil administration; and those
governments, so far from being legally and duly constituted, were not constituted at all.

[1] "It really appears to me that administration will proceed to such ex-
tremities as will terminate in the ruin of England and the colonies. It is
a capital mistake of our American friends to expect insurrections here.
There is not a shadow of hope for such an event. . . . It is said most
vigorous measures will take place in the Spring, if no offer be made on
the part of the colonists." Letter by Samuel Curwen, the loyalist, from
London; August 8, 1775.

[2] *A Defence of the Constitutions of Government of the United States of
America;* by John Adams, LL.D., and a Member of the Academy of
Arts and Sciences at Boston. London : printed for C. Dilly in The
Poultry ; M.DCC.LXXXVII.

The provincial Charters were now waste parchment. The old constitutions had perished; and in their place was anarchy, tempered by the common-sense and public spirit of the citizens. It has been said, by those who love definitions, that the end and object of human institutions is to get twelve honest men into a jury-box, and a rogue into jail. But here was a community without judge or juryman, constable or turnkey. Society could not have held together unless the colonists had been a law-abiding people, or rather a people who abode in reverential observance of a law which for the time was extinct. But the population never existed whose principles of morality could long be proof against such a strain. An event befell John Adams, trifling in itself, which threw him into a reverie tinged by profound melancholy. He met on the road a common horse-jockey, against, or in behalf of, whom he had often appeared in court; for the man had been always at law, and for the most part in the capacity of a defendant. " As soon as he saw me, he came up to me, and his first salutation was; 'Oh! Mr. Adams, what great things have you and your colleagues done for us! There are no courts of justice now in this province; and I hope there never will be another.' 'Is this,' said I to myself, 'the object for which I have been contending? Are these the sentiments of such people? And how many of them are there in the country?'"

That occurrence took place in the fall of the year 1775; and things were soon in the way of mending. Many far-sighted, and all hot-headed, patriots were eager to see the day when their country should declare herself an independent nation. America could not put forth her full strength at home, or acquire allies on the Continent of Europe, as long as Americans were content to style themselves subjects of the British Crown. Most interesting were the communications which, during that period of suspense and incubation, passed between members of Congress and their leading supporters in the provinces. James Warren, the President of the

Massachusetts Assembly, thus addressed one of his representatives at Philadelphia. "The sentiments of our
colony are more united on this great question than they
ever were on any other. Perhaps ninety-nine out of
one hundred would engage with their lives and fortunes
to support Congress in the measure. There is little left
to do but the form and ceremony; but even that is important." General Charles Lee wrote as follows to
Richard Henry Lee of Virginia. "The pulse of Congress is low. If you do not immediately declare for
positive Independence we are all ruined. There is a
poorness of spirit, and a languor, in the late proceedings
of Congress that I confess frightens me so much that at
times I regret having embarked my all, — my fortune,
life, and reputation, — in their bottom. I sometimes
wish I had settled in some country of slaves, where the
most lenient master governs." Arthur Lee despatched
from Paris to the Committee of Secret Correspondence,
whose emissary he was, a letter bound up within the
cover of a dictionary. He reported that the desire of
France to assist America was sincere, but that the Court
was timid, and the position of the Ministry precarious.
"My opinion is," he said, "that Independency is essential to your dignity, essential to your present safety, and
essential to your future prosperity and peace." [1]

Such were the incentives by which ardent and anxious partisans endeavoured to quicken the march of the
Revolution. But Congress, in those early days of the
struggle, was full of strong men who had no intention
of being hurried over a task the scope and gravity
of which they adequately measured. Although not
given to meaningless delay, they had their weighty
reasons for advancing with circumspection and on sys-

---

[1] The dictionary in question was the key to a new cipher, worked by
putting the number of the page on which the word was to be found, and
indicating the word itself by a more complicated process. "I cannot,"
said the Commissioner, "use this until I know it is safe. You can write
to Mrs. Lee, on Tower Hill, in a woman's hand. If you have both books,
say the children are well; if the first only, the eldest child is well; if this,
the youngest child is well. They will let this pass."

tem. The aspiration after national independence, however widely prevalent now, was in the main a new sentiment. The idea had long been familiar to Samuel Adams, and a few like him; but it had not begun to pervade the people at large until a very recent date. Before blood had been shed, and towns burned, and half a score of petitions thrown into the royal waste-paper basket, colonists of every shade in politics had scouted as a libel the charge that they aimed at separation from the mother country. So late as October 1774 the First Congress thus addressed the British people. "You have been told that we are seditious, impatient of government, and desirous of independence. Be assured that these are not facts, but calumnies." Among those who voted that address was George Washington; and in the same autumn he told a military friend at Boston, who had spoken of New Englanders as rebels, that it was not the wish or the interest of Massachusetts, or of any other colony, to set up for independence either separately or collectively. Washington never romanced to anyone; and, if Benjamin Franklin occasionally practised duplicity, at any rate he always spoke the truth to Lord Chatham. Franklin had resided in England since 1765, and his experience of the bent of colonial opinion was wanting in freshness; but, such as it was, that experience covered half a century. He informed Lord Chatham that in the course of his life he had travelled from end to end of the American continent, had conversed with all descriptions of people, and had never heard a hint from any individual, whether drunk or sober, that Independence was desirable or even imaginable.

Testimony to the same effect has been given by Jay, and Madison, and by Jefferson and John Adams themselves, in vigorous and characteristic phrases which have been collected and treasured by a people who never tire of reading what their great men said about the chief event in American story. But these were colonists, educated amid an atmosphere of universal loyalty to the Crown, who might be slow in noticing the symptoms of a change in that public opinion by which their boyhood and youth had been surrounded. More conclusive, therefore, is a record of the impression produced upon an Englishman belonging to the lower middle class, who had been born in the heart of our Eastern counties, and who had turned the corner of life before he emigrated to the colonies. Thomas Paine brought to the study of the American Revolution a mind neither profound nor cultivated, but agile, vivid, and impressible; quick to see into things, and marvellous in its power of stating them with lucidity, with liveliness, and with incisive force.[1] " I happened," Paine wrote, "to come to America a few months before the breaking out of hostilities. I found the disposition of the people such that they might have been led by a thread, and governed by a reed. Their suspicion was quick and penetrating; but their attachment to Britain was obstinate, and it was at that time a kind of treason to speak against it. Their idea of grievance operated without resentment; and their single object was reconciliation."

When the second Continental Congress met in May 1775 a change had passed over the mind of the American people. Their love of England was wounded deeply at Lexington, and the events of the ensuing autumn and winter had killed it outright. The party of the Revolution outside Congress was already bent on Independence; but the assembly itself was divided on the question, though in very unequal proportions. When the House first met, champions of the British connection were not many in number; but they were able, wealthy, and respected; and they enjoyed the great advantage of being on their own ground. Pennsylvania, as the most populous colony, supplied the largest number of delegates to Congress. Most of them were luke-

---

[1] This sentence is a verbal, though abbreviated, reproduction of Mr. Tyler's admirable description of Paine in the twenty-first chapter of the *Literary History of the American Revolution.*

warm patriots; and some were greater Tories than they themselves as yet knew. Enthusiasm was discountenanced by the company with whom they habitually consorted. Many leading gentlemen of Philadelphia had been attached to the Proprietary Interest, and owed their fortunes, and their municipal importance, to the favour of the Penns; and the Penns were for the Crown, although it had used them ill in the past, as against the Revolution, which was sure to use them much worse in the future. The Quakers, generally speaking, had gone as far in the direction of resistance to authority as their conscience sanctioned, and as their tastes inclined them. Fond of comfort and security, and knowing the income of every local politician, (which in some cases was no great burden on their memory,) to within a hundred dollars, they had scanty sympathy with the less solvent personages who so often push to the front in times of trouble. Their attitude towards warlike members of their own body, who were very seldom warm citizens in any sense except in that of their revolutionary ardour, was illustrated by the anecdote of a rich and cautious Friend who chanced to encounter a Free Quaker arrayed for battle. The old man inquired as to the nature and object of the implement with which his neighbour was girt, and learned, in reply, that liberty or death was now the watchword of everyone who meant to defend himself and his property. "I had not," was the rejoinder, "expected such high feelings from thee. As to property, I thought thee had none; and as to thy liberty, I thought thee already enjoyed it through the kindness of thy creditors."

The policy of hesitation gained dignity and popularity from the adhesion of John Dickinson, the author of the "Farmer's Letters." Dickinson had the virtues and the social standing indispensable for the leader of a middle party; and his political creed was compounded of such peculiar elements, and so sincerely and bravely held, as to give him unusual influence at a very special conjuncture. He was prepared to fight to the death for the rights of America, and to die twice over rather than consent to forswear his allegiance to the King. A poorer motive was attributed to him by John Adams, who never showed to so little advantage as when analysing the character of a prominent contemporary. The Quakers, (so Adams was told, and so he was willing to believe,) had intimidated Dickinson's female relatives, who continually distressed him with their remonstrances. His mother kept telling him; "Johnny, you will be hanged. Your estate will be forfeited. You will leave your excellent wife a widow, and your charming children orphans, beggars, and infamous." "From my soul," said Adams, "I pitied Mr. Dickinson. If my mother and wife had expressed such sentiments to me, I am certain that, if they did not wholly unman me and make me an apostate, they would make me the most miserable man alive." And then he went on to enumerate a list of his connections on both sides, from grandparents downwards, — names of the sort which have ever since supplied Boston society with a very passable substitute for a titled aristocracy, — and to congratulate himself on the fact that they had one and all uniformly been of his mind at every turn of the great controversy; so that, however loud the storm might rage without, he had enjoyed perfect peace at home.

Adams should have judged others by himself. If all the Quincys and Nortons in Massachusetts had been Tories together, it would not have abated a tittle of his own patriotism; and the resolution with which Dickinson maintained his antiquated constitutional attitude was proof against far severer trials than the tearful expostulations of his family. Like a Puritan country gentleman at the beginning of our Civil War, he held that to bear arms against the Crown was consistent with the duty of a loyal subject; and a loyal subject he was determined to remain. Clear and steadfast in his own views, he for a while exercised a remarkable influence over others. He kept his followers united and busy, and encouraged them to attract recruits from among their colleagues. Working with great art and assiduity, they won over to their own party the representatives from South Carolina. A visible impression was produced even upon the Sacred Band of the Massachusetts delegation, two of whom, in a weak moment, had consented to bring their wives to Philadelphia. These ladies were invited everywhere, and visited by everybody; while their husbands, tired by a long day's work, and with the cheerless alternative of an evening in hired lodgings, gladly went where there was a good cook, a choice cellar, and reception rooms decorated with an abundance of those simple and beautiful articles which now, under the title of old colonial furniture, are the chief treasures of a genuine American collector.

Strong courses were for the present unacceptable to these butterflies of politics; if such a term could be applied to any New Englander. But even the more severe statesmen of the popular party did not wish to force the situation. An assertion of national independence, extorted from Congress after protracted and angry debates, and supported by anything short of an overwhelming majority, would be of less than no value for the high purposes which those statesmen had in contemplation. Their sound policy was to wait for unanimity; and meanwhile, with excellent judgement, they conceded to the chieftain of the royalists a provisional, but very real, leadership in the conduct of their assembly. There was no danger lest warlike preparations should suffer on that account; because, in all which related to the public defence, Dickinson was far more ready to help than to impede. In September 1775 a secret Board of nine Congressmen was appointed to contract for the importation of five hundred tons of powder, forty brass field-pieces, ten thousand stand of arms, and twenty thousand " good, plain, double-bridled musket-locks; " in the following November five members were nominated to correspond "with friends in Great Britain, Ireland, and other parts of the world;"

and Dickinson sate on both those most important committees. With less expectation of a fruitful result, but
with a single-minded desire for it, Congress gave him a
free hand in his endeavour to conciliate England. He
was empowered to petition George the Third once
again; to word the document in a style which he
thought would please; and to entrust it to a messenger
chosen from that Proprietary Family of Pennsylvania
which had a nearer interest than the House of Brunswick itself in staying the progress of the disturbances.
From this step, which Dickinson was permitted to take,
and to take exactly in his own way, nothing but good
could come. "There was not a moment during the
Revolution," (so John Adams wrote, years after that
Revolution was over,) "when I would not have given
everything I possessed for a restoration to the state
of things before the contest began, provided we could
have a sufficient security for its continuance." If
Penn's mission had succeeded, that ancient peace would
have been restored; and during the remainder of his
life Dickinson would have been the first man in America, and after death would have been regarded with
something of the veneration which now is paid to the
memory of Washington. And, if the result was otherwise, (as those who had carefully watched the King
reluctantly foresaw,) the partisans of peace would themselves acknowledge that their remedy had been fairly
tried, and had hopelessly failed; and the doctrine of
non-resistance would thenceforward never be preached
except by politicians who were in favour of abject submission and unconditional surrender.

Adams, for a reason of his own, was just now not
sorry to be working unostentatiously and in the background. He had been overtaken by one of those disagreeable incidents, — more odious to their victim in
the retrospect than grave calamities, — which an impulsive and emotional man, who ventures into politics,
must sooner or later count on facing. A Boston advocate, who had served his time as clerk in a Tory

lawyer's office, found or feared that nobody would employ him at the bar; and he accordingly prayed John Adams to give him a certificate of patriotism. Adams at last was teased into drawing up letters of recommendation addressed to his own wife, and to President Warren. When once his pen was in motion, he allowed it to run. He wrote as he would have talked in the presence of the two people whom he was addressing, and poured himself out as plain as if, on that July afternoon, he had been sitting between them over a jug of cider in his verandah at Braintree. He passed a jest on General Lee's devotion to a favourite dog.[1] He inveighed against Dickinson in terms more amusing indeed, but not a whit more slighting and embittered, than those which many and many a statesman, in his private correspondence, has employed when writing about an antagonist. And, finally, he described the labours of Congress in highly seasoned language which, especially in the estimation of small critics, had a flavour of the grandiose. "My anxiety," he told Mrs. Adams, "about you and the children, as well as our country, has been extreme. The business I have had upon my mind has been as great and important as can be entrusted to man, and the intricacy of it prodigious. When fifty or sixty men have a Constitution to form for a great empire; a country of fifteen hundred miles extent to fortify; millions to arm and train; a naval power to begin; an extensive commerce to regulate; numerous tribes of Indians to negotiate with; a standing army of twenty-seven thousand men to raise, pay, victual, and officer,—I really shall pity those fifty or sixty men."

It was very much what an over-worked man of genius might be expected to write, during a scrap of leisure, for the benefit of those who loved to hear him discourse, without reserve, in obedience to the mood

[1] "You observe in your letter the oddity of a great man. He is a queer creature; but you must love his dogs if you love him, and forgive a thousand whims for the sake of the soldier and the scholar."

which was upon him at the moment. But his confi-
dences were exposed to the ordeal of an unfair and
most unpleasant notoriety. The young lawyer, when
crossing Hudson River, was intercepted by the boats
of a British man-of-war; and he was fool enough not
to destroy the letters. Admiral Graves sent them to
the Governor of Boston, as a proof that the fleet under
his command had at least contrived to capture something; and Gage, when it came to his turn, so forgot
himself as to publish them in the newspapers. General
Lee at once wrote to assure their author that, as far as
he himself was concerned, no mischief had been done.
He was pleased, he said, that his dog had got into
history; and he did not object to be called a queer
creature, since in the same sentence his name had been
handed down to posterity as that of a soldier and a
scholar. Unfortunately there was more good sense,
and less sensitiveness, in the camp than in the Congress.
Though names had not been mentioned in the letters,
everybody detected the personage of great fortune, and
petty genius, "whose fame had been loudly trumpeted,
but who had given a silly cast to the whole of the
doings" at Philadelphia. Dickinson cut Adams in the
street: and Dickinson's friends called him faithless
and slanderous because, in the postscript of a private
letter to his wife, he had complained that some among
the delegates were fidgety and conceited. But the
indignation professed to be felt over these trivialities
was a cloak for resentments more profoundly based.
Adams had written to President Warren that already,
had it not been for the timidity of certain folks, America should and would have been declared an independent nation. That was his true crime. The opponents
of Independence saw their chance, and made haste to
ruin him. They accused him openly and clamorously
of being disloyal to his colleagues; but they whispered
among themselves that he was a traitor to his King.
Mr. Adams, (so his grandson relates,) was shunned by
many as if it were contamination to speak with him.

" Even of his friends, several became infected with the general panic, and looked coldly upon him. At no time, (and he had repeated trials of this kind,) did he stand more in need of all his fortitude and self-control than upon the occasion of this sudden and unlooked-for influx of the general disapprobation." [1]

Every intelligent reader in England took the intercepted letters very seriously. They brought home to him, as nothing had done before, the far-reaching character of those political problems which had been so lightly and wantonly raised, and the stern purpose of at least one rebel statesman, who was bound to solve those problems on peril of his own life. The revelations of the inner mind of John Adams extorted respect, and even admiration, from enlightened adversaries of his cause. Burgoyne, who could relish a literary style the very opposite to that which he himself cultivated, exclaimed that the American lawyer wrote with the conciseness of Tacitus, and propounded matter for a volume in half a sentence. In something less than the half of one of his own sentences, (for, in dealing with Burgoyne, condensation must be permitted if he is to be quoted at all,) the General called Lord Dartmouth's attention to the acute and dangerous genius of Adams. " The bare effort of investigating such objects argues an aspiring and vigorous mind ; but when it is considered that, with a profligate character, — neither supported by pecuniary nor political interest, nor ascending by the footsteps of any leader or patron, — by the exercise of his parts he has cajoled the opulent, drawn in the wary, deluded the vulgar, till all parties in America, and some in Great Britain, are puppets in his string, I am persuaded your Lordship will, with me, lose sight of Catiline and Cromwell in passing judgement upon his character. Be assured, my Lord, this man soars too high to be allured by any offer Great Britain can make.

[1] *Life of Adams*, by Charles Francis Adams the elder; chapter iv. " I was avoided," (John Adams himself said,) " like a man infected with the leprosy."

America, if his counsels continue in force, must be sub-
dued or relinquished. She will not be reconciled." [1]

Adams soon regained any ground which he might
have lost in Congress. The unpopularity of an honest
man, who has done an unlucky thing, is superficial and
transient; however deeply in his own mind the sting
may rankle. For the work of the next twelvemonth
John Adams was indispensable; and he could not be
gossiped and sneered out of the secure position which
he occupied in the confidence of his fellow-countrymen.
Ill suited to be chief of a party in ordinary times, "when
much depends on a spirit of accommodation to the whims
or the longings of individuals held together by fleeting
considerations of personal or public interest, he was emi-
nently qualified to stand forth the exponent of a clear,
strong, and noble plan of action in a time of danger." [2]
So his descendant has judged him; and it was an estimate in no degree affected by family partiality. John
Adams could be politic and discreet for the attainment
of a great end; and, when a national crisis pressed, he
would forego his own claims, forget his own grievances,
and do full justice to the merit of others. His strict
and pure morality, fortified by courage and industry,
gave him a commanding influence over an assembly so
limited in number that each member of it, whether
friend or enemy, knew him exactly for what he was.
His speeches were the mirror of his character; and
each of them displayed that instinctive devotion to fixed
principles, and that solid comprehensive grasp of the
facts and particulars of the hour, which were his most
valuable qualities as an orator.

---

[1] Coarser natures than Burgoyne thought it a fit opportunity to revive
those suggestions of hanging American statesmen which had helped to
provoke the rebellion. In the Dartmouth Manuscripts there is a letter
from a Virginian Tory in London to a Virginian patriot at Philadelphia.
" I pity," said the writer, "the poor ignorant People who must be sacrificed by thousands to gratify the Pride and Ambition of that damned rascal John Adams. If you become a separate State, I hope he will turn out
another Cromwell. If Gage does not raise him *to a more exalted station*,
he won't be contented with anything less from your hands than Stadt-
holder."

[2] *Life of John Adams;* chapter iv.

Those fireworks of declamation, by which American freedom is annually celebrated, have dazzled mankind into forgetting that the edifice of the great Republic was not built up by rhetoric. The famous Virginian speaker, Patrick Henry, has sometimes been represented as a type of the statesmen of the Revolution. His contemporaries have handed down to us a tradition of his idleness and want of method, founded on truth, but not exempt from exaggeration.[1] Patrick Henry, like most public men, had enemies; and he was singularly unfortunate in his panegyrists. From them we learn that he hated the toil of composition; that he left no manuscripts, and read very few books; inasmuch as he maintained, all through life, that men were the only volumes which could be perused to advantage. His library, (we are told,) was in his youthful days the bar of his father's tavern. " The character of every customer underwent his scrutiny; not with reference either to the integrity or solvency of the individual, in which one would suppose that Mr. Henry would feel himself most interested; but in relation to the structure of his mind, the general cast of his opinions, and what may be called the philosophy of character." [2] From these studies he emerged "the orator of nature; — one of those perfect prodigies of whom very few have been produced since the foundation of the earth was laid." He spoke as Homer wrote. He was Shakspeare and Garrick combined. His biographer in title describes him as possessing a genius which designed with all the boldness of Michael Angelo, and an imagination which coloured with all the wealth of Titian. This author

[1] The Journals of Congress, and Henry's own private fee-book, have recently been subjected by Professor Tyler to a careful and intelligent examination; and they indicate that, both as lawyer and senator, the great orator was more industrious and less unpractical than anecdote has represented him.

[2] *Sketches of the Life and Character of Patrick Henry*, by William Wirt of Virginia; Philadelphia, 1818. Whatever of value Henry might have learned at the tavern in his character of son of the house, at all events he got little harm; for he was a water-drinker.

could find nothing in the material world wherewith to compare his hero except the cataract of Niagara; and the book ends with a declaration, adapted from a better writer, that we never shall look upon Patrick Henry's like again.

Jefferson, — a critic of strong perception, and immense experience, — pronounced Henry the greatest popular speaker whom he ever heard. He was, indeed, a marvellous orator; and some of his phrases still ring through the generations. It is therefore all the more worthy of note that he was held of no great account in the Continental Congress. His most devoted admirer acknowledges that, when the war had fairly begun, and the crisis demanded not words but work, it became evident that Mr. Henry was no business-man. He could not endure the labour of close thinking; and the lax habits of his early life had implanted in him an unspeakable aversion to the drudgery of detail. "I found Mr. Henry," said Jefferson, "to be a silent and almost unmeddling man in Congress. On the original opening of that body, while general grievances were the topic, he was in his element, and captivated all by his bold and splendid eloquence. But, as soon as they came to specific matters, he had the good sense to perceive that his declamation had no weight in an assembly of cool-headed, reflecting, judicious men." And so it came to pass that, a year before the Declaration of Independence, Patrick Henry ceased to be a Member of Congress, and never again took a seat upon the benches.

There seldom was an assembly which fixed its attention more obstinately upon realities, and listened less greedily to the elegancies, the subtleties, and the personalities of debate. Men repaired thither every morning as to a scene of exertion where their own lives and fortunes, and the future of their country, depended on their common labours and their mutual forbearance. Orators were at hand, if orators were wanted. Conspicuous among such was Richard Henry Lee, who almost justified those hyperboles which, according to colonial fashion, were then applied to a fine speaker. His admirers called him the Cicero of the House. His style, to their perception, bore a striking resemblance to that of Herodotus. He required to read nothing up, and to think nothing out, but was ready to handle any subject as soon as it was announced; "and his speech was copious, mellifluous, and set off with bewitching cadence of voice and captivating grace of action." But with all that, and several pages more of laudatory epithets, he had not a tithe of the influence exercised by another public man who, like himself, came from Virginia. Washington, too, had passed through a political apprenticeship in the Assembly at Williamsburg. His maiden speech was a single lame and broken sentence, stammered out when he was thanked in his place for distinguished military services rendered in the great French war. Like all men of parts and courage, he soon learned to command his faculties when addressing his fellows; but he never wasted time and breath, or appealed to the ear about a matter which could be decided by the eye. He had been known to refute a persuasive and passionate orator, on a question concerning the appropriate site for a public building, by producing a map from his pocket and indicating the exact situation of the localities in dispute.

The four men who, in the earlier sessions of Congress, had most share in guiding its deliberations and moulding its action, were Washington and Franklin, Thomas Jefferson and John Adams. Three out of the four never made a speech as long as the very shortest which, on an important evening, a front-bench man in the House of Commons would think it compatible with his dignity to make. "During the whole time," said John Adams, "that I sate with Mr. Jefferson in Congress, I never heard him utter three sentences together." Washington very seldom exceeded ten minutes, nor Franklin either; — mindful, as the latter was, of what he had written in Poor Richard's Almanack about "the Orator, with his flood of words, and his drop of reason."

Adams himself spoke extemporaneously, from stores of information which he had made his own for reasons other than oratorical, and ceased as soon as he had put his audience in possession of the facts, and of the proposals, with which it was essential that they should be acquainted.   The power of these men lay in what they knew, and did; and, above all else, in the circumstance that their brother Congressmen gratefully recognised how very much leisure, comfort, and private advantage they had sacrificed under a sense of public duty.   Washington, until he joined the army at Boston, sate on every committee where his military experience was in demand. Franklin, as soon as he returned from London to Philadelphia, afforded an example of diligence which his younger colleagues were proud to follow.   He was a Chief Commissioner for Indian Affairs, and a member of three bodies which sate every day, — the Committee of Safety, the Pennsylvania Assembly, and the Continental Congress.   When the hours, at which these bodies severally met, interfered with each other, he preferred to attend Congress; not because the work done there was more showy, but because it was more urgent.   And, as for Adams, from four in the morning until ten at night he did not find a minute which he could call his own.   New Englander that he was, he kept a pretty exact account, both in Colonial and British money, of the value of the time which he gave to the service of the State.   There were lawyers, (he said long afterwards,) who made five thousand guineas a year, and many who earned ten thousand dollars; but not one of them went through as much business for all his emoluments as he himself had undertaken and discharged during those eighteen months when he was Chairman of the Board of War and Ordnance, and a frequent and most weighty, although no lengthy, speaker in the Continental Congress.

The Reverend William Gordon was a very familiar figure in American political circles during that anxious and busy session. He was a Congregational minister at Roxbury near Boston, and the self-destined historian of the American Revolution. Piercing the mists of the future with a confident glance, Gordon foresaw a theme which demanded a Thucydides; and, as early as the year 1774, he commenced to gather together his materials according to methods recommended by the practice of that immortal writer. In order to qualify himself for his large task, (we are told,) Gordon began by making his purpose widely known.[1] He was in and forth of Congress daily, jotting down the heads of speeches, and button-holing the Committee-men who were the real rulers of the country. He travelled up and down in the wake of the armies, examining the ground where actions had been fought, and plying the generals with questions about the strength of their forces and the meaning of their strategy. It was the function of history, (so Gordon wrote,) to oblige all who had performed any distinguished part on the theatre of the world to appear before mankind in their proper character, and to render an account of their actions at the tribunal of posterity, as models of what ought to be followed, or as examples to be censured and avoided.[2] With such a prospect before them, few commanding officers, who had any care for their reputation, ventured to refuse Gordon admission to the inmost recesses of head-quarters. His principal informant on military matters was General Gates, to whom he wrote as his " dear Horatio," in a long series of letters containing a good deal less wit and insight than we are accustomed to associate with observations addressed to a person of that name. The Commander-in-Chief himself was persecuted by Gordon with demands for private interviews, for a sight of confidential documents, or for information on military and political points of interest. The patience with which, for many years, Washington endured this infliction was exemplary, and almost inexplicable. The truth

[1] Tyler's *Literary History;* Vol. II., chapter 39.
[2] Preface to Gordon's *History* in the edition of 1788.

seems to be that the great Virginian, who knew his own multifarious business well, was very cautious about forming an unfavourable judgement with regard to the qualifications of people who practised arts outside the scope of his experience. He had no difficulty when the question was one of selecting a brigadier-general, or a Secretary of State, or an ambassador, or a land-agent, or the foreman of a tobacco factory; but he was content to accept historians at their own valuation, until the world had pronounced a definite verdict upon their merit.

Gordon's head was perpetually filled by consciousness of his high mission; and he set an extravagant value on the favour which he conferred by his bodily presence. In the fall of 1776 he pompously announced himself as intending a visit to both the armies. He did not doubt, (he said,) that he would meet with a hearty welcome from Gates and Washington, and see them in the happy character of glorious conquerors, loved and admired by all about them for having been instrumental in saving the liberties, as well as the necks, of the Americans. But there was one statesman in Philadelphia who never was sorry when the minister of Roxbury for a while transferred himself and his note-book from the city to the camp. Parson Gordon's indiscreet prate, (said John Adams,) was a mischievous element in politics. Although zealous in the cause, and well-meaning, he was an eternal talker, — vain, inaccurate, and injudicious, and, (beyond all,) not sufficiently alive to the claims and merits of the province of which Boston was the capital.[1] On that head Adams was hard to please; for, sooner or later, Gordon was at the trouble to read near thirty folio manuscript volumes of the records of Massachusetts Bay.

But, in order to write like a great Athenian master in the age of Pericles, something more was required than diligence in collecting facts. Gordon, in an unhappy hour, invented for himself the very worst historical

[1] *Diary of John Adams;* November 16, 1775.

vehicle that misdirected ingenuity ever constructed or conceived. He composed his book in the shape of detached letters professing to have been posted from America, to correspondents in Europe, at dates immediately subsequent to the occurrences which they narrated. By this process, (to employ his own exact words,) he intended that a present ideal existence of past events should be created in the mind, similar to what is felt when a well-executed painting is examined.[1]

A complete history, industriously composed on these strange lines, was ready for publication as soon as the war ended. But the author, on reviewing his work, had come to the conclusion that America was far from a safe place in which to publish. Gordon's fellow-citizens were not just then in a mood to bear criticism meekly, or to read with pleasure an impartial recapitulation of events many of which they chose should be forgotten. They were proud and exultant, and unwilling to be reminded by a too faithful monitor how often in the course of the war they had been foiled and dispirited; not a few politicians and generals, moreover, had risen to fame and power whose past career had occasionally been marked by failures and blunders; and twenty continuous years of political commotion had habituated the Americans to very rough modes of vindicating public or private honour against anyone whom they regarded as a traducer. Liberty, property, and character, (so Gordon had persuaded himself,) were

[1] Gordon, after reporting the famous outrage in Boston Harbor as a piece of thrilling news, goes on to anticipate that the destruction of the tea will issue in the destruction of the Provincial Charter, which will make the inhabitants of the colony furious beyond expression. The letter relating to what passed at Lexington is dated on the day week after the battle. The account ends by expressing an apprehension that Massachusetts will be crushed unless the other colonies come to her assistance. Gordon's correspondent, however, would be interested to hear that, at all events, the inhabitants of the threatened province will act their part with firmness and intrepidity, knowing that slavery is worse than death. This solemn trifling was kept up through four thick volumes, published many years after the consequences, so gravely and specifically foretold as being still in he future, had all come to pass.

safer in Great Britain than in the States ; and the historian could use the impartial pen with less danger in
the old Kingdom than in the new Republic.[1] He accordingly resolved that his book should appear in London.

It was a desperate hope. The Americans might
be intolerant from the insolence of success ; but the
British were very sore. When Gordon arrived on the
other side of the water, he was given to understand
that his story of the war abounded in statements which
the Law-courts at Westminster would regard as libels
on some of the most respectable characters in the
British army and navy ; that the Admiralty and the
War Office would never even contemplate the notion of
permitting him to examine their archives for evidence
to make good his allegations ; and that, if he possessed
the fortune of the Duke of Bedford, he would not be
able to pay the damages which would be recovered
against him. And so, having omitted what would give
umbrage to Americans, Gordon next proceeded to strike
out all that might offend Englishmen ; and his original
manuscript was docked of at least a hundred pages,
which were somewhat less dull and pointless than the
rest. Under such conditions Thucydides himself would
have failed to produce a work deserving to be classed
as a possession for ever : and, for poor Gordon, the
publication was not even a source of present profit.
John Adams, who then was Envoy at the Court of St.
James's, had some while before informed a friend at
home that neither history, nor poetry, nor anything but
painting and music, balls and spectacles, was in vogue
in London. Serious study had gone out of fashion ;
and, if ever people went back to books, they would not
begin with a narrative of the most disastrous undertaking in which their country had for centuries been
engaged. "It is a story," (said Adams,) "that nobody
here loves to read."[2]

[1] Gordon to Horatio Gates; October 16, 1782.
[2] Gordon's pretensions, the docility with which they were recognised
by his countrymen while the history was still in preparation, and the utter

The group of statesmen who, in 1775 and 1776, inspired the tactics of the advanced party in Congress, were disinclined to rush a declaration of Independence against the resistance of what was still a compact and not insignificant minority; but they had a stronger reason yet for postponing a project on which the mind of every man amongst them was by this time unalterably set. As things then stood, they did not feel themselves justified in committing their own generation, and posterity likewise, to a step which would be ruinous in case they failed, and irrevocable if they succeeded. Congress was a mere collection of individuals, sent to Philadelphia by self-appointed constituents for the purpose of making head against a great and sudden peril, but with no right or title to construct a nation. In order to approach such a scheme with moral authority, and even a show of legality, the central assembly must receive a definite and specific commission from the regular governments of the several colonies; and at present no such governments existed. The pedestal had to be completed before the statue of liberty was erected; and the hewing out of each block of the granite which composed the substructure was not less necessary, and even tougher, work than the shaping of the marble. To that work the craftsmen of the Revolution addressed themselves boldly and betimes. On the third of November, 1775, Congress resolved that it be recommended to the Provincial Convention of New Hampshire to establish such a form of government as in their judgement would best produce the happiness of the people, and most effectually secure peace and good order in the Province, during the continuance of the present dispute between Great Britain and the colonies. Next day the same advice was given to South Carolina. Six months elapsed; and in May 1776 Congress recorded its earnest desire that any colony, which had not already pro-

collapse that followed its appearance, are notably illustrated by Washington's correspondence, as may be seen in the First Appendix at the end of this volume.

vided itself with a new constitution, should forthwith proceed to remedy the omission. "This resolution," said Adams, "I considered as an epocha, a decisive event. It was a measure which I had pursued for a whole year, through a scene and a series of anxiety, labour, study, argument, and obloquy which was then little known, and is now forgotten by all but a very few." The ingratitude of oblivion is the common lot of public men. Those are fortunate whose private complaints and sorrows over the fickle memories of mankind never see the light; and happier still is he who does not trouble himself about the matter at all.

Both before and after the Resolution of May 1776 the reorganisation of local government was going on rapidly throughout the colonies; and those proceedings were extraordinarily impressive to English politicians who watched them from across the ocean. There was something very formidable in the coolness and determination of men who could thus legislate under fire.[1] Massachusetts, with her hands full, and the enemy inside her gates, had no time to spare for the niceties of constitution-making, and pursued a short cut to freedom. She contented herself with re-enacting, almost in block, those ancient rights and privileges which the Parliament at Westminster had temporarily extinguished; and it may well be believed that no respect was paid to that clause in the British statute which made the revival of the Charter dependent on the gracious initiative of the Crown.[2] Other New England colonies took the same course as Massachusetts. They had lived under forms of government so liberal that few and superficial changes were needed in order to place them in a position to carry on business as republics. In each province the King's name disappeared from the headings of public Acts; and provision was made for the discharge of functions which hitherto had belonged to royal Governors who had left their State-houses vacant, and who, under the

[1] The Hon. C. J. Fox to Lord Ossory; White's, September 24, 1776.
[2] *The American Revolution;* chapter v.

existing circumstances, were in no hurry to re-inhabit them. The new Constitutions of the Northern states had nothing monarchical about them, except a solemn announcement of allegiance to the King of Kings by which their publication was generally accompanied; but on the other side of the Potomac supreme executive power was for the most part entrusted to an individual. South Carolina built up afresh from the foundation an elaborate system, with a General Assembly, a Legislative Council of thirteen, a Privy Council of seven, and a President whose assent was required before laws became valid. Virginia, in her stately fashion, set forth the lines on which she proposed to govern herself in a Declaration of Rights, thoughtfully framed and nobly worded. "No free Government," (so that instrument ran,) "can be preserved but by a firm adherence to justice, moderation, temperance, frugality, and virtue, and by frequent recurrence to fundamental principles."

That last phrase would have had an ominous sound if employed by men of certain other races. There have been republics in the Southern continent of America where recurrence would be had to fundamental principles every time that the party in opposition had scraped together enough dollars to purchase a few thousand muskets. But the Virginian Declaration of Rights was faithfully and literally construed by all who gave it their adherence. On the abstract doctrines therein laid down was founded a system of government which called forth the enduring affection of a proud and steadfast population. Eighty-five years afterwards, — when in 1861 the South seceded from the Union, and a controversy, insoluble except by arms, arose between the State of Virginia and the central administration, — it became evident that the Old Dominion, in the view of a vast majority of its citizens, had a first claim on their loyalty. And so it was from the very commencement. The generation which made the American Revolution witnessed a brilliant proof that the local patriotism of Virginians was already an absorbing and sufficing passion. Patrick Henry, — who always drew force and purpose from contact with his native soil, where his early triumphs had been won, — took a part in creating a constitution for Virginia, and was chosen her Governor. That office he filled so often that there was some excuse for French officers in the allied army who addressed him on the cover of their letters as His Royal Highness.[1] At such times as he was not the chief ruler of his State, Henry preferred to all other honours that of remaining one of her private citizens. In after years, as a notability of the Revolution, he had only to choose between the elevated employments which were pressed upon his acceptance. He was elected to the Senate of the United States; and he declined to serve. Washington offered him successively the great posts of Secretary for Foreign Affairs, and Chief Justice of the Supreme Court; but he refused them both. The political party of his adoption urged him eagerly, and all in vain, to have himself put forward as candidate for the Vice-Presidency in succession to John Adams. He lived to the end at his home in Virginia; — pleading causes in her law-courts; and electrifying her public meetings, on rare and momentous occasions, by outbursts of an eloquence to which advancing years added dignity, while they did not quench its fire.

The more deliberate, — or in some cases, it may be, the half-hearted, — among the colonies were occupied during many months in perfecting their organic laws. It was not till April 1777 that New York, last of the thirteen, promulgated her Constitution. Nevertheless at a much earlier date the event had justified those statesmen who insisted that the national fabric should be built up in solid layers of masonry from below. When once the problem had been solved of converting each separate colony into a self-governed and independent state, it followed as an axiom, intelligible even to the humblest and worst educated citizen, that a federa-

[1] Tyler's *Patrick Henry;* chapter xvi.

tion composed of those states must be emancipated from external control. John Adams, in a string of precise and homely sentences, had sketched out the course which the Revolution thenceforward was bound to follow. "A few important subjects," (he wrote to his friend William Cushing,) "must be despatched before I can return to my family. Every colony must be induced to institute a perfect government. All the colonies must confederate together in some solemn bond of union. The Congress must declare the colonies free and independent States; and ambassadors must be sent abroad to foreign courts, to solicit their acknowledgement of us as sovereign states, and to form with them, at least with some of them, commercial treaties of friendship and alliance. When these things are once completed, I shall think that I have answered the end of my creation, and sing my *nunc dimittis*, return to my farm, ride circuits, plead law, or judge causes, just which you please."

That programme was played out to the last letter. On the twelfth of April, 1776, the Convention of North Carolina expressly ordered its representatives in Congress to join in a declaration of Independence. Massachusetts and Rhode Island next renounced their fealty to the Crown; and on the fifteenth of May the Convention at Williamsburg directed their delegates at Philadelphia to propose separation from Britain, and communicated that resolve to the other colonies in a circular letter. All through June the provincial assemblies were declaring their concurrence with the course taken by Virginia. Connecticut acceded, and New Hampshire, and Maryland. New Jersey, cautious in theory, drafted her Constitution in such a form as not to exclude the possibility of a reconciliation with the Crown; but at the same time she gave a very practical indication of her sentiments by throwing the royal Governor into prison, and intimating to her delegates that they had better "pass the Rubicon, and vote plump."[1] Delaware

[1] Letter of Jonathan D. Serjeant from Burlington; June 15, 1776.

K 2

still hesitated; and the adhesion of New York to the party which favoured uncompromising and immediate action was of an informal character. South Carolina and Georgia had issued instructions to their representatives which implied a recognition of national independence, without directly naming the word. The Georgian congressmen, who were patriots to the core, found the terms of their commission quite explicit enough for their guidance; but the South Carolinian delegates were backward in the cause of the Revolution, and would not stir an inch unless they were given a lead by Pennsylvania.

CHAPTER XVI

THE PENNSYLVANIAN REVOLUTION. "COMMON SENSE." THE DECLARATION OF INDEPENDENCE

PENNSYLVANIA was passing through a political crisis, the issue of which had a dominating effect upon the future of America. The colony extended across what was then, to all intents and purposes, the whole continent, from Lake Erie to Delaware Bay. Her western territories afforded abundant room, and a hearty welcome, for emigrants in any multitude and of every nationality. Her eastern districts were well populated and carefully tilled, and replete with accumulated wealth, and a solid comfort which in some cases had begun to assume the aspect of luxury. Commanding the landways and waterways then habitually in use, Pennsylvania could connect, or separate, at pleasure the group of Southern colonies on the one hand, and New York and New England on the other. But the material advantage which she could bring, or refuse, to the Revolutionary cause was small as compared with the moral effect of whatever action she chose to take at this precise juncture in American history.

It is difficult to over-estimate the influence necessarily exercised upon a great national movement by the city in which the earlier stages of that movement are conducted. The attitude of Philadelphia in 1775 and 1776 had an importance, not so great indeed in degree, but the same in kind, as the attitude of London during the first sessions of the Long Parliament, and of Paris between the meeting of the States General and the fall of the Directory. A handful of strangers, lodg-

ing wherever they can find shelter in the various quarters of a large town; dependent on its hospitality;
unable to escape the contagion of its enthusiasm, or
withdraw themselves from the alarming consequences
of its paroxysms of excitement; hooted or cheered up
to the very portals of the senate-house, and only too
glad if they are allowed to deliberate, safe and uninter-
rupted, within the precincts;—the makers of a revolution
would be more than human if they did not come to regard the local opinion immediately surrounding them
as the general opinion of the nation. It is true that
Congress was not exposed to insult or impertinence,
and still less to open violence. Philadelphia respected
herself, and honoured her guests; but the threescore
delegates, who lived scattered up and down among her
thirty thousand inhabitants, could not preserve themselves from being sensibly affected by her political
atmosphere. It mattered to them much what were the
inclinations of the province and the provincial capital,
and whether a Constitutional machinery existed for
making those inclinations felt.

The Pennsylvanian Assembly, which held its sittings
within a few yards of the hall where Congress met,[1]
was not in sympathy with the Revolution. In that
Assembly the Quakers had no longer, as of old, a majority; but their power was still great out of all proportion to their numbers. Twenty years before, when the
Friends were reckoned at forty thousand, or about a
sixth part of the population resident within the colony,
twenty-eight assemblymen, in a total of thirty-six, were
members of their body. But in 1756, for a most honourable reason, they deliberately renounced their monopoly of the representation. The Governor and Council
had embarked upon an Indian war which according to
the Quakers was unjust, and waged it after a fashion

[1] "The Pennsylvania assembly in 1775 gave up its room, (now Independence Hall,) East of the main Entrance of the State House, to the
Continental Congress, and moved across to the West side, to the Judges'
Room; where I believe it finished its existence." Letter to the author
from the President of Haverford College, Pennsylvania.

which, even to others than Quakers, appeared to be inhumane. Many of the more rigid Friends could not find it within their consciences to vote taxes that in their view were wickedly misspent, and resigned their places in the Assembly. The void was filled by Episcopalians attached to the party of the Proprietors; for the descendants of William Penn, (with as little sense of historic fitness as was displayed by Queen Christina, the daughter of Gustavus Adolphus, when she became a Roman Catholic,) had for the most part gone over to the Church of England. A standing contention existed between the Friends and the governing family; and Franklin had commenced his ten years' mission to England in the character of an emissary charged to make interest with the Ministry and Parliament in London against the claims and pretensions of the Proprietors. But in 1772 the murmur of an approaching revolution warned the two parties, which ruled Pennsylvania, to sink their differences, and combine in defence of institutions no change in which could by any possibility tend to profit, or aggrandisement, for either of them. They already held between them most of the property in the colony, and all the privileges. The Friends, moreover, thought it wrong to fight with anybody; and the Proprietary family and their adherents were altogether averse to bearing arms against the Crown.

An assembly so composed, and with such proclivities, found the leader that suited it in John Dickinson. Born of Quakers, — and as prosperous, as virtuous, and as order-loving as the best of them, — he hung loosely on the Society, and was regarded by its members as an eminent and respected man of the world, whose aberrations from their strict rule they did not feel called upon to reprehend. Writing, not in Quaker language, he had opposed Townshend's financial policy with closely reasoned prose, and in spirited verse which was read or chanted by everyone who objected to the tea-duty. As a poet, Dickinson was trammelled by the difficulty of expressing in a popular chorus the precise constitutional relations which ought to exist between American tax-payers and the British Treasury;[1] but the " Farmer's Letters " had deservedly established his fame, at home and abroad, as a literary champion of colonial rights.   Those rights he was willing to defend sword in hand, or, (if his countrymen would not trust him with a command,) gun at shoulder; but all that large class who were partisans of royalty, without venturing so to declare themselves, felt a comfortable assurance that hostilities, with Dickinson as war-minister, would not be ruinous to the interests of the Crown.

By April 1776 revolutionary feeling had grown so hot in the colony that it became necessary for the Assembly to make a demonstration of patriotism; and a course was adopted which in Dickinson's view was righteous, and to his followers appeared comparatively innocuous.   Under his inspiration a bill was passed increasing the members of the Pennsylvania legislative body by seventeen, in order that those new ideas, which had become prevalent since the last general election, might find spokesmen within the walls.   A Resolution was carried, — which the Quakers could not support, but were well able to obey, — approving the military association of all who had no scruples against bearing arms.   Three battalions of regular infantry, and a large issue of paper money, were voted; and then it was decided by a great majority to maintain unaltered the instructions which, from the very first, had been imposed upon the Pennsylvanian delegates in the Continental Congress.   The last paragraph of those instructions was conceived as follows: "Though the oppressive measures of the British Parliament have compelled us to resist their violence by force of arms, yet we strictly enjoin you that you, in behalf of this colony, dissent from and utterly reject any proposition

---

[1] "In Freedom we're born, and in Freedom we'll live.
　　Our purses are ready,
　　Steady, friends, steady!
Not as slaves, but as freemen, our money we'll give."

that may cause, or lead to, a separation from our mother-country, or a change in the form of this government."

Dickinson's political platform was too narrow, and too delicately balanced, to accommodate any large part of the heterogeneous population which swarmed in Pennsylvania. In the seventeenth century three thousand Germans, who had escaped from French barbarities in the Palatinate, had found their way to America. Repulsed from other colonies, they were accepted with open arms by a community which had learned tolerance and generosity from the precepts and example of its founder. Securely planted in the rural districts of Pennsylvania these fugitives attracted thither a constant stream of industrious workmen, and good Protestants, from Suabia and Switzerland. The German immigrants were soon counted by scores of thousands. Unambitious, and not so sure of their English as to venture on airing it in debate, they did what gratitude bade them, and very generally sent a Quaker to the Assembly as their representative. They took this course the more readily because, being mostly poor and always thrifty, they trusted the Friends as economical administrators of the provincial finances. But of late years the case was altered, and the same motives of parsimony made German farmers intensely hostile to the claims of the British exchequer. Those claims, (said one who knew Pennsylvania well,) very forcibly appealed to the pocket, and impelled the great body of foreign settlers to side with the patriots. "And as for the genuine sons of Hibernia, it was enough for them to know that England was the antagonist."[1]

Those sons constituted a large and extremely formidable family; — although their genuineness as Hiber-

[1] *Memoirs of a Life chiefly passed in Pennsylvania within the Last Sixty Years;* Edinburgh, 1822. Much curious, and quite unprejudiced, information on the lighter aspects of the American troubles, and on the composition of both armies in the war, may be found in this volume, which was edited, with a preface of warm appreciation, by no less a writer than John Galt.

nians would have been disputed by Roman Catholics in the south of their native island; for they were Scotch-Irish from Ulster. With both the ruling sects of the colony they maintained an irreconcilable feud. Their fathers and grandfathers had been driven across the seas by the vexatious treatment, petty in all but its insanity, which as Presbyterians they had endured at the hands of Bishops of the Established Church in Ireland. And, again, the memories of ancient persecution stood between them and the Quakers; although in that case the relation was inverted. Presbyterians had been tyrannised over by Episcopalians in Tyrone and Londonderry; but the Friends had suffered cruelly, both in England and Massachusetts, from the peculiar antipathy with which they were regarded by Presbyterians. That antipathy originally sprang from a controversy about one of those theological points which formerly men thought vital, but which are meaningless now. Already in 1776 people required, in order to hate each other, something besides a divergence of view about the question whether, or not, there was a limitation to the effect of Saving Grace; but Quakers and Presbyterians in Pennsylvania had a more recent and acute motive for mutual dissatisfaction. The Scotch-Irish to the west of the Susquehanna resided, isolated and armed, on farms which they themselves had cleared; and they had no defence against a raid of savages except their own vigilance and courage. A fierce and resolute race, they lived not indeed in the fear, but in the contemplation, of a probability that their families might be butchered, and the fruits of their labour destroyed, in the course of one bloody night. It was hardly in human nature, — it most certainly was not in theirs, — to feel charity towards such an enemy. To the Quaker, in his beautiful country-seat among the groves which skirted Philadelphia, the red man presented himself in the light of a distant and appropriate object for evangelising efforts; but the proverbial saying that the only good Indian was a dead Indian, (a grim doctrine which cut at the very root of missionary enterprise,) represented the creed of all but a few among the backwoodsmen. For these reasons there was no love in Pennsylvania between the Ulstermen and the partisans of the Crown; and, as soon as a quarrel arose against the Crown itself, the Presbyterians of the western districts were revolutionists almost to a man. The German settlers in America, when once emancipated from those stringent military obligations which they leave behind them at home, have never shown themselves a particularly martial people; but the North Irish colonists had brought over with them an ineradicable conviction that opinions worth holding were worth fighting for. A record has been preserved of the nationalities in a company of Pennsylvanian volunteers which marched to join the army of Washington. Out of seventy-three privates, two were from Germany, twenty from Ireland, and six from Great Britain; while forty-five enlisted under the designation of Americans.

Among those Americans some were Quakers; though they did not remain Quakers long. There was searching of heart, and trying of spirit, for all brave men in America; and of such the Society in the main consisted. The early history of the Friends is one long record of invincible fortitude displayed in the presence of atrocious malevolence and unsparing ridicule. Theirs was a courage of the sort which the world calls passive, and not active. The distinction is an idle one; for nobody who has seen the Friends working in the thick of a famine or a fever, directing the operations of the life-brigade on a stormy sea-coast, or immersed in the heat and turmoil of a contested election, will ever doubt that they are potentially the keenest fighters. Those Pennsylvanian Quakers, who belonged to the popular party, found themselves in a grave predicament; for they had to resolve whether they would stand idle and unarmed at a time when the country of their selection was in danger. A considerable number of them rallied to the defence of the Revolution, and were expelled from the

Body as persons unfaithful to its principles. Their cases were considered at the Monthly Meetings in the city of Philadelphia; and all who furthered, or even remotely abetted, warlike proceedings lost their birthright in the Society. Recreant Friends were "disowned" by dozens and scores on a great variety of charges; — for assuming a military appearance; for joining the American army, and attending a stage-play; for fitting out an armed vessel; for making weapons of war to the destruction of their fellow-men; for being in an engagement where many were slain; for selling prize rum which their relatives had captured when privateering. As against four hundred, who were faithfully dealt with on account of help given to the American cause, twenty only were punished for taking open part with the British. That disproportion in the numbers of the outcasts by no means represented the balance of political opinion in the Society; for Quakers who were Patriots had a much stronger motive for declaring themselves partisans than Quakers who were Loyalists. People must be audacious, busy, and much in evidence if they desire to help on a revolution; whereas a man may do something to hinder one who stays quietly at home, grumbling against the members of the provisional government, throwing difficulties in the way of their tax-gatherer, and refusing to pay for a substitute in the militia until his bed is sold from under him.[1]

That was the course taken by the great majority of Quakers; and the neighbours among whom they lived were at no loss to interpret the inward sentiments which their attitude betokened.[2] Paine roundly called them dishonest respecters of persons, who addressed all their

[1] A Quaker, drawn for the militia, was bound to see his goods actually seized and sold, under pain of disownment. That penalty was inflicted on one offender for "Purposely placing money before a person who was about seizing his effects to satisfy a fine imposed on him in lieu of military service," and on another for "Countenancing the payment of a demand for the releasing of his cow."

[2] "The official position was one of neutrality; but individually the Friends could hardly be neutral. It seems almost certain that the men of property and social standing in Philadelphia, like the wealthy mer-

sermons about the wickedness of war to one party in the quarrel. "If," he cried, "ye really preach from conscience, and mean not to make a political hobby-horse of your religion, convince the world thereof by proclaiming your doctrine to our enemies; for they likewise bear arms. Give us proof of your sincerity by publishing it at St. James's. Preach repentance to your King; and do not spend your partial invectives against the injured and insulted only, but, like faithful ministers, cry aloud and spare none." The Quakers, however, had no mind to rebuke their Sovereign; with whose proceedings, indeed, they were very fairly satisfied. On First Month Twentieth, 1776, the Meeting for Sufferings, — a council hardly inferior in weight and authority to the Legislative Assembly of the Colony, — issued a general address defining the position of the Friends. The closing paragraph of this document expressed unqualified abhorrence of all such writings and measures as indicated a design to break off the happy connection hitherto enjoyed with the Kingdom of Great Britain, and to impair the just and necessary subordination to the King and those who were placed in authority under him.

The creed formulated in these antique phrases was very little to the taste of all, or most, Philadelphians. When the news of Lexington had arrived in the city, the flame of patriotism blazed hot and high. Two thousand volunteers were soon at drill. Townsmen as they were, they knew the use of their limbs and their weapons; for manly exercises had long been of great account in the community. Philadelphians enjoyed every facility for becoming expert swimmers and oarsmen; they prided themselves, with some show of reason, on being the most elegant skaters in the world; and,

chants of New York and Boston, were loyalists, though in their case passively so." That is the account given by Mr. Isaac Sharpless, the President of Haverford College, in his *History of Quaker Government in Pennsylvania*. Mathieu Dumas, bringing a fresh mind from France, very soon detected that "the Quakers, with an outward show of indifference, at the bottom of their hearts inclined towards the party of the King."

when a lad was in cash, his first thought was to buy powder and shot, and hire a skiff in which to hunt duck and water-rail along the sedgy banks, and among the reed-clad islets, of the Delaware. The enthusiasm of war was not confined to the less wealthy classes. One company of light infantry went by the title of the Quaker Blues. Another, recruited from the gilded youth of a town where gold was in plenty, called themselves the Greens, and were spoken of by everybody else as the Silk Stockings. The frugality and austerity, which had been the fashion in New England ever since the outbreak of the Revolution, took a modified form in the easy-mannered capital of Pennsylvania. There, we are told, the serious aspect of affairs brought temperance into vogue; and, instead of frequenting tavern suppers, young men of family generally spent their evenings among their female acquaintance. They flirted more, and drank less; but even so their abstinence stopped short of asceticism. The captain of the Green Company owned a noted cellar; and "capacious demijohns of Madeira" were set out in the court-yard where his men mustered, for their refreshment before marching to parade. It was a jolly time; in marked contrast to the hardships that were in store for them all, and to the humiliations of defeat and captivity which soon befell very many among their number.

The worse educated and more boisterous votaries of the Revolution could not repress their pugnacity until they had an opportunity of displaying it on the field of honour. In Philadelphia, as elsewhere, they carried on irregular and most unchivalrous hostilities against those who disagreed with them. One Tory lawyer received a box with a halter coiled inside it. Another, who noticed a volume entitled Trials for High Treason on a bookseller's counter, "asked the gentleman who kept the store whether it would not be a proper book for Mr. Adams to peruse." Next day the unfortunate loyalist was carted round the streets, and only escaped worse treatment on account of the meekness with which, at every stopping-place on the route, he thanked the crowd for their forbearance and civility. He was the father of Leigh Hunt. In 1813 the son paid a heavy penalty for bantering an elderly Regent; and the father, in 1776, had found it not less dangerous to laugh at an infant, or rather an embryo, Republic. Physicians, as usual, were allowed to think as they pleased without being molested; but even they were expected to repay lenity by discretion. Doctor Kearsley, who talked loud in disparagement of the Revolution, and was most inconsequently suspected of plotting secretly against it, was seized by a party of militiamen, and hustled, bleeding and indignant, into "the Tory cart." His profession was so far respected that he escaped being tarred and feathered, and was supplied with as much punch as he wished to drink. The poor man, however, did not long survive his ride, and died with a mind disordered by the shock.

The only conceivable excuse for these detestable practices was that they were perpetrated by men who had no voice in deciding into which scale of the balance, at a supreme national crisis, the vast weight of their native province should be thrown. In May 1776 the additional members of the Pennsylvanian assembly fell to be chosen; but the electorate was narrow, and in no sense entitled to speak for the colony. The franchise was denied to every man who could not show fifty dollars. Many thousand Germans, zealots for liberty, were not allowed to vote unless they were naturalised; and they could not be naturalised without taking the oath of allegiance to the King. Many hundred energetic politicians were fighting in Canada, or living in tents at the military stations along the Hudson river, while civil power was left "to the timid who remained at home."[1] The Proprietary party easily held their own at the poll in the country districts; and only one Patriot was returned among the four representatives allotted to the capital.

[1] Bancroft: Vol. V., page 240, of the Centenary edition.

Multitudes of excellent citizens, who had never soiled their hands by participation in terrorism and outrage, had looked forward to the election as a slender chance of bringing constitutional pressure to bear upon the action of the Assembly; and that hope was now gone. The prospect was indeed appalling. Far the largest army that had ever been sent across the ocean by the most powerful nation in the world was drawing near their shores from day to day. Hordes of foreign mercenaries had already been enrolled for their destruction; and the supply would never be exhausted as long as there was a venal prince in Germany, or until the British Treasury had lost credit to borrow. On every frontier the savages were waiting, armed and painted, until their Great Father should speak the word which would turn them loose upon his disobedient sons and daughters. Populous and flourishing seaside places had been laid in ashes under orders, still in force, which expressly enjoined that towns should be destroyed at that season of the year when the houseless inhabitants would suffer the most severely. And, — more alarming than all besides, — a humble petition, dictated, (it is true,) by a well-wisher of the King, but subscribed by the most eminent among the opponents of the King's policy, had elicited no response. That ominous silence had been broken only for the purpose of proclaiming that every colonist who took a part in the civil government of America, or who aided its defence, was a rebel and traitor, liable, just as much as in days of old were the fugitives from Sedgemoor or Culloden, to the extreme penalty of the law.

Those were the circumstances under which the voice of Pennsylvania was stifled, and her sword-arm paralysed. It was a situation like that of France in August and September 1792, when the terror and wrath of a threatened and bewildered people deluged Paris with blood, and blackened history with a stain which time will never efface. But the Philadelphians of 1776, though exposed to the same trials and temptations, comported themselves in a manner which left nothing to regret. A population of Englishmen, and Northern Irishmen, they were not inclined to sit quietly down, and wait for the day when they would learn which of them were to be hanged, and which pardoned. It was a work of necessity to disentangle themselves from the trammels of the existing Constitution; but they set about that work decently and in order. No life was taken; no store was plundered; not a coat was torn, or a pane of glass broken. There assembled in the State-house yard a crowd too large to count, and guessed by various witnesses at from four to seven thousand householders. It was nothing more nor less than an exceptionally large Town-meeting. The gentlemen who summoned it had defined their position in a spirited manifesto, putting forward no official claims to public obedience, but describing themselves as watchmen for the province, who perceived, and were prepared to combat, the dangers of the hour.[1] The meeting unanimously voted that the Instructions issued by the Assembly to their delegates in the Continental Congress were of a nature to withdraw Pennsylvania from a happy union with other colonies. It was then moved that the present House of Assembly, not having the authority of the people for that purpose, could not, without usurpation, proceed to form a new government for the province. From that proposition only one person dissented; and the Committee of the City and Liberties of Philadelphia was accordingly directed to summon a conference of the committees of every county in the province, and to make arrangements for a Constituent Convention, which should be chosen by the people.

[1] " Friends and fellow-countrymen, the question before you is short and easy. You will be called upon to declare whether you will support the Union of the Colonies in opposition to the Instructions of the House of Assembly, or whether you will support the Assembly against the Union of the Colonies. We have declared for the former; and we will at the hazard of our lives support the Union. We have been open in our affairs. The sense of this city hath been publicly taken, and we will not be belied by Tories. Our situation makes us a kind of sentinels for the safety of the Province." *American Archives:* Series IV., Vol. VI.

That day extinguished the self-confidence and self-respect of the Pennsylvanian Assembly. Its sittings thenceforward were infrequent, and its proceedings nugatory. The members gladly found engagements which kept them elsewhere; and, when a quorum was obtained, they could resolve upon nothing more dignified than neither to advise, nor forbid, a Declaration of Independence, inasmuch as they trusted " the ability, prudence, and integrity" of their delegates. That trust was not shared by the majority of their countrymen. On the eighteenth of June the committees of Philadelphia, and of the several counties, met in a provincial conference; and the Legislative Assembly made its final exit from the political stage. The members confessed, in a formal vote, their despair of being able to attend in sufficient numbers for the due discharge of business. They adjourned for a couple of months; and the announcement of the adjournment was intended, and accepted, as an abdication. The provincial conference was held in Carpenter's Hall; a fine, simple, brick building, with a bold pediment and a deep cornice, most appropriate for the sober, durable work which was being done within. There, at all events, no difficulty arose about a quorum. In the presence, and with the approbation, of a hundred and four members, the government of the colony was declared incompetent, and a new one was ordered to be formed on the authority of the people only. For the purpose of obtaining that authority it was determined to revive William Penn's " Great Law" of December 1682, and to confer upon every tax-payer the right of voting to elect a convention charged with the duty of making a reformed Constitution for Pennsylvania; and, before another week was out, "the Conference, with perfect unanimity, all its members giving their voices one by one, pronounced their willingness to concur in a vote of Congress declaring the united Colonies to be free and independent States." [1]

[1] Bancroft ; Vol. V., page 309. The proceedings of the Assembly, and of the conference, are recorded at length in the *American Archives.*

The Pennsylvanian revolution had been accomplished; and meanwhile the larger movement was rapidly approaching to its consummation. A prodigious impulse had of late been given to the national sentiment of the colonies by a colonist of such recent adoption that he had been an Englishman for twice as many years as he had been an American for months. Paine emigrated to Philadelphia at the end of 1774, bearing a letter of introduction from Doctor Franklin which described him as an ingenious worthy young man. He seemed young, no doubt, to Franklin, who was vainly endeavouring to feel old at seventy; but Paine was already eight and thirty, and had left behind him in England a wrecked career and a ruined home. He was separated from his wife; and the Commissioners of Inland Revenue had ejected him from the employment by which he earned his bread. Nor can it be said that his antecedents pointed him out as a leader of the popular party in America; for his misfortune had arisen from his having been too outspoken a champion of the claims and interests of excisemen. On the other hand, enemies of the Revenue might account it in his favour that he had passed among his official superiors for a notoriously lax and inefficient gauger.

Far from immaculate, Paine was not without his excuses. The constitution of society in the country from which he came was ill suited to humble men who were more desirous to express their political opinions than to improve their material fortunes. For their views on public questions no demand existed; and, if they tried to create one, the Court of King's Bench, and the Sergeant-at-Arms of the House of Commons, might soon have had a good deal that was very unpleasant to say to them. Cut off from more congenial opportunities of intellectual expansion, Paine's energies had hitherto been directed into sordid, and even vicious, channels; but there was in him something higher and better than had been called forth by the circumstances in which the prime of his life was passed. Franklin asked his correspondents in America to put the newcomer into the way of obtaining the post of a clerk, or assistant surgeon, or usher in a school; but Paine turned his attention to literature. His articles were the making of a publication which had lately been started in Philadelphia; and he soon became the editor. He conducted the magazine with great and ever increasing success, which was the more remarkable and honourable because he never shrank from the defence of novel, and sometimes most unpopular, principles. He condemned duelling, and the deliberate or thoughtless ill-treatment of animals. He spoke up against negro slavery quite as emphatically as against hereditary privileges and religious intolerance. He advocated international arbitration; international and internal copyright; and justice to women, especially in the form of increased facilities for divorce. Many causes which, for good or otherwise, have since prevailed in America, had their first, or very nearly their first, exposition in the pages of the "Pennsylvania Magazine." During eighteen months, (so a competent judge has pronounced,) there probably never was the same amount of good literary work done on a salary of fifty pounds a year.[1]

In the second week of January, 1776, a pamphlet called "Common Sense" appeared in Philadelphia. The production had those merits which the title indicated. The author, whoever he was, made no pretence to guide his readers through the Dismal Swamp of the financial controversy, — that intricate and slippery region where even Edmund Burke had confessed himself afraid to tread.[2] But he was familiar with

[1] The *Life of Thomas Paine*, by Moncure Daniel Conway; chapter iv.
[2] " Sir, I think you must perceive that I am resolved this day to have nothing at all to do with the question of the right of taxation. I do not examine whether the giving away a man's money be a power excepted and reserved out of the general trust of government; or whether, on the contrary, a right of taxation is necessarily involved in the general principle of legislation, and inseparable from the ordinary supreme power. These are deep questions, where great names militate against each other; where reason is perplexed, and an appeal to authorities only thickens the confusion.

public transactions, and in touch with popular opinion;
and he gave forcible and glowing expression to the
thoughts and aspirations which surged around him in a
hundred thousand souls. The poet has been described,
by a poet, as one who expresses that which is only
thought by others;[1] and the same is the secret of
the orator and the publicist. Learned men, a century afterwards, construct an elaborate catalogue of
the reasons and considerations which ought to have
governed, whether they did or not, the actors in
historical events; but the true motives, that once
swayed great multitudes, have to be sought in those
speeches and writings which stirred them at the time.
The author of "Common Sense" has not unfrequently
been criticised as superficial; and ill-educated and inexperienced perhaps he was. But he saw beyond pre-
cedents and statutes, and constitutional facts or fictions,
into the depths of human nature; and he knew that,
if men are to fight to the death, it must be for reasons
which all can understand.

America, (so the writer declared,) would flourish as
much, and probably much more, if no European power
had anything to do with her government. The articles
of commerce by which she had enriched herself were
not articles of fancy and luxury, but the prime necessaries of life; and she would always have a market in
Europe for her produce while eating was the custom of
that continent. She gained no profit from the English
connection, and she suffered in her dignity. A greater
absurdity could not be conceived than three millions of

For high and reverend authorities lift up their heads on both sides, and
there is no sure footing in the middle. This point is
> 'The great Serbonian bog,
> Betwixt Damiata and Mount Casius old,
> Where armies whole have sunk.'

I do not intend to be overwhelmed in that bog, though in such respectable
company." Burke's Speech on his Resolutions for Conciliation with America; March 22, 1775.
[1]   " You tell
    What we felt only."
        The Last Ride Together, by Robert Browning.

people running to their sea-coast, every time a ship arrived from London, to know what portion of liberty they
should enjoy. Let alone the humiliation, Americans
endured great practical inconvenience by their subjec-
tion to a nation so far distant from them, and so very
ignorant about all which concerned them. To be for
ever travelling three or four thousand miles with a tale
or a petition, and waiting four or five months for an
answer which, when obtained, wanted five or six more
to explain it, would in a few years be looked upon as
folly and childishness. There was a time during which
such a condition of things had been proper; there was
a proper time for it to cease; and that time was the
date when the first shots were fired at Lexington. "The
period of debate is closed. Arms, in the last resource,
must decide the contest. A new era for politics is
struck. A new method of thinking has arisen. All
plans and proposals prior to that nineteenth of April
are like the almanacs of last year."

That was the way to write, if a man wanted to be
read; and "Common Sense" was read to some purpose.
It would be difficult to name any human composition
which has had an effect at once so instant, so extended,
and so lasting. It flew through numberless editions.
It was pirated, and parodied, and imitated, and translated
into the language of every country where the new Republic had well-wishers, and could hope to procure
allies. Parisians were of opinion that it had a greater
run in France even than in America.[1] It was reprinted
in all the colonies with a frequency surprising at a time
when colonial printing-houses were very few. Three
months from its first appearance, a hundred and twenty
thousand copies had been sold in America alone; and,
before the demand ceased, it was calculated that half a
million had seen the light. Demosthenes has said that
the power of oratory is as much in the ear as in the
tongue. The extraordinary success of this famous
pamphlet proved, if it needed proving, that the power

[1] *American Archives;* August 1776.

of authorship is as much in the reader as in the writer. "In the elements of its strength it was precisely fitted to the hour, to the spot, and to the passions. It was meant for plain men in desperate danger, and desperately in earnest." [1]

According to the contemporary newspapers, "Common Sense" turned thousands in New York to Independence, who could not endure the idea before; in Pennsylvania and the Carolinas it was read by all, and few put it down unconvinced; it had done wonders in Maryland, and worked nothing short of miracles, for, all over the province, it had made Tories into Whigs; while even in Massachusetts, where the margin for conversion was small, it added a perceptible amount of heat to the fire of patriotism. Authoritative testimony to the amazing influence of "Common Sense" remains on record in the private correspondence of innumerable individuals. Mrs. John Adams, in a letter which must have less than half pleased her husband, confessed herself charmed with the sentiments of the piece, and unable to imagine how an honest heart could hesitate one moment at adopting them. General Charles Lee, whose heart was as honest as his vanity would permit, owned that its perusal had brought him round to a belief in the necessity of separation; and Washington placed its "sound doctrine and unanswerable reasoning" on a level of importance with the "flaming arguments" which went up from the burning houses of Falmouth and Norfolk. "My countrymen," he wrote, "will come reluctantly into the idea of independence, but time and persecution bring wonderful things to pass; and, by

[1] Tyler's *Literary History;* chapter xxi., section vii. Professor Tyler, who always writes with force, but always with measure, thus introduces the subject of the pamphlet: "In one sentiment all persons, Tories and Whigs, seemed perfectly to agree: namely, in abhorrence of the project of separation from the empire. Suddenly, however, and within a period of less than six months, the majority of the Whigs turned completely round, and openly declared for Independence. Among the facts necessary to enable us to account for this almost unrivalled political somersault, is that of the appearance of 'Common Sense.'"

letters which I have lately received from Virginia, I find
'Common Sense' is working a powerful change there
in the minds of many men."

The authorship was attributed to some of the most
distinguished names in America. It was reported that
the Prince of Wales was caught by his mother reading
"Dr. Franklin's pamphlet 'Common Sense'" in a corner of the Palace, and stoutly refused to confess how
it had come into his possession.[1] The credit of the
book was frequently given to Samuel Adams, who had
been a literary gladiator, and no lover of monarchy,
from his youth onwards. While still at college, in
presence of all the Harvard dignitaries, he had defended the thesis that it was lawful to resist the Supreme Magistrate, if the Commonwealth could not be
otherwise preserved. His talents were acknowledged
by friend and foe. With his own party he passed for
"the most correct, genteel, and artful pen in America;"
and Governor Bernard had declared, with a round oath,
that every dip of that pen stung like a horned snake.
Bostonians, whose business or pleasure kept them late
out of bed, seldom failed, however far the night was
spent, to see a light in a certain window which indicated
"that Sam Adams was hard at work writing against the
Tories." The most aggressive of controversialists, he
laid it down as a canon so to conduct a dispute as always
to keep your adversary in the wrong: and thousands of
people, who were acquainted with his polemical methods
and his political creed, would have it that the Junius of
America was Samuel Adams, and no other.

In the House of Commons, and in some other

---

[1] The belief that Franklin had been the author of *Common Sense* was
still held in 1824 by Paul Louis Courier. "Happy was Franklin, who
saw his country free, having done more than anyone else for her freedom
by his famous *Common Sense*, that tract of two sheets of print. Never did
any portly volume effect so much for the human race. Rallying all hearts
and minds to the party of Independence, it decided the issue of that
great conflict which, ended for America, is still proceeding all over the
rest of the world." So wrote Courier in his *Pamphlet of Pamphlets*, —
the latest in date of those exquisite productions which were the first-fruits
of the great harvest of French nineteenth century literature.

quarters, the book was ascribed to John Adams.[1] **More** than three years afterwards, when he landed on Gallic soil, he was hailed as the famous Adams, the celebrated member of Congress, whose wonderful pamphlet France, and all Europe, had received with rapture. The first half of the compliment lost something in value when he became aware that fashionable Paris, which never mistook Benjamin Franklin for anybody else, was not very clear in its mind as to whether the famous Adams was John or Samuel. And to be credited with the paternity of "Common Sense" was still less acceptable, inasmuch as he disagreed with two-thirds of the volume, and could not abide the real author.

That personage had been in no haste to disclose himself. In some editions the book was announced on the title-page as having been composed by an Englishman. In others it was described as the work of a man unconnected with any party, and under no sort of influence, public or private, except that of reason and principle; but, by the summer of 1776, it was generally known that Paine was the writer. He was accused by John Adams, (as if it mattered,) of having been furnished by others with his more telling arguments, and especially with his title, which was the best portion of the book. One of the recommendations contained in "Common Sense" Adams held to be so impolitic that he published a brief, and rather timid, protest,[2] the appearance of which procured him a visit from Paine. Considering that Adams regarded Paine as "a disastrous meteor," and his literary style as suitable for an

---

[1] On the twenty-fourth of April, 1776, Rigby argued that the Americans aimed at Independence. "He deduced this opinion from Mr. Adams's pamphlet called *Common Sense*, in which he without scruple talked of everything short of Independency as ridiculous, and wrote in such a style that no man here could lay claim to common sense, and not see the drift of the writer."

[2] "*Thoughts on Government, Applicable to the Present State of the American Colonies;* In a letter from a Gentleman to a Friend; Philadelphia, 1776." It was a reply to Paine's advocacy of a single legislative Chamber.

emigrant from Newgate,[1] the interview was sufficiently amicable. Before it ended, Paine confided to Adams that he had some thoughts of publishing his views on religion, but believed that he had best postpone it to the latter part of life; — which, if he desired to retain the confidence of New England Puritans, must in his case be called a judicious resolution. The hold which he had acquired over American opinion remained unimpaired for many years to come. His reputation gained, rather than lost, by the attempts of Tory writers to refute him. A whole first edition of the most able among the answers to his pamphlet has perished, and is said to have been burned by the Sons of Liberty. The incendiaries, however, showed their discrimination; for they spared another reply to "Common Sense" entitled "Plain Truth, by Candidus," which is so forlorn a production that in our own day more than one admirer of the American loyalists has been at pains to prove that his own special hero had no hand in the writing of it.

Paine got nothing from his book except celebrity, and a consciousness that he had powerfully promoted the spread of opinions which he sincerely held. It was said in South Carolina that the author of "Common Sense" deserved a statue of gold; but none of that metal reached him as the reward of a performance which still is the high-water mark of success in ephemeral literature. He was denounced in the "Pennsylvania Gazette," in a communication signed by Cato, as an interested writer, and a stranger meddling with American affairs. Cato was pretty well known to be the Reverend Doctor William Smith, Provost of the

---

[1] *Autobiography of John Adams.* Adams disliked Paine from the moment that he first met him; but the contemptuous expressions quoted in the text are of much later date. The Autobiography was written after Paine had published *The Age of Reason,* and *The Rights of Man;* and when he was a notorious partisan, and Adams a prominent adversary, of the French Revolution. In 1776 an American patriot would hardly have ventured, even in the privacy of a journal, to handle the author of *Common Sense* so disrespectfully.

University of Philadelphia; a man altogether devoid of sympathy with those who do public work gratis. To that untiring and ubiquitous solicitor for Church preferment Paine replied that Cato was a stranger nowhere, and a slave everywhere. So much revenge he allowed himself to take; but he did not condescend to repel the unworthy imputation, which had been levelled against his motives, by vaunting, or even mentioning, his own disinterestedness. He sold his book at a price that constituted a renunciation of all personal profit; and he subsequently followed the same course with regard to other publications which had only less vogue than his first pamphlet. He surrendered a fortune in the case of that pamphlet alone; and "notwithstanding this experience Paine also gave to the States the copyright of his 'Crisis'; was taunted as a gazetteer; ate his crust contentedly; and the peace found him a penniless patriot, who might easily have had fifty thousand pounds in his pocket."[1]

John Adams, — a good workman, but one who quarrelled with his tools, — decried the merits of " Common Sense "; and yet that book rendered the main exploit of his own life possible, and in the later stages almost easy. The direction in which ideas had been set marching showed itself first, according to the custom of the colonies, in the tone of the sermons. So late as February 1776, Provost William Smith, who had been invited by Congress to deliver a funeral eulogy in honour of General Montgomery, had taken that curious opportunity of announcing that the sentiments of the body which he addressed were opposed to Independence; and a considerable number of the members, (though not a majority,) were in favour of thanking the orator, and requesting him to print the oration. But already in the

---

[1] Conway's *Paine;* chapter vi. The publisher of *Common Sense* sent in a bill to the author of nearly thirty pounds for presentation copies. That amount appears to have represented the final balance on the whole transaction.

ensuing May, when John Adams went to hear a discourse on the signs of the times, the preacher treated
him to a comparison between George the Third and
Pharaoh, and an assurance that Providence, which had
liberated the Jews, would do as much for the Americans. The part which man had to play in that enterprise was all the more likely to be successful because
the chief of the actors regarded himself as a chosen instrument. "Is it not," Adams wrote to his wife, "a saying of Moses, 'Who am I, that I should go in and out
before this great people'?   When I consider the great
events which have passed, and those greater which are
rapidly advancing, I feel an awe upon my mind which
is not easily described."   For some weeks more, such
thoughts as these fermented in the heads of the patriots; and on the seventh of June Richard Henry Lee,
in the name and with the authority of Virginia, called
upon Congress to resolve in favour of declaring the
thirteen colonies independent. After several days of debate it was arranged that an interval should be allowed
for the purpose of enabling the delegates of the central
provinces to consult their constituents; but that, to prevent loss of time, a small committee should be charged
with the duty of preparing a Declaration in harmony with
the proposed resolution. And then Congress dropped the
subject for a while, and reverted to the endless routine
of administration, which was always going forward behind the scenes of that great drama; — providing muskets for one battalion, and stopping the price of uniforms
out of the pay of another; fixing the salary of the Secretary of the Board of War and Ordnance at a hundred
and sixty pounds a year; voting John Bruce the sum of
thirteen dollars as the balance of his bill for cartridge-
boxes, and twelve dollars to Margaret Thomas for nurs-
ing two soldiers in the small-pox.[1]

The Committee was composed of Roger Sherman and
Robert Livingston, Benjamin Franklin, John Adams,
and Thomas Jefferson.   Congress chose them by ballot;

[1] *Journals of Congress* for June 1776.

and most votes were cast for Jefferson. He was a young man, and an unobtrusive legislator; but an independent fortune had given him leisure for self-culture, and he had not wasted his privilege. Congress was a practical assembly, and selected men for posts which they were qualified to hold. They appointed Washington Commander-in-Chief because he could fight; they sent Franklin to Paris because he had culti-vated the art of turning great people round his finger; and they entrusted the Declaration of Independence to Jefferson because, both in style and substance, his writings betokened the lawyer, the statesman, and the student.[1] The spirit which he brought to the task is displayed in a private letter, dated six months before he received a commission to be the exponent of his country's wrongs. "There is not," he said, "in the British empire a man who more cordially loves a union with Great Britain than I do. But, by the God that made me, I will cease to exist before I yield to a con-nection on such terms as the British Parliament pro-pose; and in this I think I speak the sentiments of America."[2] That was no vain boast, as a century and a quarter of Fourths of July have already shown. Jefferson wrote off the Declaration, without looking inside a book or a pamphlet. So representative an American as Franklin found nothing to add or to ex-punge; and the other members of the committee were not less speedily and entirely satisfied. Two or three verbal corrections were suggested; and then Jefferson made a fair copy in his own hand, which was laid before Congress on the twenty-eighth of June.

[1] "The Sub-Committee met. Jefferson proposed to me to make the draught. I said, 'I will not.' 'You should do it.' 'Oh no.' 'Why not?' 'Reasons enough.' 'What can be your reasons?' 'Reason first, — You are a Virginian; and a Virginian ought to appear at the head of this business. Reason second, — I am obnoxious and unpopular; you are very much otherwise. Reason third, — You can write ten times better than I can.'" John Adams to Colonel Timothy Pickering; August 6, 1822.

[2] Thomas Jefferson to John Randolph; Philadelphia, November 29, 1775.

The discussion of the Virginian resolution was re-
sumed on the first of July. The names of the speakers
are known, and the sides which they took, and, (in a
few cases,) the impression which they produced upon
their audience. There our information stops. In those
days, (said John Adams,) there were no stenographers;
speeches were never printed; and all that was not
handed down orally, like the harangues of Indian orators, was lost in air.[1] The Chevalier Botta, an historian
of the American war, constructed imaginary declama-
tions in choice Italian, and put them into the mouths of
the statesmen at Philadelphia. A lifelike picture of
Congress, however, must not be sought in the pages
of a Piedmontese who, when recording debates in the
Parliament at Westminster, made English public men
address each other as Honourable Senators and Dear
Fellow-citizens, instead of the Worthy Alderman and
the Noble Lord in the Red Ribbon. Nor was the text
of speeches made by the Revolutionary leaders to be
found among the papers which they left behind them;
for their colleagues in the State House of Philadelphia,
during the summer of 1776, were in no mood to listen to
the eloquence of manuscript. Dr. Witherspoon of New
Jersey, who had preached in a Scotch pulpit, was said
never to have addressed Congress without committing
his observations to memory; but the most telling sentence which he uttered on this historical occasion could
not have taken very long to compose. In his judgement, (he said,) the country was not only ripe for Independence, but was in danger of becoming rotten for
want of it. That went to the root of the matter. It
was in vain that the friends of the British connection
exerted themselves to the utmost against a foregone
conclusion. Dickinson fired a parting salvo in defence

---

[1] John Adams to Henry Niles; Quincy, January 14, 1818. In a letter
to Thomas McKean, in 1815, Adams says: "The debates and deliberations of Congress, from 1774 to 1783, were all in secret, and are now lost
for ever. Mr. Dickinson printed a speech, which he said he made in
Congress against the Declaration of Independence; but it appeared to
me very different from that which you and I heard."

of his own position, which had always been illogical, and had now become untenable; but that position was stormed and carried by the irresistible onset of John Adams. Not a word of his speech had been considered beforehand; not a word has reached posterity; but every person there present pronounced it to be above criticism, and beyond praise. According to Jefferson, his deep conceptions and nervous style, (and, it may safely be added, the faith that was in him,) gave him a power of thought and phrase which moved his hearers out of themselves. A Congressman from the central colonies, not specially given to classical allusions, exclaimed that Adams had stood forth as the Atlas of Independence; and the Virginian delegates paid him the unique tribute of admitting that nothing better had ever been heard at Williamsburg. The expression of views and convictions, which had so long been rolling up and down in his mind, seemed to Adams himself a small matter. In a private letter, written that evening, he described the debate as time misspent; because nothing was said but what had been repeated, and hackneyed, in that room a hundred times over for six months past.[1]

The Resolution was carried, with the adherence of only nine among the thirteen colonies; and it was understood that a final and decisive vote would be taken on the morrow. But the season for debate came suddenly to a close. That very afternoon, while Dickinson was still speaking, a hundred and thirty-seven sail were counted in the channel north of Sandy Hook, within three leagues of New York; and heavy firing of cannon was heard at four o'clock on the next morning.[2] Before the sitting of the first July came to an end, a despatch from General Washington had been read aloud at the table, reporting that the English ships were dropping in by threes and fours; that an attack was imminent; and that, with the slender forces at his

---

[1] John Adams to Samuel Chase; Philadelphia, July 1, 1776.
[2] John Cortenhoven to the President of Congress. *American Archives.*

command, it would require all his exertions to prevent the ruin and destruction which appeared to be impending. It was the sort of argument which turns votes wholesale wherever Anglo-Saxons are concerned. South Carolina came round at once; — for the sake of unanimity, as the delegates alleged; but in reality because the fighting blood in their veins neutralised the effect of all the Quaker claret which they had imbibed since Congress met in the fall of the preceding year. Delaware acceded to the Resolution; and enough Pennsylvanians stayed away to enable the suffrage of their colony to be cast on the same side. New York was still in the throes of constitution-making, and her representatives, who had not yet received an authoritative mandate, sate apart while the vote was being taken; but it had been ascertained that all of them, except one, were personally in favour of Independence. Congress affirmed, — and none of the thirteen provinces dissented, — that the united colonies were, and of right ought to be, free and independent States; that they were absolved from all allegiance to the British Crown; and that the political connection between them and Great Britain was dissolved. "Thus," said Adams, "was decided the greatest question which ever was debated in America; and a greater, perhaps, never was, nor will be, decided among men. The Second day of July, 1776, will be celebrated by succeeding generations as the great anniversary festival. It ought to be commemorated as the day of deliverance by acts of devotion to God Almighty. It ought to be solemnized with pomp and parade, with guns, bells, bonfires, and illuminations from one end of this continent to the other, from this time forward for evermore."[1]

It was a veracious prophecy, although the date named was wrong by eight and forty hours; for the Declaration of Independence had not yet been submitted to Congress for revisal, correction, and approval. So much still remained to do; and that the pressure of

[1] John Adams to Mrs. Adams; Philadelphia, July 3, 1776.

necessity required it to be done quickly was well both for the merits of the composition, and the feelings of the author. Even as it was, Jefferson suffered, as man must ever suffer, from the excision of some among his most glowing periods. Franklin, who sate next him, and perceived that he "was not insensible to these mutilations," comforted him by a homely apologue, in queer disproportion to the magnitude of the occasion.[1] But Congress used a sparing hand; and the alterations made were all in the direction of the accuracy, the conciseness, and the discretion on which the literary excellence of a State-paper depends. In the original draft George the Third had been taken to task for withdrawing his governors, and thereby depriving the colonists of his favour and protection. The list of charges against that monarch was sufficiently voluminous without the insertion of any such preposterous imputation; for the royal governors had withdrawn themselves to the shelter of the nearest British frigate, without orders from Whitehall, and not a moment before it was necessary. Indeed, the only one of them still resident at the capital of his province was the governor of New Jersey, whose late subjects had got him safe under lock and key.

Jefferson, again, had written, and somewhat overwritten, a denunciation of the King for having refused his sanction to the successive endeavours which the Virginian assembly had made, in all honesty, to suppress the importation of negroes. The accusation in itself was just; since George the Third had exerted his Veto in defence of the slave-trade with unusual zest, and with strong resentment against the authors of the proposal which he thought fit to negative. But Jefferson's treatment of this burning question was, (to use his

---

[1] " I have made it a rule," (Franklin told his younger colleague,) " to avoid becoming the draftsman of papers to be reviewed by a public body. I took my lesson from an incident which I will relate to you." And then he told, with a perfection of native humour, his tale of the hatter who composed an inscription for his shop-front, and invited his friends and neighbours to criticise the wording of it. The story is given in full by Jared Sparks, in the ninth chapter of his *Life of Franklin.*

own imposing words,) " disapproved by some Southern gentlemen, whose reflections were not yet matured to the full abhorrence of that traffic." And some Northern gentlemen rightly apprehended that the world outside the United States, and very probably their own descendants likewise, would fail to distinguish between the guilt of keeping, and the guilt of importing, slaves. Their American sense of humour was already sufficiently developed for them to perceive that allusions to negroes should be sparingly introduced into a document which proclaimed it a self-evident truth that men were created equal, and endowed by their Creator with an inalienable right to liberty and the pursuit of happiness.

The most important change was the conversion of the paragraph, addressed to the people of Great Britain, from a bitter impeachment to a friendly and pathetic remonstrance. That change was highly politic in view of passing events ; and it saved future generations from a situation which would sometimes have been ludicrous, and at others most embarrassing. George the Third has long passed away ; although America annually denies him the benefit of the kindly Latin proverb which bids us be silent about the dead, where we cannot praise them. But the British people is as much alive as ever ; and it is a good thing that every township between the Atlantic and the Pacific Oceans does not listen once a summer to Jefferson's thrilling sentences about the last stab that had been given to agonizing affection, and the duty of forgetting the love which the colonists formerly entertained towards their unfeeling brethren in England.

Under the amending touch of Congress the Declaration of Independence assumed, and kept, the shape of an indictment against the King. The framers of that indictment did not act in ignorance. Eager readers of history, with an especial fondness for its dry and legal aspects, they had all been nurtured on the doctrine that the King could do no wrong, and that, when an account had to be exacted, his ministers were answerable. But they were not inditing a treatise on the theory of the British Constitution. They were contending for their lives and fortunes against a practical abuse of that Constitution which those English writers, who more than others are careful to weigh their words, have denounced with the most telling vehemence. Mr. Lecky, stating the case shortly but comprehensively, relates how George the Third habitually declined to call into his counsels any statesman resolute and conscientious enough to insist that the policy of the country should be directed by its responsible ministers, instead of being dictated by an irresponsible sovereign. At a notable crisis, which occurred later on in this very war, the King refused to dismiss North, Wedderburn, and Sandwich, and to place the administration in the hands of Chatham and Rockingham. That refusal is declared by Mr. Lecky, — a judge who charges with rare impartiality, and as a rule gives light sentences, — to be as criminal as any of the acts which led Charles the First to the scaffold. The author of that " Short History of the English People" which, to their advantage, the English people have found time to read, devotes an uncomplimentary page to the Government that held office continuously for fourteen years after the retirement of Chatham in 1768. Mr. Green there says that the influence of the King was predominant in the Cabinet from the first, and was supreme in the later and more disastrous days when North had gone to the Treasury. "George was in fact sole Minister during the eight years that followed ; and the shame of the darkest hour of English history lies wholly at his door."

The King was his own prime minister, and as autocratic a prime minister as Whitehall had ever seen. To prove and illustrate that position is an act of superfluity. It would be pedantry to multiply authorities. There are none on the other side. If learned men, writing securely in their libraries a century after date, could not restrain the expression of their righteous indignation, is it a matter for wonder that the Ameri-

can colonists, between two great campaigns, with the
King's sword at their throats, and his German mercenaries and Indian allies almost at the threshold of their
homes, should have spurned the conventionalities of the
law-books, and arraigned the monarch instead of casting
blame upon the nation?   Save and except for the
system of personal government, which George the Third
had laboriously built up ever since 1760, Americans and
Englishmen would not have been slaughtering each
other in 1776.   The King's policy caused the war; the
King kept it going, long after everybody except himself was weary of it; and in 1782 that war was terminated, against his will, by nothing except a peremptory
injunction from the English people, who, if they had
been properly represented in Parliament, would have
brought it to an end long before.

The stock charge against the Declaration of Independence, — repeated in a hundred shapes ever since it
appeared in print, — has been that it lacked originality,
and that its author was a plagiarist.   It was imitated,
(so we are informed,) from the State-papers of the Long
Parliament; it owed much to Locke, and much to
Milton, and more still to Rousseau; and some of the
ideas were taken without acknowledgement from one of
Mrs. Aphra Behn's indecorous comedies.[1]   More recent
sources, on which Jefferson had largely drawn, were
detected in a Charge delivered to the Grand Jury of
Charleston; in the Virginian Declaration of Rights;
and in a mythical document, said to have been issued
as early as May 1775 by the citizens of Mecklenburg
County in North Carolina.   John Adams, great at great
moments, but with a mind too active and uneasy for the
prolonged leisure of his later days, six and forty years

---

[1] *The Widow Ranter, or The History of Bacon in Virginia,* which
Dryden honoured with a prologue, contains a very full-flavoured description of the horrors of Indian warfare.   As if a Virginian of 1776, who had
lived through a real Cherokee war, could not find words to protest against
the treatment which his country-people were likely to endure from hired
savages without having to look in a foolish play written in London more
than a century before!

afterwards explained to a correspondent that there was nothing new in Jefferson's paper.[1]   Jefferson lived to see the letter of his old colleague, and his remarks on it were as sensible as they were good-tempered and dignified. " I did not," he said, "consider it as any part of my charge to invent new ideas, and to offer no sentiment which had ever been expressed before.   Had Mr. Adams been so restrained, Congress would have lost the benefit of his bold and impressive advocations of the rights of Revolution.   For no man's fervid addresses, more than his, encouraged and supported us through the difficulties which, like the ceaseless action of gravity, weighed on us by night and by day.   Yet, on the same ground, we may ask which of his elevated thoughts was new, or can be affirmed never before to have entered the conceptions of man ? "

An American author has argued powerfully and truly that, for such a paper as Jefferson was commissioned to write, the one quality which it could not properly have possessed would have been originality.   Was he to regard himself as a literary essayist, set to produce a sort of prize dissertation on history and politics with a particular application to Anglo-American affairs ? Was he not rather the mouth-piece of a people who had deliberately exposed themselves to perils, the gravity of which they all had measured, under the influence of motives by which they one and all were swayed?[2]   The wiser world has recognised that there

[1] " As you justly observe, there is not an idea in it but what had been hackneyed in Congress for two years before.   The substance is contained in the Declaration of Rights and the violation of those Rights, in the Journals of Congress in 1774.   Indeed, the essence of it is in a pamphlet, voted and printed by the town of Boston before the first Congress met, composed by James Otis, as I suppose, in one of his lucid intervals, and penned and polished by Samuel Adams."   John Adams to Timothy Pickering ; August 6, 1822.   Jefferson's observations on this letter were addressed to James Madison in August 1823.

[2] Tyler's *Literary History;* chapter xxxiii., section 6.   Professor Tyler disposes of the allegation of plagiarising from the early champions of English liberty in a passage which Fox and Macaulay would have liked well to read.   "In the development of political life in England and America there had already been created a vast literature of constitutional

are certain productions which stand in a class apart. To that class belong Elizabeth's speech at Tilbury, and the Declaration of William of Orange, and President Lincoln's discourse in the Cemetery at Gettysburg. The excellence of such pieces is to be judged, not by the ordinary rules of criticism, but by the character and extent of the response they evoked from the nation to which they were addressed. An English member of Parliament, in the following autumn session, said that Jefferson's style was full of faults, and possessed no merit except that of captivating the people. He was told in answer by John Wilkes that he had paid the American a high compliment; for the people would have to decide the controversy, and, if they were captivated, the end had been attained.[1] The people, (said Samuel Adams,) seemed to recognise the Resolution of Congress as if it were a decree promulgated from heaven. The Declaration of Independence went straight to their hearts, because they found in it their own conceptions, put into words which few or none of them were capable of writing. Jefferson had "poured the soul of the Continent" into his manifesto; and therefore, (as a Congressman, who had signed it, joyfully exclaimed,) "it produced a glorious effect and made the colonies all alive."

To be read aloud is the severest test of a literary composition; and the least favourable critic of the Declaration of Independence will not assert that it has been insufficiently subjected to that ordeal. The public listened to it for the first time on the eighth of July, 1776, when it was delivered, slowly and very impressively, in the State-house yard, from a platform which in peaceful times had been erected for the purpose

progress,—a literature common to both portions of the English race,—pervaded by its own stately traditions, and reverberating certain great phrases which formed, as one may say, almost the vernacular of English justice, and of English aspiration for a free, manly, and orderly political life. In this vernacular the Declaration of Independence was written."

[1] *Parliamentary History.* Debate on the Address of October 31, 1776.

of observing the planet Venus.[1] The Pennsylvanian
militia paraded on the Common, and fired away an
amount of powder most discomposing to members of the
Secret Committee charged with importing ammunition,
and collecting sulphur and saltpetre. The welkin, (we
are told in good old English,) was rent with cheers.
The bells were rung, all day and all night, by relays of
the best chimers in the city. To these joyous accom-
paniments an election of members for Philadelphia, in
the new State Assembly, went briskly forward; and
Benjamin Franklin was returned at the head of a list of
sturdy patriots, containing a note-worthy infusion of
German names. The royal coat of arms was taken
down from the Court House, and burned amidst the
acclamations of a throng of spectators. Scenes of this
nature were successively renewed in every colony, or
rather, (for that word was now out of use,) in every
State,[2] as the slow posts came travelling in with the
intelligence of what had passed in Philadelphia.
Throughout Massachusetts the Declaration was read
in all the churches, and entered at full length in the
records of the towns. In the sea-ports of Rhode Island
the news was greeted by loud huzzas for " Free Trade
with all the world," from crowds of hardy mariners who
for some years back had taken very good care that
Rhode Island, in any case, should enjoy the blessings of

[1] "One unseen auditor there was who has left us an account of that
day. Deborah Norris, then a girl of fifteen, had climbed her garden wall
to catch a glimpse of what was going on. The reader was hidden from
her by the side of the Observatory; but she heard distinctly from her high
perch every word he uttered, and was awed into a childish terror as the
grave voice repeated slowly those memorable words, the full significance
of which she was too young to understand." *Philadelphia ; The Place
and People ;* chapter xii.

[2] In November 1775 Congress considered the Instructions to New
Hampshire. "By this time," wrote John Adams, "I mortally hated the
words *Provinces, Colonies,* and *Mother-Country,* and strove to get them
out of the Report. The last was indeed left out ; but the other two were
retained even by this Committee, who were as high Americans as any in
the House." The two first terms have long been obsolete in America ;
but there are pleasant symptoms of the third expression once more coming
into fashion.

free trade between ten at night, and three in the morning. There were bonfires in one city, and illuminations, with rockets and crackers, in another; every locality contributing some additional suggestion towards the programme of jubilation, which everywhere, and ever since, has been observed with all the sanctity of a ritual. The Assembly of South Carolina, which was among the latest converts to Independence, accepted the proclamation of it "with unspeakable pleasure." The ragged fever-stricken garrisons, who were guarding the northern passes along the Hudson river and the line of lakes, assembled to shout over the tidings that they now had a country to sicken and to die for. At New York the Declaration was read at the head of the brigades in what was still a well-nourished and self-confident army. The same evening a mob of soldiers, their blood curdled by the recitation of that portentous catalogue of George the Third's iniquities, pulled down his equestrian effigy on Bowling Green. Horse and man were soon in the melting pots, and re-appeared as bullets of the same material, (so a city humourist declared,) as the brains of those rulers who to gain a pepper-corn had lost an empire.[1] Washington rebuked the riot in a General Order; but, as a work of art, the statue was beyond recovery. The lead had already been distributed among a thousand cartouch-boxes; and portions of it must to this day be embedded in the heart of forest trees which shade the old battle-fields of Long Island and the Jerseys.

And so the United States of America were started on their career duly equipped with a *journée;* — a national possession of the sort which France has inherited in too great abundance, and England only in the somewhat questionable shape of the Fifth November.[2] There have

[1] The statue yielded 42,500 bullets. *Life of Major General John Paterson*, by his great-grandson Thomas Egleston, LL.D.

[2] It is characteristic of the indifference of our forefathers to historical anniversaries that the most important reason for keeping the Fifth of November, — the landing of William of Orange, — was soon as good as forgotten. We ran a near chance of a *journée* on the Tenth of April,

been very famous Fourths of July. One of them, which promised to be gloomy, was brightened by the victory of Gettysburg and the capture of Vicksburg. Another was signalised by the destruction of the Spanish fleet outside the harbour at Santiago. But there is one anniversary of the Declaration of Independence the interest of which can never be surpassed. John Adams lived to a great age. He heard, or read, forty-five orations on the anniversary of the Boston Massacre, and he might have been present at many more; but, when turned of eighty, he ceased to take pleasure in " young gentlemen of genius describing scenes they never saw, and descanting on feelings they never felt, and which great pains had been taken that they should never feel." [1] His wife died old, but long before him; and he waited very quietly, and not unhappily, till the time came to rejoin her.[2] A cheerful account of his closing years has been left by his grandson, — the taciturn, much-enduring, diplomatist whose presence in London from 1861 to 1865 did no little to avert a desolating war between England and America. We are told how the ex-President lived on till his sight almost failed, taking his daily ride; and sitting at home, with his arms folded over the head of his cane, straight upright in an old colonial arm-chair, and in the old colonial attitude. He never tired of listening to the latest and most admired works of contemporary literature, — the Waverley novels, the sea-stories of Fenimore Cooper, and the

1848 ; but the good fortune of England prevailed ; and we have secured the most valuable among those constitutional reforms, to obtain which the Chartists rose, without being under an obligation to observe the day.

[1] John Adams to Dr. Morse ; Quincy, January 5, 1816.

[2] The Ambassador speaks thus of the letters which, in 1763 and subsequent years, passed between his grandfather and grandmother. " With what a mixture of feelings do I look over these old papers ! They contain the secret history of the lives of a single couple ; joy and sunshine, grief and clouds, sorrow and storms. The vicissitudes are rapid, the incidents are interesting. Happy are those who pass through this valley with so much innocence ! " The quotation is from a *Life of Charles Francis Adams*, published in 1900 by his son, C. F. Adams, — a veritable masterpiece among short biographies.

poetry of Byron.   In February 1825 he received a letter
from his old friend, the Marquis of Lafayette, wishing
him joy on the election of his son, John Quincy Adams,
as sixth President of the United States.   He was still
susceptible to the emotions which such events excite in
a father's breast.   "Never," he wrote, "did I feel so
much solemnity as upon this occasion.   The multitude
of my thoughts, and the intensity of my feelings, are
too much for a mind like mine, in its ninetieth year."

One other founder of the Republic still breathed
American air.   Twenty-five years had elapsed since
John Adams was President, and seventeen since Thomas
Jefferson left the Executive Mansion at Washington
after a second term of office.   The Fourth of July,
Eighteen Hundred and Twenty-six, was the Jubilee of
Independence ; and the eyes of all spontaneously turned
to the two veterans, — so long divided by political differences, more recent indeed than the Revolution, but
already of ancient date.   It was hoped that they might
meet once again, to shake hands over their life's work in
the presence of an immense assemblage ; some of whom
might speak of it in the twentieth century as the most
memorable sight an American ever witnessed.   But
they both were very feeble, and the hope was abandoned.   A few days before the festival, Adams was
invited to suggest a toast which his neighbours might
honour at their banquet with the knowledge that it
came from him.   "I will give you," said he, "'Independence for ever!'"   He was asked if he would add
anything to it; and he replied, "Not a word."   The
great day arrived, and the old statesmen, for all that
they were absent, were not forgotten.   "From one end
of the country to the other, wherever Americans were
gathered together, the names of Adams and Jefferson
were coupled in accents of gratitude and praise.   Party
passions were completely drowned in the flood of national feeling which overspread the land." [1]   All day
long Adams was sinking rapidly, and without pain

[1] *Life of John Adams ;* chapter xi.

His last audible remark is said to have been: "Thomas Jefferson still survives." But such was not the case. Jefferson died at noon on that Fourth of July, and Adams shortly before sunset. There are few more striking circumstances, and no more remarkable coincidences, in history.

CHAPTER XVII

WASHINGTON IN BOSTON.   WASHINGTON'S NEW YORK
ARMY.   THE AMERICAN SOLDIER

ALTHOUGH America had now defined her attitude in
the face of England and of Europe, she required something beside State-papers, however resolutely worded, in
order to stem the tide of war which was surging in upon
her confines.   She possessed a victorious army and a
popular general; but they had still to prove what they
were respectively worth under an ordeal far more arduous than that by which they had hitherto been tested.
On the twentieth of March, 1776, Washington made his
entry into Boston; and the people, whom he had rescued, gave him the very choicest entertainment which
their town afforded.   He attended the Thursday Lecture, the social event of a New England week; and he
there listened to a prophecy, truer than most, that the
city was thenceforward a tabernacle that should never
be taken down, of which not one of the stakes should
ever be removed, nor one of the cords be broken.   He
was gratefully welcomed by the Selectmen of Boston,
and by the two branches of the Massachusetts Legislature.   Charles Lee, then commanding in Virginia,
wrote him a letter of congratulation.   That letter contained four sentences about the grievances of General
Lee for every one which related to the glories of General Washington; but it freely testified to the esteem
felt by friends and neighbours for the great soldier
whom Virginians loved to call their "countryman" in
the limited sense in which provincial patriots then employed the term.[1]   The Congress at Philadelphia, on

---

[1] " Go on, my dear General ; crown yourself with glory, and establish
the liberties and lustre of your country on a foundation more permanent

the motion of John Adams, voted thanks to their army and its leader ; and Washington acknowledged the compliment on behalf of his troops. They were, (he said,) at the first a band of undisciplined husbandmen ; but it was, under God, to their bravery, and attention to their duty, that success had been due. Congress, moreover, struck a gold medal inscribed with some brave Latin mottoes. It bore on one face a fleet, sailing out of a harbour beneath the cannon of a besieging force ; and on the other a head of Washington, whose features lent themselves readily to artistic treatment. They did well to take some pains over the design ; for that medal was the only coin which their general consented to receive from them in payment of his services.

The confidence which Washington inspired among his fellow-citizens contributed more than any other circumstance to carry America safe and triumphant through all her difficulties ; but, for the present, the somewhat premature splendour of his reputation was not without its dangers. Congressmen could not bring themselves to believe that any tasks whatsoever were above his capacity ; and, at the same time, they had not learned to resist the temptation of indicating to him, peremptorily and persistently, what those tasks should be. Even when the Committees at Philadelphia refrained from direct interference, the unbounded admiration with which the general was regarded proved a source of embarrassment to himself, and of peril to his cause. Public opinion relied upon the liberator of Boston to surrender no American town, and yield no

than the Capitol Rock. My situation is just as I expected. I am afraid I shall make a shabby figure, without any real demerits of my own. I am like a dog in a dancing-school. I know not where to turn myself, where to fix myself. The circumstances of the country intersected by navigable rivers, the uncertainty of the enemy's designs, who can fly in an instant to any spot they choose with their canvas wings, throw me, and would throw Julius Cæsar, into this inevitable dilemma. I may possibly be in the North when, as Richard says, I should serve my sovereign in the West." It was a private letter ; but, unfortunately for Washington, Lee had only one style for his private letters and his official despatches.

square mile of American territory; and during the coming months the pressure of that opinion exercised a baneful, and very nearly a fatal, influence over Washington's strategy. It was a weakness of which he was cured before the year ended; and his countrymen, too, received a lesson which they never forgot. From that time forward they allowed him his own way, — all the more because it became evident that his own way was the one which he meant to take. During the remainder of the war the men, money, and provisions supplied to Washington by Congress often, indeed, fell far short of his requirements; but in the military disposal of the resources at his command he was as unfettered as any royal captain of the old world at the head of his own army.

There had been a moment, earlier in the Revolution, — and, during the evil days now close at hand, there was another such moment, — when some faint-hearted colonists turned their glance in search of a leader outside their own borders. It was suggested that America, after the well-known example of England, should apply for a monarch to Central Germany. Her security would be assured if the hero of Rossbach and Zorndorf would extend to her the protection of his sword and sceptre. The notion, as any one who knew Frederic the Great would have foreseen, struck him as exquisitely comic. Whatever turn affairs might take, (such was his comment on the proposal,) he should refuse any offer of Transatlantic sovereignty, and cede, without hesitation, all his rights to the King of England.[1] Nothing more was heard of that fantastic scheme; but on the first week of December, 1776, — when America was in dire straits, — Silas Deane sent to the Committee of Secret Correspondence at Philadelphia a despatch of which one paragraph, for intelligible reasons, was not allowed to be seen in print until the writer, and the recipients, of the letter had long been in their graves. For in that

[1] Le Comte de Maltzan au roi Frédéric, 10 Février 1775; Le Roi Frédéric au Comte de Maltzan, 21 Février 1775.

paragraph the envoy at Paris urged his masters at home to direct their thoughts towards engaging a great general, of the highest character in Europe, such as Prince Ferdinand or Marshal Broglio, to take command of the colonial armies.[1]

That was how some men felt when the war was first impending, and again at a subsequent period, when it appeared likely to terminate in a rapid and complete disaster for America. But, in the weeks which immediately followed General Howe's retirement from Boston, Washington's compatriots were so far from wanting to borrow a marshal from France, or a prince from Germany, that they would not have exchanged their own Virginian for Hannibal or Alexander. There was, however, one American who did not over-rate George Washington; and that was George Washington himself. He put in no claim to the possession of a heaven-born genius for war, — a term which historians have so freely applied to certain conquerors the nativity of whose military talent might not unfairly be assigned to a very different region. "Who would have thought," (wrote an author of the seventeenth century,) "that Spinola, soe young and unexpert as he was, should begin his prentiship in armes with taking Ostend, and of the suddaine become soe great a captaine? Some men grow up to be famous generalls before they have scarce learnt the dutyes of souldiers; and others that spend their whole time in the exercises of military discipline, — to whom fights, sieges, batteryes, approches, and underminings are as familiar as the wearing of their corsletts, — are yet cleane to seeke how to manage the highest command of an army."[2] To neither of those two classes did Washington belong. Of him was true

[1] *The Revolutionary Diplomatic Correspondence of the United States ;* Edited under Direction of Congress by Francis Wharton: Washington, Government Printing Office, 1889. The passage mentioned above does not appear in the earlier collection of State documents arranged for publication by Mr. Sparks, under resolution of Congress of March 27, 1818.

[2] *History of the War in Ireland,* 1641 to 1673, by Richard Bellings, Secretary of the Irish Confederation.

what a famous writer said of a famous warrior, that his proficiency in military science was the proficiency which a man of vigorous faculties makes in any science to which he applies his mind with earnestness and industry.[1] Before the summer of 1776 Washington had seen plenty of hard service; but he had never conducted an extensive campaign in the open field. The sense which he entertained of his own deficiencies stands recorded in a generous letter referring to a gallant officer who had given his chief some trouble already, and was destined to give him more in the future. "General Sullivan," wrote Washington, "does not want abilities; but he has his wants, and he has his foibles. His wants are common to us all. He wants experience to move upon a large scale; for the limited and contracted knowledge, which any of us have in military matters, stands in very little stead."[2]

During five or six weeks before Washington's arrival at New York, the city and district were committed to the care of one of his brigadiers who went by the name of Lord Stirling. The apparition of a nobleman on the rolls of a Republican army is startling enough to call for explanation. William Alexander's father had been a gentleman of old Scottish family, who, after the Jacobite rebellion of 1715, had taken refuge in America; where he became an important official, a leading advocate, and the husband of a rich woman. In 1756 the son went to England on public business of some moment, and was recognised by society as a colonist of good position and repute, and a scion of the noble house of Stirling.[3] Before returning home he put

---

[1] Macaulay on Frederic the Great.

[2] Washington to the President of Congress; New York, June 17, 1776.

[3] The following sentence, relating to Stirling, is taken from a London newspaper: "Great respect was shewn, and court paid to him, by the Scotch, particularly by Mr. Alexander Wedderburne, Drummonds the bankers, Lord Aberdeen, and others of Scotland; as well as by the late Lord Northampton, Charles Townshend, and many more considerable people on this side the Tweed; every one of whom advised him by all means to take up the title."

in a claim to the Earldom, which already was extinct. The prize was of a nature to inflame the imagination of an American. The first Earl was the poet, the tutor of Prince Henry, who helped James the First in his translation of the Psalms; and who would have received the profits of the work, if profits there had been, and if the whole British people had not stoutly refused to sing the Royal version. But that was the least of the favours showered upon him by the Crown. He was made Secretary of State for Scotland, and a Judge of the Court of Session; and he obtained the privilege of issuing a copper coinage. In 1621 James endowed him with the whole territory of Nova Scotia, as well as the County and the Lordship of Canada; and the grant was accompanied by the duty of recommending gentlemen to be created Baronets at a hundred and fifty pounds a head. The Charter was confirmed by Charles on his accession to the throne; and in course of time Alexander was invested with the titles of Earl of Stirling, and Viscount Canada. But to him, as to others of the great American Proprietors, his concessions and monopolies brought little besides vexations and embarrassments; and in 1640 he died bankrupt.

That was a matter of indifference to the William Alexander of 1760, who did not need money, and who would willingly have paid the price of a score of Nova Scotia baronetcies in order to become the Sixth Earl of Stirling. The case was tried. An Edinburgh jury found for the claimant, and he was proclaimed as Earl of Stirling at the Market Cross; but the decision was over-set by a Committee of the House of Lords. Alexander returned to America, which was a country where a man was at liberty to call himself anything he pleased, except a Bishop; and thenceforward he was Lord Stirling, not only to his provincial neighbours, but to the Royal generals and administrators, who treated him with marked civility. His mother, seeing no reason why an heiress should be idle, had set up a thriving business. She made herself notable among women by selling thirty pounds worth of goods on the day after her son was born; and, when he reached the proper age, she took that son into partnership. The pair lived in a community where people who kept a store were the equals of people who bought at it; and Stirling held his head high among the best. When he was forty years old an English officer, who supplied friends in London with New York gossip, opined that Lord Stirling, if he played his cards prudently, might rise to be Governor of the province. He adhered to the Revolution from the very first, and brought strength to the cause which he adopted; for he was very popular with his own party, and supremely indifferent to what might be said or written about him by his opponents. He had his share in the personal abuse which was poured forth by the Loyal poets and poetasters in enormous quantities; although the entire mass of their rhymes made fewer converts among a grave and hard-headed people than any five pages of " Common Sense," or a single one of the Farmer's Letters. The ablest, and perhaps the most ferocious, of these satirists, the Reverend Jonathan Odell, has lampooned Stirling as an habitual drunkard; but it must be remembered that the same pen denounced Washington as a perjurer and a liar, and applied to Jay, — who was a purist among statesmen, and in after life a revered magistrate, — the epithet of " Satan's Darling Son." [1]

The worst that could be told about Stirling might be conveyed by a quotation taken from verses of a very different order. When seated at the head of his own table he did not love

> [1] " Or what if Washington should close his scene,
>   Could none succeed him ? Is there not a Greene ?
>   Knave after knave as easy we could join
>   As new emissions of the paper coin."

That is a very mild sample of Odell's judgements on his prominent contemporaries. Such strictures, even when proceeding from a Church of England clergyman, cannot fairly be received as evidence against character. John Jay became the first Chief Justice of the Supreme Court of the United States.

> "a lingering bottle
> Which with the landlord makes too long a stand,
> Leaving all claretless the unmoistened throttle ;
> Especially with politics on hand."

Politics were always on hand in America from the passing of the Stamp Act onwards; and they were talked with jovial emphasis and unanimity around Stirling's well-spread board. He was celebrated for his hospitality in town and camp alike; and no staff-officer, with a message to deliver, ever grudged a long ride if only the last stage of it brought him to Stirling's quarters. These quarters were all the more attractive to youthful chivalry because Lady Stirling, who never left her lord for long, was everywhere attended by a bevy of girls as clever and engaging as any in America.[1] Stirling was a careful and watchful commander, who prided himself on his acquaintance with the technical side of his profession, and who, as the war progressed, shook off the martinet, and became a practical soldier of considerable value in the field. He was in most of Washington's engagements; and there was sure to be plenty of tough and steady fighting in the quarter towards which Stirling and his division had been ordered. He showed a burly figure, and a fresh-coloured visage, in the front of battle. "My Lord Stirling," said a Hessian Colonel, "looks as much like my Lord Granby as one egg does like another;" and every Englishman, who cares for a good portrait by Reynolds, knows how Lord Granby looked. Stirling died just at the moment when peace was arranged between England and the United States, deeply regretted by his chief, whose beautiful letter to Lady Stirling may well stand in history as her husband's epitaph.[2]

[1] Lady Stirling was the mother of Lady Mary Watts and Lady Kitty Duer. She herself was a sister of Governor Livingston of New Jersey ; and his three daughters had a home in their aunt's household. One of them married Chief Justice Jay, and in after days gave the law to New York drawing-rooms. Indeed, all the five ladies belonged to that first dynasty of American fashion which came into power when the war was over. *Life of Martha Washington*, by Anne Hollingworth Wharton, New York, 1897 ; chapters 7 and 9.

[2] Washington to Lady Stirling ; Newbury, January 20, 1783.

Within twenty-four hours after Boston became his own, Washington began his arrangements for the defence of the middle colonies. On the eighteenth of March a strong advanced guard was despatched by land to Norwich in Connecticut, and thence by water to New York. The rest of the army followed, in divisions; and on the thirteenth of April the Commander-in-Chief himself arrived, and established his headquarters within the city. He left General Ward in charge at Boston; — an easy billet, if the old man still had a mind for employment. One antique hero, at any rate, was now provided for as honourably to himself, and with as little disadvantage to the public service, as if he were a time-worn British veteran installed in the Governor's house at Chelsea Hospital. Far other was the lot which awaited Washington, who was at once confronted by the necessity for a decision which brought to the test his moral qualifications for the supreme direction of a great war. The American army in Canada could not be saved unless it was speedily and largely strengthened; and Congress begged Washington to reinforce it without delay. He was asked to denude himself, when he had nothing to spare, in order to promote operations of which the success, purchased at his expense, would redound to the credit of another. Excuses were at hand, such as it would not have been difficult to present in the form of weighty reasons. The temptation was great, and the mental struggle severe; but that was the sort of conflict from which George Washington never came off a loser. He detached ten regiments, as good as the best he had, and embarked them on their voyage up the Hudson under the orders of General Sullivan. When the last battalion had sailed northwards, Washington was left with the prospect of having the main British army at any moment upon his hands, and with only six thousand infantry fit for duty.

These were Continental soldiers; regulars in name, although enlisted for a single twelvemonth, and devoid of the very slightest intention to remain under arms a day longer than the end of December 1776. But the pressing dangers ahead of them made it necessary that their numbers should be supplemented from any source which was immediately available; and Congress ordered out to their assistance a multitude of raw recruits, compared with whom, whatever their own defects in point of discipline might be, they were as the palace-guard at Potsdam, or the Musketeers of the French Household. Washington spared a fortnight towards the end of May for a journey to Philadelphia. He represented to people in authority the fearful risk of entrusting New York, the grand magazine of America, — as well as the mouth of the Hudson river, which was the military highway of the Continent, — to a mere handful of defenders. Men of some sort had to be procured; and none were forthcoming unless he was empowered to draw freely upon the militia of the neighbouring provinces. It was a poor resource at the best. Months before, when it was suspected at Boston that Howe, instead of making for Halifax, might sail straight for New York, three thousand of the Connecticut and New Jersey militia had been called in to garrison the city. There were no funds in the Treasury to pay them; and they had gone back grumbling to their villages, whence it would not be easy on a second occasion to induce them, or their neighbours, to stir. The personal influence of Washington, as always, quickened the resolve of Congress. It was agreed to increase his army at New York by thirteen thousand eight hundred militiamen, and to form in the vicinity a flying camp, (an ominous expression,) of ten thousand more.

Late in August, on the eve of his first collision with the enemy, Washington had collected a very considerable gathering of fighting men; or rather of men who came out for the purpose of fighting if a battle was not put off too long to suit their convenience. Armed, half-armed, and unarmed; young and old; loyal and disaffected;[1] engaged to serve for five more months, for

[1] The militia of some counties laid hands on the local Tories, and brought them along to be employed as fatigue-men, on the plea that they were less dangerous in camp than at home.

six weeks, for four weeks, or for as long as they felt inclined;—the American levies of all sorts and descriptions were reckoned at something between twenty and twenty-five thousand. Three thousand of these were on detached service; and five thousand, (the most constant quantity under any heading in the official returns,) were reported as sick. It was probably the largest army that Washington ever commanded; and it certainly was the worst, from causes which reflected little discredit on him or on his compatriots. Indeed, the contrast between the troops who were mustered at New York in August 1776, and the troops who were disbanded at New York in December 1783, was in a high degree honourable both to the leader and to the followers. They never wearied out his patience; and he at length obtained from them, after more than one disappointment, obedience and devotion in the fullest measure. There have seldom been better soldiers, of every arm and in every rank, than those Americans who, after the war was over, divested themselves of their ragged uniforms, and became civilians at the first moment when their country had no longer need of them as professional warriors.[1]

It is difficult to pronounce in general terms upon the value of the American militia during the War of Independence. Some of their feats, if we take into consideration the quality of their opponents, have seldom been surpassed except in legendary warfare; but at other times they fought poorly, and proved themselves hopelessly unequal to the demands of a long and trying campaign. New England farmers, aided by backwoods-

[1] " You know the steps by which Washington succeeded in forming an army. At first, men engaged for a single campaign, mixed with militia and volunteers; then paid soldiers, their mutiny, the new regulations, and at length the military constitution unanimously accepted by the United States. The excellent condition of the Continental troops, as we saw them at the review of King's Ferry, before our departure for France, will remain in our eyes as not the least among the triumphs of the hero of America." This is a passage from a letter written by General Mathieu Dumas, and published after he had served many years, and with great distinction, in Napoleon's Grand Army.

men of the Pennsylvanian border, captured at Saratoga a splendid army which had advanced beyond its depth into an ocean of primæval forest. In October 1780 a similar victory, on a smaller scale, was achieved at King's Mountain in North Carolina by bear-hunters and wild Indian fighters from the regions which afterwards were known as Kentucky and Tennessee. It was an occasion when the North Carolina militia performed their share of the work; and yet that very militia could not be trusted to keep their place in line when it came to a ranged battle on an open ground.[1] American minute-men did well, and sometimes did wonders; but they required two conditions in order to show themselves to advantage. It was essential that the circumstances should be favourable to their method of fighting, and that they should have begun with a success. Both those conditions prevailed during the earlier phases of the Revolutionary War. Lexington had put the colonists in heart; Bunker's Hill did anything rather than discourage them; and, after those two affairs were over, they had but to sit quiet behind solid earthworks, eating varied and ample rations, and speculating on the date when the British inside Boston would be reduced to eat horses. Lafayette, after long experience, reported to the French Ministry that American regulars had as much courage and true discipline as their adversaries, and were more hardy and patient than any European troops with whom he was acquainted; but that their militia, on the other hand, were only armed peasants, who had sometimes fought, but who would be most usefully employed in the works of a siege.[2]

Their first campaign had been a long siege, and little

---

[1] Nathanael Greene, who always asked and got from his soldiers the utmost of which he thought them capable, promised these Carolinians at Guildford Court House that, if they would stand long enough to fire two volleys, he would engage that his Continental troops should do the rest. But, as soon as Lord Cornwallis sent his people forward, the militia broke and ran, and never stopped retreating until, (to use the words of their disgusted General,) they had gone home to kiss their wives and sweethearts.

[2] Letter of 1781 from Lafayette to the Count de Vergennes.

else; but they were now to have a taste of all the operations, incidents, and emergencies of active warfare.
The host which had been assembled to oppose the invasion of the central colonies had many characteristics of
a tribe in arms. " A number of aged gentlemen, of the
first society in the town of Waterbury, embodied themselves, and nominated their officers. When they were
ordered to New York, this company was the first that
reached the place of rendezvous. They were twenty-
four in number; and their united ages reached one
thousand. They are all married men, and left behind
a hundred and fifty-nine children and grandchildren."
That account came from Connecticut; and at another
town, nearer to the field of action, the announcement of
National Independence evoked an equally remarkable
ebullition of martial ardour. An effigy of George the
Third, with a crown of feathers like that of an Indian
chief, was solemnly hanged and burned; and then the
older citizens of the locality, "to the age of seventy and
upwards, formed themselves into a company, determined
at the risk of their lives to defend the free and independent States. May such a shining example stimulate
every father in America to follow their aged brethren
here!" It would have been well for General Washington if all his patriarchs had arrayed themselves in
special and separate companies, so that they might
have been sent back to their firesides after their inspir-
ing story had gone the round of the newspapers, and
before they had caught their deaths of cold. Unfortunately, grandfathers were impartially enlisted throughout every militia battalion of the continent; and the
case was sometimes all the worse when they brought
their grandsons with them. An English officer, who
spent several years as a prisoner in one State or another,
had leisure and opportunity for observing the weak sides
of the American military system. You would see, (he
said,) in the ranks of the militia a soldier of sixty
marching next a boy of sixteen; a sturdy negro, and an
old decrepit white man limping by his side; most of

them wearing great bushy wigs, and presenting a spectacle to which nothing could do justice except the pencil of Hogarth.[1]

These veterans, according to one of their admirers, were a theme for Homer; and undoubtedly they resembled the Nestor of that poet in the facility for copious dissertation by which they enlivened the camp, and the comparisons which they drew between the generals of their youth and the degenerate race of strategists by whom they now were commanded. But, whatever might be their failings, at all events they brought with them respectability; — an attribute the largest possible infusion of which was needed in order to counteract those baser elements which, for the first time, were disagreeably prominent in the colonial army. The men who swarmed in upon Lord Percy's line of retreat on the memorable nineteenth of April, and who then stayed with the colours until they had taken Boston, were the pick of the population, — true volunteers, actuated by public motives. But in the summer of 1776 the institution of a compulsory ballot had swept good, bad, and indifferent into the State militia. Not a few men of questionable antecedents, whom the fortune of the lot had spared in their own persons, entered the ranks as hired substitutes; for there already were plenty of timid and slothful householders eager to purchase exemption from service, and prepared to satisfy the demands of a tariff which, as the war proceeded, rose to famine prices.[2] The contrast between the force which had lain in front of Boston, and the force which at present occupied New York, soon became painfully visible. Colonel Reed, the Adjutant General, informed President Hancock that the army was composed of a greater mixture than any which had yet

[1] *American Archives*, July 23 and November 29, 1776. *Travels through the interior parts of America by an Officer ;* Letter XCVIII.

[2] " A rich and well-to-do militia man does not serve himself. He hires a substitute, and pays for two months as much as a thousand French Crowns." Baron de Kalb to the Count de Broglie; Valley Forge, December 1777.

been collected, and was full of crime.   There were men,
(he wrote,) to whom thirty-nine lashes was a con-
temptible punishment.   When they had received that
allowance, they would offer in the hearing of their
comrades to take as much more for a pint of rum.[1]

In the case of a people endowed with valour, and
not deficient in volubility, the experience of active
service soon makes it evident that those two qualities
are not always united in the same individual.   In
America especially, where national self-knowledge is
stimulated by a national sense of humour, men discover,
at an early period in every successive war, that heroes
of the tavern and the street corner are in a large proportion sluggards on the march, and skulkers in action.
"When I see," wrote Colonel Reed, "how few who
talked so largely of death and honour are around me,
and that those who *are* here are those from whom it
was least expected, I am lost in wonder and surprise.
Your noisy Sons of Liberty are, I find, the very quietest
in the field.   An engagement, or even the expectation
of one, gives a wonderful insight into character." [2]
Loud politicians often showed themselves tame soldiers ;
and professional bullies were invariably among the very
worst.   A Federal general, eminent in the War of the
Secession, expressly says that champions who had been
the terror of their native place in time of peace, — whose
features were disfigured by traces of the prize-ring, or
of conflicts with a rival volunteer fire company, — were
no better than cringing cowards in an honourable
encounter where death stared them in the face.[3]
The relative worth for military purposes of a ruffian,

[1] Colonel Joseph Reed to the President of Congress ; New York, July 25,
1776.   *American Archives.*
[2] Colonel Reed to his wife ; September 6, 1776.
[3] "The Philosophy of Courage," by General Horace Porter ; a paper
which, perfect in its class, appeared in the *Century Magazine* of June
1888.   General Porter justly contrasts these noisy braggarts with the men
who, on the evening before the assault at Cold Harbor, were seen calmly
and silently writing their names and home-addresses on slips of paper,
and pinning them to the back of their coats ; so that next morning their
bodies might be recognised, and their fate made known to their families.

and of a plain quiet man, is an old story, — as old as war.[1] In the summer of 1776 a Pennsylvanian captain, (for the drudgery of enlistment, in the American Army, devolved not upon the sergeants, but on the commissioned officers,) had got hold of a recruit who entertained his comrades with stories of the race-course and the cock-pit, and froze their blood by dark hints of the fate reserved for any one who ventured to trifle with him, and with his like. "There," he would say, "is a fellow that has not his match in the country. See what a set of teeth he has! A man's thumb would be nothing to them." This worthy had been introduced to the regiment by a sporting gentleman, who recommended him for a soldier on the ground that he would be no loss to the countryside, and that he would stop a bullet as well as anybody. That however, as soon as shots began to fly, proved to be the very last thing which he had an idea of doing; and thenceforward, whenever his company advanced to skirmish, he was left behind to guard the colours.

But, though there were more black sheep than could be wished among the American militia, the great majority of them were as decent, worthy people as ever marched out of step. They had the virtues of civilians; and many of them, when they joined the camps around New York, to all intents and purposes were civilians still. Some battalions arrived at the front without having learned the rudiments of training. In Virginia, the most military community of the whole continent, a spectator who had seen one of the independent companies put through what, at that distance from Berlin, was called the Prussian exercise, spoke of the perform-

[1] Tacitus states it as a recognised fact that gladiators made a poor figure among the swordsmen in a Roman battle. Xenophon tells of a noted Thessalian boxer, who, during the Retreat of the Ten Thousand, distinguished himself only as a marauder, a mutineer, and a malingerer. And, as long ago as the Iliad itself, a pugilist, to whom no one in the whole Grecian army before Troy could stand up for five minutes, confessed without reserve, and apparently without shame, that he was of very small count in the line of spears.

ance as a mere burlesque.   The General Orders, which Washington issued in rapid succession to his New York army, dealt for the most part with very elementary points of discipline.   Captains were instructed, over and over again, to see that, in the presence of the enemy, every man had twenty-four cartridges in his pouch, and a good flint well fixed in the lock of his piece; colonels were informed that they must break sentries of the habit of sitting down, and laying by their muskets, before they could shoot them for sleeping at their posts; and subalterns were desired, when the line was turned out on ceremonial occasions, to salute by taking off their hats, until they had mastered the correct method of presenting their fusees.

A very diligent reader of American annals has remarked that it must always prove a source of wonder to the scientific soldier, and of mystery to the historical student, how the Revolutionary war could ever have been carried through.[1]   At the critical moment of each campaign the militia habitually evinced a desire to go back to their homes; and they belonged to a people who usually take the shortest way to get whatever they may want.   It must be admitted that a military life presented itself to them under the least seductive aspects. The pride and pomp of war were often represented in their case by a strip of cloth, which once had been red or yellow, sewed on to the sleeve of their upper garment.   Comforts they had none.   The men of the contingent, which marched for Canada under General Sullivan, possessed one shirt apiece, and often not a waistcoat in a company; and that expedition was fitted out as lavishly as the slender resources at the command of Washington would admit.   The pay which the militia received, — or rather, to speak more accurately, the pay which was in arrear to them, — was computed on a lower scale than that of the Continental troops. They were unprovided with blankets, tents, or shoes;

---

[1] Introduction to the private papers of George Clinton, by Hugh Hastings, State Historian: New York and Albany, 1899.

and, at the end of the severe campaign which now was opening, an English officer observed, not without a touch of sympathy, that the few coats which they had among them were out at elbows, and that a whole regiment seldom could display a whole pair of breeches. They were often in hot quarrel with their military superiors. Officers of a company were chosen by the company, under a system which ensured the most absolute freedom of election. Indeed, wherever coercion took place, it did not come from above. A Maryland colonel had called his regiment together, in order to poll for a field officer. They met on another day from that which he had appointed; they refused to let him be present at the counting; and, when he insisted on his right to inspect the votes, they threatened to throw him over an adjoining fence. In fine weather, and commodious quarters, the relations between all ranks were pleasant enough. The Adjutant General of the army mentioned in a letter to his wife that he had seen a captain of the Connecticut Light Horse shaving a trooper on the parade-ground. But, when the service became hard, and the discipline severe, privates were apt to regard their officers as constituents view a representative whose political conduct has deceived their legitimate expectations. "Captain Watkins and his men," (thus ran an official report,) "are on very ill terms. The Captain has beat some of them. He says he has great cause. They say he has none. Some of the men have said that nothing shall induce them to stay in the company under him." [1]

It did not, however, require a special or a personal grievance to turn the thoughts of American militiamen in the direction of their homes. The peculiar conditions of their service were well known to British Ministers, and ranked high among those circumstances which encouraged the Cabinet to believe that the colonies would soon be brought to terms. Mr. Paul

[1] Letter to the Maryland Council of Safety; September 1776. *American Archives.*

Wentworth, a steadfast partisan of the Crown, exposed the weakness of New England in a series of extremely able letters addressed to Downing Street. The most cultivated parts of the country, (this gentleman wrote,) contained no spare labourers; so that the farmers and their families mutually assisted each other to reap their harvests. He had remarked, too, that there were more females than males among them; and, from their prolific nature, and the plenty of food and raiment, a great proportion of children was to be found in every farm. From those facts the writer deduced the cheering conclusions that the devastation of the rural districts would cause acute and wide-spread suffering, and that the militia would be for ever running off to get in their crops, and protect their wives and little ones. Each of the two inferences was correct by itself: but in the long run the one neutralised the other. The horrible misery inflicted in the Jerseys by British foragers, and Hessian plunderers, did more than all the proclamations of Congress, and all the sermons of militant Whig clergymen, to convince the farmers that the only method of safeguarding their property and families was to remain together in the front, and keep the invader well outside their borders.

But, in the summer and fall of 1776, that truth had not been taken to heart by those it most concerned. The colonists gratefully acknowledged that it was a wonderful harvest with which Heaven had blessed their land;[1] and to an honest militiaman, who could cut his swath much more neatly than he could do his facings, it savoured of impiety that the precious gifts of a bountiful Providence should not be duly reaped and garnered. "Their complaints are without number;" (the colonel of a regiment wrote). "Some have got ten or twelve loads of hay cut, and not a man left to take it up. Some have got a great quantity of grass to cut. Some have not finished hoeing corn. Some, if not all, have got their ploughing to do, for sowing their

[1] *American Archives;* November 1776.

winter grain. Some have all their families sick, and not a person left to take care of them."[1] In the absence of the farmers, the work was mainly done by women; a sight strange, and almost unnatural, to a people which already had begun to consider that sex as too good to be employed on field-labour. General Greene told Washington that the harvest throughout New York and Connecticut had been generally got in by wives and daughters, assisted by the men whose advanced age rendered them unfit for the army; — and, to judge by those who thought themselves young enough to serve, that age must have been advanced indeed. Ladies of the first consideration, without regard for their dignity or their complexions, set the example of self-help to those around them. Towards the end of August, at the Forks of Brandywine, girls were harnessing the ploughs, and preparing fallows for the seed, on the very fields where, a twelvemonth from that date, a costly crop of human life was reaped.[2]

Militiamen, whose families were domesticated near the Indian border, had a more poignant motive for going home to keep watch and ward beneath their own roof-trees. The riflemen, indeed, who came from the Southern colonies, were spared one most serious anxiety; for danger was not apprehended from the slaves. Lord Dunmore, the Governor of Virginia, — apparently forgetting that George the Third had upheld the slave-trade against the earnest wish of the colony, — did his utmost to provoke a servile insurrection. He proclaimed freedom to all negroes, appertaining to rebels, "who

[1] Colonel Fitch to Governor Trumbull of Connecticut; August 1776. On the 12th of the same month Hezekiah Howell, of Blaggs Clove, wrote to General Clinton what may be regarded as a specimen letter. "By your calling Captain Woohul's Company I am entirely stript of Hands to carry on my business, having but one Negro and a boy left with me, and the most of my hay to get, (no hands are to be had for hire,) besides if they are continued long I shall be unable to sow any winter grain. If it is anyways consistent with your duty I should take it as a favour to let either my son or grandson Return home as soon as possible."

[2] Greene to Washington; July 25, 1776. Private letter of August 27, in the *American Archives*.

would take arms against their masters "; and Virginians never forgot or forgave the threat.[1] The Governor's invitation, however, was not heeded by those to whom it was addressed. The negroes refused to rise, continued to eat their rations peaceably, and even made a show of working; but, although they remained loyal to their owner, nothing except his bodily presence could keep them from being lazy. It was a poor life for a small planter, distracted by the thought of his tobacco left unhoed, and of his field-hands revelling in idleness and rude plenty, while he was marching wearily from defeat to defeat, empty and barefoot, and with a gun longer than himself on his aching shoulder.

It was the most difficult thing in the world, (so Washington declared,) to know in what manner to conduct himself with respect to the militia. "If you do not begin to raise them many days before they are wanted, you cannot have them in time. If you do, they get tired and return, besides being under but very little order or government while in service."[2] A general complained that the army was mainly composed of raw levies, perpetually fluctuating between the camp and their farms. According to another officer, they had come and gone in such shoals that His Excellency could never tell for two days together the strength which he had at any

---

[1] A letter from Antigua, in a London newspaper, relates that Lord Dunmore's offer to emancipate and arm the slaves of Virginia "had incensed the whole continent, and inflamed the minds of many who before were pacifically inclined." The Governor's former subjects dwelt with satisfaction upon the real, or supposed, details of his exit from the province. "A nine-pound ball from the Lower Battery entered the ship's quarters, and beat in a large timber, from the splinters of which Lord Dunmore got wounded about the legs, and had all his valuable china smashed about his ears. It is said that his Lordship was exceedingly alarmed, and roared out; 'Good God, that I should have come to this!'" *American Archives;* July 1776. The opinion entertained about Lord Dunmore by American loyalists was the same as that held by American rebels. "The unimportant, insignificant, fribbling Governor of Virginia has gone back to England." So Judge Curwen remarks in his *Journal* of December 1776.

[2] Washington to the President of the New York Convention; New York, August 30, 1776.

given post. One element of uncertainty was soon removed from Washington's calculations ; for, after the first success of the British, his numbers no longer fluctuated, but sank steadily by thousands every week. The militia altogether ceased to come; and they went in larger parties than ever. There was no stopping them; and it was useless even to talk of recovering them by force.[1] All through September they departed by whole regiments, by half regiments, and by companies. They carried away their arms, and their ammunition too, at a time when it was almost worth its weight in silver; as well as other Government stores which, to their artless fancy, seemed likely to conduce to the comfort of the folks at home.[2] Within a fortnight after fighting commenced, the Connecticut militia had been reduced from six thousand, to less than two thousand, rank and file. Washington bitterly exclaimed that to place any dependence upon such a force was resting on a broken staff. "Men just dragged from the tender scenes of domestic life, unaccustomed to the din of arms, and totally unacquainted with every kind of military drill, are timid, and ready to fly from their own shadows. The sudden change in their manner of living, particularly in their lodging, brings on sickness in many, impatience in all, and such an unconquerable desire of returning to their respective homes that it not only produces shameful desertions among themselves, but infuses the like spirit into others."[3]

[1] "By the enclosed return of my brigade, you will observe that there are wanting, to complete, 596 men. I know it is my duty to cause deserters to be apprehended. I can't. If I send officers and parties of faithful men after them, I thereby weaken the army. The deserters hear of them in their neighbourhood, know their business, and, (I am sorry to add,) are too frequently aided in evading my guards." General George Clinton to Washington; September 8, 1776.

[2] One of the fugitives was detected in possession of a cannon-ball, which he intended as a present to his mother, for the purpose of pounding her mustard.

[3] Public Papers of George Clinton, Vol. I. *Memoirs of a Life chiefly passed in Pennsylvania.* Washington to the President of Congress; September 2 and 24, 1776.

The militia would have done less ill if it had been better commanded. "We want men of knowledge to instruct us," was the prayer of those among the rank and file who aspired to become real soldiers;[1] but the officers, who should have been the teachers, in many cases had nothing of value to impart. European Governments already recognised in theory, though by no means uniformly in practice, that military commissions ought to be conferred upon men who had been carefully picked, and minutely and rigorously trained. That, however, was a counsel of perfection which, in the hurry of a sudden war, the Americans held themselves excused from even attempting to attain. Congress made a Colonel or a Major with little regard to his professional acquirements, or his personal qualities. The result sometimes astonished French generals belonging to a service in which the field-officers were young noblemen of high spirit and courtly manners; or veterans, scarred at Fontenoy, who had spent half a lifetime in putting the regiments of the Bourbonnais, or the Royal Deux-ponts, through their complicated and stately manœuvres. "One risks nothing," said Baron de Kalb, "in calling 'Colonel' a stranger who accosts you. The army swarms with them."[2] And the Baron then proceeded to enlarge upon certain details amply justifying the taunt which these gentlemen occasionally applied to each other in their cups; "Did Congress see you before they appointed you?" Captains and Lieutenants were elected by the soldiers; whose choice, in a bad regiment, was dictated by unwarlike, and often very unworthy, considerations. The process had unpleasant features even in the most virtuous and patriotic communities. The journal of a New England minute-man, himself a true hero, faithfully depicts the strong and the weak sides of the American military character. On Sunday the twenty-third of April, 1775, Amos Farns-

---

[1] Address to the Virginian Convention; July 29, 1775.
[2] Baron de Kalb to the Duc de Broglie. Henry Stevens's *Facsimile of the Correspondence during the American Revolution.*

worth, of Groton in Middlesex county, heard a fine discourse on the words, "Thou therefore endure hardness, as a good soldier of Jesus Christ." On Sunday the thirtieth the Reverend Mr. Goodridge, in an excellent sermon from a stirring text, "incoridged us to go and fite for our Land and Contry, saying we Did not do our Duty if we did not stand up now." And yet the intervening week was apparently spent neither in prayer nor in drill, but "a Strugling with the offisers which shold be the hiest in offise." [1]

Quarrelling too often did not cease when the election was over. Officers were for ever bickering about questions of rank and promotion, with the susceptibility of military men, and the breadth of language familiar to civilians whose vocabulary had been invigorated by the constant pursuit of local politics. Discord within the ranks was sometimes very little mitigated even by the most imminent danger from without. When Howe began his forward movement in Long Island, the officers of a New Hampshire battalion were not on speaking terms in consequence of a disagreement as to whether the companies should be marched to public worship on Sunday morning together or separate.[2] That same summer a gentleman in the South Carolina militia informed his State authorities that the Indians were in arms on their frontier, along the banks of the river Saluda. "I am afraid," he said, "the burden of the war will fall on this regiment. The people over the river will do

---

[1] Amos Farnsworth's Diary; published in the *Proceedings of the Massachusetts Historical Society for* 1899. Mr. Goodridge preached from Judges xx. 22 and 23: "more particularly the last Clause in the 23rd verse." That verse runs: "And the children of Israel went up and wept before the Lord until even, and asked counsel of the Lord, saying, Shall I go up again to battle against the children of Benjamin my brother? And the Lord said, Go up against him." They had already gone up against him once, on the 19th of April, when Farnsworth "came to Lexington, whare much hurt was done to the houses thare. But they was forsed to retreat, tho thay was more numerous than we. And I saw many Ded Regulars by the way."

[2] "Our Colonel," (the Major wrote,) "will not talk with me on the subject, but a great deal about me."

nothing.   They grumble at being commanded by a
major.   If Williamson is fit to command an expedition,
he certainly ought to have a much higher rank than any
of these chaps."   In the course of a month the whole
district had been over-run by savages, and the unfortunate writer of those lines had been shot down, and
scalped while still alive.[1]   Towards the end of August
one of Washington's brigadiers represented himself as
having shifted his quarters from New York to Eliza-
bethtown Point, " to be with the men, and enure them
to discipline; which, by my distance from the camp,
considering what scurvy subaltern officers we are like to
have while they are in the appointment of the Mo-
bility, I found it impossible to introduce.   And the
worst men, (was there a degree above the superlative,)
would still be *pejorated* by having been fellow-soldiers
with that discipline-hating, good-living-loving, to eternal fame damned, coxcombical crew we lately had from
Philadelphia."[2]

That letter was one among a hundred others which
betokened a condition of feeling productive of endless
scandal, and immeasurable danger.   At the moment
when every effort was required to check Carleton's
advance from Canada, General Schuyler reported that
he saw with deep affliction the unhappy jealousy occa-
sioned by those colonial differences which reigned in
the Northern army.[3]   Washington, in a General Order,
entreated officers and soldiers to consider that they
could not more effectually assist the enemy than by
making divisions among themselves; that the honour
and success of the army, and the safety of their bleeding country, depended upon their harmony; and that
things would only go well if the provinces were sincerely
united in a common cause, and all local distinctions

---

[1] Letter from Francis Salvador; July 18, 1776.

[2] This officer who used, the more forcibly to express his disgust, a Latin
compound which he had never found in Johnson's dictionary, was William
Livingston, Brigadier General of the New Jersey Militia, and afterwards
Governor of his State.

[3] General Philip Schuyler to the President of Congress; July 17, 1776.

sunk in the name of an American.[1]   The earnestness
of the Commander-in-Chief's appeal is explained by the
peculiar composition of the force under his immediate
orders, which included contingents from the entire continent.   Throughout that army provincial prejudice was
unusually bitter, and exceptionally vocal; and it took
the form of reflections cast by the officers of one State
upon the social standing of officers who were natives of
another.   New York was a colony which had a plentiful
supply of rich and leisured proprietors; while it contributed very few battalions to the defence of the Revolution.   It was acknowledged on all hands that the
officers of those battalions were men of the world, who
knew how to impress upon those beneath them a sincere
belief that levelling principles were incompatible with
good soldiership.   A New York officer, people said,
might be distinguished without a badge; but among the
tents of the New Jersey, and Maryland, and Pennsylvania regiments, an observer, with an eye to race and
breeding, looked around in vain for the gentry of the
country.[2]   It was even remarked that, — while the aristocracy of the Old Dominion might be found on the
staff, and, (at a later period of the war,) in the cavalry,
— a Virginian infantry colonel was marked out by the
colour of his cockade rather than by his address and his
appearance.   That was asserted, or rather was whispered, because Virginians were accustomed to use a
short way with critics; but, if the idleness which preceded active hostilities had been much prolonged, captains and subalterns from the most pacific colonies would
have been sending challenges like so many Southern
planters.   A few days before the General Order exhort-
ing to unity and mutual tolerance was published,
Nathanael Greene informed Washington that two officers had fallen out, and had appointed the next
morning to fight.   They knew that he knew it; and
he was perplexed what course to adopt, inasmuch

[1] Orderly Book of August 1, 1776.
[2] *Pennsylvanian Memoirs*, chapter vi.

as duelling contravened all law, whether civil or military.[1]

While the Southern and Middle Colonies had their own dislikes and preferences among themselves, they all joined in decrying the New Englanders. These latter complained, with as much dignity as such complaint admitted, that Georgians and Carolinians habitually spoke of them as damned Yankees.[2] One Southern general treated New England regimental officers with scanty deference, going so far as to refrain from offering them a drink under circumstances when they had every right to expect one. A court martial, comprising a majority of Southern judges, acquitted with honour a Maryland lieutenant who had been wanting in becoming respect, and prompt obedience, towards a Northern brigadier.[3] Even General Putnam, on horse-back in his summer costume, with a hanger belted across his brawny shoulders over a waistcoat without sleeves, excited hilarity rather than enthusiasm in a martial dandy from Baltimore, blazing in scarlet and buff, like a British line-officer, and distinguished "by the most fashionably-cut coat, the most *maccaroni* cocked hat, and the hottest blood of the Union." Putnam, (so the talk ran,) was brave, and had a certain honest manliness about him; but he was not what the time required. There was justice in that observation, and not much ill-nature. The part of the farmer-captain was already played out, and the exigencies of more regular warfare now demanded another type of leader; but the old

[1] General Greene to Washington; July 25, 1776.

[2] Charles Cushing to his brother; July 8, 1776. Authorities on this point are painfully abundant.

[3] The privates from the various colonies got on together more pleasantly than their officers. "A traffic was soon established between the common soldiers from the East, and the Pennsylvanians. This consisted in a barter of the ration of rum for that of molasses. The Yankees did not care for the first, and our Irishmen could very well dispense with the latter." Chapters v., vi., and vii. of the *Pennsylvanian Memoirs* provide a curious and authentic account of what men thought about each other at the moment, in contrast to much that is written of them in history.

man's fame is indissolubly connected with that stage of
the contest when he performed, in every meaning of the
term, yeoman's service to his country.

The Northern, (or as New Yorkers and Pennsylvanians usually called them, the Eastern,) provinces
had, at the call of duty, poured forth enormous masses
of armed men from every class except the wealthiest.
Those who came from that class were singularly well
read in military history, and displayed a remarkable
aptitude for utilising in the field the ideas which they
had thought out in the study; but they were very few.
The higher education, especially in Massachusetts, was
mostly on the other side of politics. Of loyalists who
sailed from Boston, in the wake of Howe's retreat, one
in five had been at the university. It may be doubted
whether, among the officers of the militia regiments
which were besieging the town, one in fifty had been a
Harvard man. Harvard showed quite another record
during the war of the Secession. In the four years
following the spring of 1861 twenty-nine of her sons
died of exposure and camp epidemics, and sixty-nine
by the enemy's fire. In dead alone, her contribution
towards the maintenance of national unity as nearly as
possible equalled what was then a full year's entry of
her students. But in 1776 the spirit of the place was
altogether different. Harvard, up to the very eve of
the Revolution, was a temple of privilege, in which the
scholars were ranked according to the dignity of family.[1]
This system, — the closest imitation which a colony
could produce of the institution of fellow-commoners
and gentlemen-commoners at the English universities,
— survived, but not for long, the up-turning of Ameri-

[1] John Adams stood fourteenth in a class of twenty-four; and he would
have stood lower still but that, although his father was a hard-working
farmer, his mother had been a Boylston of Brookline. A much more
exalted academical position was allotted to the son of a colonel, who
belonged to no less a family than the Chandlers of Worcester; but of
whom nothing is recorded except that he emigrated to Halifax, and left
behind him at his death seven pairs of silk stockings and two pairs of
velvet breeches.

can thought which was caused by the agitation against the Stamp Act. The Harvard class of 1770 was arranged in alphabetical order; and the change was regarded as a pregnant indication that society was tending towards republican principles.

Two Americans very soon discerned the danger which could not fail to subsist until military rank was closely connected with individual worth, and well-founded social consideration. So long, (said Washington,) as the only merit that a captain possessed was his ability to raise recruits, the privates treated him as an equal, and, in his character of a commander, regarded him no more than a broomstick.[1] John Adams, in season and out of season, (if such teaching can ever be ill-timed,) urged the doctrine that officers, whether or not they belonged to an aristocracy of birth, should constitute an aristocracy of talent and instruction. In October 1776, — while the British and American armies were at grips around New York, — he carried through Congress a motion for the appointment of a committee to consider a plan for the establishment of a military academy. The project fell through, at a crisis when every young fellow of courage was wanted in the front as soon as he had learned how to judge distances and deploy a company. But the author of the scheme kept it constantly in mind; and a quarter of a century afterwards, as President of the United States, he enjoyed the satisfaction of creating that celebrated college on the river Hudson which has been surpassed by none in the world as a nursery of great soldiers.[2]

These poorly organised battalions were the component parts of a loose-jointed and unwieldy whole. The Commander-in-Chief found it necessary to remind all and sundry that, when every officer exerted himself in

[1] Washington to the President of Congress; September 24, 1776.

[2] The Military Academy at West Point was incorporated in 1802; whereas Adams ceased to be President in 1801. He was, however, the real founder of the college. The details of its organisation, and the selection of its first professors, were his favourite occupation during his last year of office.

his own department, an army moved like clockwork; but that otherwise it was an ungovernable machine, which perplexed and distracted those who attempted to conduct it. In July 1776, twelve quires of paper were served out to each regiment, on which it was intended that the colonel should write reports; but which he too frequently used for writing letters to his representatives in Congress about the injustice of his not having been made a major general.[1] Washington proclaimed it as a melancholy truth that returns, essentially necessary for a Commander-in-Chief to govern himself by, and which ought to be prepared in an hour after they were called for, were obtained with the greatest difficulty; and that, in regiments where the men were allowed to straggle from quarters, instead of being called over three times a day on the parade-ground, no account whatever of their numbers was forthcoming.[2] A brigadier general had, indeed, the excuse that his staff was deplorably short-handed. Nathanael Greene now learned, with the docility of a valiant and modest man, that a hero's business was more complex, and vastly more tiresome, than any conception which he had formed of it from his reading of Plutarch. His experience was akin to that of the adjutant in Sherman's corps, who passed his days filling up Army forms in triplicate "in order to stamp out the rebellion." Greene at length was reduced

---

[1] The Commander-in-Chief got his share of complaints from officers who had been passed over for promotion. A Colonel thus addressed him in August 1776 : " My disgrace is unalterably fixed by conferring the *detur digniori* upon those of inferior standing, without the least competition of superior merit. The variety of incidents, that may happen in an engagement, will possibly demand my submission to the orders of a Brigadier General whose standing till lately has been subordinate to mine. Disobedience may lose a victory which is courting our embrace. How cruel the alternative to be obliged to submit to my own infamy, or, by refusing, incur the penalties of death ! " The writer then proceeds to console himself, and if possible to touch Washington, by quoting a saying of Sertorius, and three most harrowing lines from Young.

[2] Washington to Colonel Gay ; September 4, 1776. General Lee, in the South, experienced the same difficulty in getting punctual and accurate reports. "I cannot send a return of our strength just now ; " he wrote ; " for the Adjutant General, who is in love, has forgotten a whole regiment."

to apply for a secretary. " The science and art of war," (as he pathetically represented to Washington,) "require a freedom of thought and leisure to reflect upon the various incidents that daily occur, which cannot be had where the whole of one's time is engrossed in clerical employment. If your Excellency thinks I can promote the service as much in this employment as any other, I shall cheerfully execute the business without a murmur." Washington's generous heart foresaw in his correspondent a competitor in fame, who under no stress of rivalry would cease to be a loyal brother in patriotism. Within twenty-four hours an official notice was circulated that, General Greene being particularly engaged at present, passes signed by Lieutenant Blodgett were to be allowed sufficient to enable people to cross the ferries.[1] Washington himself had only three aides-de-camp ; or four, if he counted in his secretary. John Adams remarked that they all came from the Southward, were young gentlemen of letters, and thought full as highly of themselves as they ought to think, and much more disrespectfully of New England and of Congress than they ought to have thought.[2] Fine energetic fellows, they must have brought with them from their plantations a large outfit of conceit if there was any remaining after they had resided six months at headquarters. They were miserably remunerated ; and, as the only set-off against their bad pay, they were so continuously worked as to have no opportunity of spending a cent on their private diversions.[3]

In European campaigns of the eighteenth century it frequently happened that the defects of an infantry,

[1] Order of July 26, 1776.
[2] John Adams's *Autobiography* for October 1, 1776.
[3] " I give in to no kind of amusements myself ; and those about me can have none, but are confined from morning to evening, answering the applications and letters of one and another. If these gentlemen had the same relaxation from duty as other officers, there would not be so much in it. But to have the mind always on the stretch, and no hours for recreation, makes a material odds." Washington to the President of Congress; New York, April 22, 1776. As a consequence of this letter the pay of these aides-de-camp was raised from thirty-three dollars a month to forty.

which was not all that a general could desire, were compensated by the excellence of the auxiliary arms; but that resource was denied to Washington. In 1780 and afterwards, when active hostilities were in a large degree confined to the Southern colonies, a fine cavalry formed itself by a natural and spontaneous growth among populations which almost lived on horseback. It was said that a poor Virginian would walk a league to catch, or borrow, a horse which should carry him a mile to church. A rich planter, when once he had stepped outside his verandah, liked to feel between his knees a hunter which could run a four-mile heat in ten minutes, or a "pacer," (the ancestor of the true American race-horse,) which trotted its fourteen miles within the hour. In the Northern colonies, however, animals were kept, not for speed and show, but for work; nor were their masters such skilled equestrians as to be able speedily to train roadsters and cart-horses into chargers. The only cavalry in the army around New York consisted in some regiments of Light Dragoons from Connecticut. They traversed the city, five hundred strong, amidst the respectful sympathy of the New England militia, and the undisguised amusement of Southerners. Even to Pennsylvanian eyes they appeared old-fashioned men ; " heads of families, many of them beyond the meridian of life " ; carrying fowling-pieces and even duck-guns, in place of carbines and sabres ; while here and there, in their long and disordered line of march, might be noticed triangular laced hats and dingy scarlet regimentals, redolent of glories which had gained in lustre by the lapse of time. "Some of these worthy soldiers," (an admirer wrote,) "assisted in their present uniforms at the reduction of Louisburg; and their lank lean cheeks, and war-worn coats, are viewed with more veneration by their honest countrymen than if they were glittering nabobs from India." [1]

Washington surveyed the quaint procession something too much in the spirit of a country gentleman who rode

[1] Letter from New York of July 10, 1776.

to hounds.   There was plenty of capability, and some youth, in those heterogeneous ranks; and he might well have picked out eight or ten score of the best horses and smartest men, and subjected them to as much discipline and practice as time permitted.   Six weeks still remained before the fighting began; and Captain Henry Lee, or Captain William Washington, would have got a small body of cavalry into shape soon enough to be of essential service.   On the twenty-seventh of August, 1776, a couple of troops of yeomanry, posted and handled by two such officers, would have saved many hundred Americans from capture.[1]   A less judicious course was adopted.   The Commander-in-Chief had not the money to purchase the horses from their owners, and declined to be at the expense of feeding them. He proposed to dismount the brigade, and employ it on fatigue work; but the men statedly refused to have anything to do with "the pick-axe, the shovel, or the wheelbarrow."   They lingered a while in camp, pasturing out their horses at their own cost, and reminding each other that it would be cheaper to be carrying their hay at home, instead of consuming other people's grass at the rate of a dollar a fortnight;[2] and then they returned to Connecticut, having marched across the stage at a moment so critical, in the history of a nation which dwells so minutely on its own past, that posterity has been told a great deal more about them than about the hussars of Seidlitz, or the cuirassiers of Murat.   One of them found his way to Long Island, and fell into the hands of the British, who made merry at his expense, and would not be satisfied until they had put him through his cavalry exercise.   When questioned about the nature of his duties in the rebel army, he replied that he could flank a little, and carry tidings.

[1] There is a very just remark to this effect in an article by Mr. Charles Francis Adams, the younger, on the Battle of Long Island.

[2] Washington's despatches of July 9, 10, 11, and 17, 1776.   On July 11 the Colonel wrote : "The men are principally farmers, and have left their grass, their grain, and other affairs, much unprovided for ; and they hope every method will be taken for their speedy relief."

The language seemed uncouth to a professional ear; but the poor trooper, according to his lights, had in this matter shown more wisdom than his famous general.

Washington was very ill provided in another arm, second in importance to none on account of the peculiar nature of the region which he had undertaken to defend. To man the batteries of New York, to garrison the forts along those vast estuaries which embraced the city, and to work his field-guns in line of battle, he had but five hundred artillerymen present for duty.[1] Howe commanded four times that number, perfectly equipped and disciplined, and concentrated under his hand for every purpose of war.[2] On the side of the Americans in the earlier battles, round-shot and grape did little to supplement the musket-balls; and of muskets there was a poor show. Late in June, Washington's Adjutant General reported that two thousand soldiers were destitute of arms, and nearly as many more had arms "in such condition as rather to discourage than to animate the user." Three weeks afterwards, at a review of New York militia where the men were drawn up four deep, the entire rear rank in some regiments, and a great part of the centre ranks, had no firelocks. And again in August, when the same State called out its last reserves to line the river-front and guard the ferries, the Convention ordered that each man, who had not arms, should

[1] In August 1776 the Returns of the Army under General Washington show 585 artillerymen. In the same month, out of 27,000 American infantry, only 19,000 were present for duty. The effective artillerymen cannot have exceeded the number named in the text.

[2] In 1777 Howe marched to Philadelphia with eight companies of the British Royal Artillery; and the war strength of a company was 250 men. There was still some German artillery left; and it must be remembered that, in the summer and autumn of 1776, the Hessian guns and gunners, whom Washington captured in December, were still at the disposal of the English General. For information relating to the strength of the British forces I am greatly indebted to the courtesy of Colonel Gerald Boyle; the extent of whose researches into the military statistics of the Revolutionary war I am enabled to measure by the circumstance that he has never failed to solve any question on which I have consulted him.

bring with him a shovel, a spade, a pickaxe, or a scythe straightened and fixed upon a pole.[1]

The raw levies of America were subjected to an ordeal which has proved too severe for many a veteran army. From the first it was impossible to adapt their victuals exactly to their taste; and, later on in the campaign, it often happened that no food whatever was issued under circumstances when it was most wanted. The husbandmen of New England, (we are told,) "used to feed plentifully, on excellent viands, and almost literally on milk and honey. The great harvest in Massachusetts and New Hampshire is Indian Corn, which they boil plain, and with milk, two or three hours into a hasty pudding, and mix it with molasses or with finer syrops. They mix also this Flour with Wheat; but the Bread, unless split and baked like ship Biscuit, will not keep three days. These are no provisions for a campaign."[2] Nevertheless the ostensible ration, though not precisely what a farmer liked, was all that a soldier had any right to claim; — bacon and mutton; butter for the sick; a daily quart of spruce beer and cider, or molasses for those who had a sweet tooth; peas, beans, potatoes, vinegar, and salt, — all of the very best, unless the contractor was prepared to have his goods returned upon his hands; with three pounds of candles a week to every company, as well as four and twenty pounds of soap. It was to the honour of New England housewives that they had educated their sons and husbands into a keen appreciation of the blessings of cleanliness even under the most adverse conditions. General Greene made it a personal favour that his troops should receive a double allowance of the means for washing clothes when they were occupied in digging trenches; and a Colonel, — who had inter-

[1] Colonel Reed, June 28; Egbert Benson to the New York Convention in the middle of July; and a note subjoined by Jared Sparks to the letter of General Washington, August 12, 1776. In May a new colonel had written to his Provincial Congress: "Gentlemen, I want arms. I have no more than 110 in the regiment. For God's sake exert yourselves."

[2] Letter from Paul Wentworth; *Auckland MSS.*

cepted a British mess-train laden with six pipes of what he had ascertained to be Madeira, some hundred dozen of a liquor conjectured to be Teneriffe, and a chest of soap, — requested that his men might have some of the wine, but earnestly begged that they might keep all the soap.[1] Such was the comfort and abundance officially promised to the militia; but experience unfolded another tale when the fat weeks around New York were succeeded by the lean months of marching and countermarching on the shores of North River, and along New Jersey byways.

The Staff departments of the American army were sparely manned, and feebly conducted. Among them all, that of the Quartermaster General was in lowest repute. The office had been conferred upon Colonel Mifflin, who was brave and not corrupt; but more of an orator, and very much more of a party manager, than of a military administrator. He was appointed Quartermaster General, as a man is appointed anything and everything at the outset of a Revolution, on account of a reputation mainly founded on his having been the author of a sentence which embodied the popular faith in few and telling words;[2] but his aptitude lay elsewhere than among his professional duties, and his short official career was a hopeless struggle against insuperable difficulties. Colonel Mifflin's misfortunes, as head of the transport, began early. When he became Quartermaster General in October 1776, many of his waggons, and those the best, had been left behind on Long Island; and nearly all that remained had fallen

[1] Greene to Washington, July 11; Colonel Huntington to General Heath, December 4, 1776.

[2] "Let us not be bold in declarations and cold in action, nor have it said of Philadelphia that she passed noble resolutions, and neglected them." The words were spoken at the town meeting held in Philadelphia on receipt of the news from Lexington. Mifflin, before the campaign was over, rendered some brilliant and remarkable service, though not in his own department. He soon afterwards retired from the Staff, and betook himself to politics. After no long while he was chosen President of Congress, and occupied the Chair on the fourteenth of January, 1784, when that body ratified the final treaty of peace with England.

into the hands of the British when they took New York. Without waggons, (so General Lee pronounced,) it was sometimes as impossible to march a hundred miles, although the fate of a Colony depended on it, as if the soldiers wanted legs. But there are times in warfare when, at a vast expense of human misery, the impossible has to be accomplished, or at least attempted. Needs must when a victorious enemy is driving; and the American army retreated, and turned round to fight, and retreated again, throughout an autumn, and half a winter, in which the weather began by being bad, and became atrocious. The Commissariat broke down. Supplies of food were less than scanty. The Continental troops, according to a belief current among the Provincial regiments, obtained more than their wretched share of the pittance that was forthcoming; and the swarms of militiamen, who had gathered round the standards in July, melted away under starvation and exhaustion, and by the end of December had almost totally disappeared.

Such, in its weak points, was the American army: but it had merits even more peculiar than its imperfections; and those imperfections care and time might remedy, while its more valuable attributes were of a kind which no mere military training could create. In many of the infantry regiments two companies, out of ten, were armed with rifles; and from almost every homestead along the Western border came a backwoodsman carrying a weapon which was the pride of his eyes, and a main implement of his industry. "Over every cabin door hung a well-made rifle, correctly sighted, and bright within from frequent wiping and oiling. Beside it were a tomahawk and knife, a horn of good powder, and a pouch containing bullets, patches, spare flints, steel, tinder, and whetstones, with oil and tow for cleaning." All these appliances were of the very best; because the sustenance of the family, and, (when the Indians were out and about,) its existence and its honour, depended upon straight shooting. A boy of the wilderness, at an age when in England he would have been scaring crows, was sent to kill squirrels, under penalty in case the number of the squirrels did not tally with the number of bullets that he expended. So soon as he had passed his twelfth birthday, he was recognised as part of the garrison of the farm, and was allotted his loophole in the stockade which encircled it. In the more settled districts, many of which were wild enough, the country folk spared no pains to keep up the standard of marksmanship that ruled among their grandfathers when their township was still a frontier district. They exercised themselves assiduously with the rifle; just as an English yeoman under the Tudors, jealous for the departing glory of the long-bow, made it his duty to practise at the butts. A shooting match formed part of the programme in all colonial festivities, and drew more spectators than the horse-race, the auction, the raffle, or the dance. But every American, who boasted pioneer descent, preferred a living target. The time had passed when venison was everywhere a staple food, with which the population were surfeited;[1] but deer roamed in the Southern forests; and, where deer ran, wolves were seldom absent. Wild turkeys were killed with the bullet, and afforded a repast of which no epicure ever wearied; and an incautious sportsman might at any moment find himself in startling proximity to a wildcat.[2] There were New Englanders, who, (as if they could not fail, even in their pastimes, to outrage the aristocratic sentiment of the old country,) had shot as many as ten foxes of an evening. In the most civilised provinces water-birds, from geese to teal, were in enormous abundance; wood-pigeons, when the season for their

[1] There was a time when one planter's household in Maryland was said to have had eighty deer in ninety days. The inmates at length preferred dry bread to venison.

[2] A British officer, a prisoner in the interior of the country, was in real danger from one of these animals. A colonist, who was fortunately at hand with his rifle, put a bullet through its brain. *Travels through the Interior Parts of America;* Letter LXIX.

P

slaughter came, might be bought in the Boston market for a few pence the hundred; and a rustic, although his gun was nothing more than a fowling-piece, had at all events learned the habit of shooting with intent to kill.

That habit did something to supply the want of a professional training in the American artillerymen. When a British fleet bombarded the Charleston forts on the twenty-eighth of June, Carolinian officers, laying down their pipes to point the guns, waited patiently for the smoke to clear away that they might aim with more precision. Seldom, in so fierce an engagement, was so little powder consumed by the victors, or so much tobacco. When the fire opened, the colonists had less than thirty rounds for each cannon; and only seven hundred pounds of powder were sent into the batteries during the conflict. And yet the British flagship was hulled no less than seventy times; the squadron lost over two hundred killed and wounded; and the two largest men-of-war were reduced to little better than a couple of wrecks. General Charles Lee, who commanded the defence, had issued orders that, if it came to a fight on land, no field-pieces should be discharged at a distance over four hundred, and no rifles over a hundred and fifty, yards. He addressed willing ears. A colonist, in the first years of the war, was often prone to run away if he was very much afraid of being killed himself; but, when he stood his ground, it was with an express purpose of killing some of his opponents. The deadly, personal, character of American sharpshooting was for the British an unexpected and disconcerting phenomenon, and would have altogether daunted less brave troops than those against whom it was directed. "This war," said an English officer, "is very different to the last in Germany. In this the life of an individual is sought with as much avidity as the obtaining a victory over an army of thousands."[1]

Nothing like it had ever been witnessed on the other side of the Atlantic. Marshal Saxe, — whose exploits,

[1] *Travels through the Interior Parts of America;* Letter XXXI.

experience, and natural ability gave him high rank as an authority, — stated that he had more than once seen a regiment in action fire a volley without killing four men.[1] The musketry instruction vouchsafed to a European fusilier was most elementary. He was taught to point his weapon horizontally, brace himself for its vicious recoil, and pull a ten-pound trigger till his gun went off ; if, indeed, it did go off when the hammer fell. French powder was bad ; and the flints used in the English army were execrable. A most indifferent character is given them by one of our colonels, who had fought in America and the West Indies. On the day of a grand review, (he said,) a captain, who had the credit of his company at heart, would buy them flints at his own expense. The pebbles supplied by Government were good for five or six shots, but after that they could not be trusted ; and the springs of the lock were too stiff and strong for convenient handling.[2] Under those circumstances it was no wonder that even a cool and courageous soldier let off his piece at the mass of uniforms opposite him without distinguishing between the individuals.

The slaughter in the commissioned ranks at Bunker's Hill, as is sure to be the case with an unpleasant novelty, excited moral disapprobation in English circles. "How far," one gentleman wrote, "the Bostonians can justify taking aim at officers with rifled muskets, I am

---

[1] Article VI., page 21, of *Reveries or Memoirs on the Art of War*, by Field Marshal Count Saxe ; English Translation, London, 1757. When serving under Prince Eugene, at the battle of Belgrade, the Marshal saw two battalions give a fire upon a large body of Turks at thirty paces ; instantaneously after which the Turks rushed through the smoke, and with their sabres cut the whole to pieces upon the spot. "I had curiosity enough," he wrote, "to count the number of Turks which might be destroyed by the general discharge of two battalions, and found it amounted only to thirty-two." The Marshal, in his observations, discriminated between the many nations whom he had led, or met, in battle. A British volley at near hand, as no one knew better than the victor of Fontenoy, was sometimes a deadly performance.

[2] Vol. II., page 47, of a *Military Miscellany*, by the Honourable Colin Lindsay, Lieutenant Colonel of the Forty-sixth Regiment.

not military jurisprudent enough to determine. It seems to be contrary to justice." [1] There was no question of justice, but of physical and mental custom which had become an ingrained instinct. Many a colonist had never in his life fired off a charge of powder without singling out something or somebody, whether it was the chief with the largest bunch of feathers in a rush of Indian warriors, or the drake in a string of wild-fowl. In the later stages of the war, proficiency with their weapon was still retained by troops whom Washington had by that time brought under the influence of the best traditions of British discipline. The old military precept, by enforcing which General Wolfe gained the battle of Quebec, — that the line should reserve its fire until the enemy was within forty paces, — produced a terrible effect when, as was the case with the American army, at least one private out of every three in that line had been a marksman from his boyhood upwards. [2]

American soldiers possessed another most valuable qualification for war which, from that day to this, they have never lost. The multifarious labours of the farm in a thinly peopled country had taught them to construct intrenchments quickly, out of the materials that lay closest to hand. On the evening after the engagement at White Plains, Washington's officers exultingly declared that their men were the most expert in the world in making breastworks. In an hour or two they had built an amazingly long stone fence, and covered it properly with earth. On the same day, in another

---

[1] *Historical Manuscripts Commission;* Fourteenth Report, Appendix, Part IX.   MSS. of James Round, Esq., M.P., of Birch Hall, Essex.

[2] In the eighteenth century the ideal of every good colonel, who gave the word of command in English, was that his battalion should deliver " one close well-directed fire at the distance of eight or ten rods."   *American Archives;* October 27, 1776.

While writing the last four paragraphs I have been especially indebted to two articles in American periodicals; — " Social Life in the Colonies," by Edward Eggleston, in the *Century Magazine* for July 1885; and "The Birth of the American Army," by Horace Kephart, in *Harper's Magazine* for May 1899.

part of the same position, lay a field of Indian corn which the soldiers pulled up by armfuls. The roots of the stalks, with the great lumps of soil adhering to each bundle, were arranged "in the face of the works, and answered the purpose of sods or fascines. The tops having been placed inwards, as the loose earth was thrown upon them, became as so many ties to the work, which was carried up with despatch scarcely conceivable." When more time was at the disposal of the Americans, and when the neighbourhood happened to be well wooded, their field-works attained a perfection of solidity. The fortifications on Long Island consisted of timbers a yard thick, laid side by side to a breadth of ten or twelve feet, and a height of twenty; and a hedge within gun-shot of the rampart was deftly converted into an abattis which ought to have been sufficient to delay the assailants while a half dozen rounds were being fired by the defenders. Wherever, as in the siege-works outside Boston, there was a continuous front which could not be turned, the rank and file of the army might be trusted, almost without superior direction, to render that front impregnable; but it was another matter when the work to be done was beyond the scope of spadesmen, wood-cutters, and mechanics.

The American had not yet been discovered who was equal to the task of locating, and laying out, an isolated and self-contained fortress which might confidently be esteemed defensible. In November 1775 Washington had informed his Government that the camp could not furnish one good engineer; and he was no better provided in May 1776, when necessity called upon him to occupy the shores of New York Island, and the dominant headlands along the Hudson River, with strongholds upon the maintenance of which the very existence of the Republic, to all appearance, depended. His Chief Engineer was Colonel Rufus Putnam, nephew to the Major General. Fashionable and fastidious officers objected to him because he had been seen carrying his own ration of meat to his quarters. When speaking about the gorge of a redoubt, Colonel Putnam was rumoured to have pronounced the word as if it were the name of the King with a view to whose discomfiture that redoubt was in course of erection; which, indeed, would have mattered little if only the work had been so planned as to keep the monarch's soldiers outside its walls. But the science of Vauban, even more than others, demands the acquisition of exact knowledge as an indispensable preliminary to the inspirations of natural genius. Putnam's citadels were death-traps for their garrisons; and not Putnam's only. General Arnold wrote from St. John's that his Engineer was a perfect sot; and indeed he appears to have taken so little account of water as a beverage that one stockade in the Northern district did not include a well or a spring, although the space walled in was too large for any force that could be spared to hold the post. "The thing called a fort," (such is the testimony of an eye-witness,) "baffles all description. It is an irregular polygon; — irregular indeed, and indefensible with a vengeance." [1]

After a while Colonel Putnam resigned his position, on the respectable plea that Congress had refused to sanction the formation of a separate corps of sappers and miners. He took command of an infantry regiment, which every Major General was soon eager to have attached to his brigade; for Putnam made his people skilful boatmen and good workmen, and he himself, like a true American, had been instructed, and not disheartened, by his own failures as an engineer. Washington was in no hurry to replace him either by a native amateur, or by one of those numerous foreigners who, to hear them talk, were as good as anything that had appeared since Archimedes; but whose only ascertained qualifications were that they could not speak English, and stood in urgent need of a salary. At length he secured the services of four excellent French officers,

[1] Washington's letters of November 2, 1775; *Pennsylvanian Memoirs*, chapter vi. ; Arnold to Sullivan, June 10, 1776; and Bernard Romans to Gates, November 1776.

regularly bred to their business, who came to the United States with the knowledge and approbation of their own Government. Soldiers and men of science, these gentlemen were neither martinets nor pedants. They knew how to encourage the cleverness, and stimulate the exertions, of an American working-party; and in return they freely acknowledged that better sappers and military artificers did not exist than the farm-hands of Rhode Island and New Hampshire, and the lumberers from the forest-camps on the banks of the Kennebec and the Penobscot.[1]

The military successes of the colonists were in part due to a special circumstance with reference to which their ardent, and in other respects sympathetic, well-wishers in Parisian philosophical circles regarded them as sadly behind the times. Patriotism and religion existed in other countries; but the colonies had not passed the stage when, in many minds, these two sentiments were inextricably mingled. Religious doctrine in America was more reasonable and milder, and far less intellectually tyrannical, than among English Puritans and Scotch Covenanters during the great period of their history; but not John Lilburne, or Baillie of Kilwinning, had a stronger and more present faith in the personal government of the universe than that which, in the year 1776, animated the congregations of America. Those congregations never doubted that the Almighty dealt directly with nations as with individuals; and it was a belief which, (as in other virile and thoughtful communities, when profoundly excited by momentous events,) took shape in a persuasion that their own interests and for-

---

[1] "I have to mention," (so Washington wrote from Trenton on December 20, 1776,) "that for want of some establishment in the department of engineers, agreeably to the plan laid before Congress in October last, Colonel Putnam, who was at the head of it, has quitted, and taken a regiment in the State of Massachusetts. I know of no other man tolerably qualified for the conducting of that business. None of the French gentlemen whom I have seen appear to me to know anything of the matter." The Chevalier Duportail was appointed Chief Engineer in the latter part of the year 1777, and retained that employment until the war had ended.

tunes were, in some sort, His peculiar care. Such a persuasion, when sincerely held, is a political, and still more a warlike, force of remarkable potency. So far from tempting those who entertain it to relax their efforts because the final result of those efforts is ordained on high, it makes them diligent in preparation, valiant in action, and, above all things, patient and resolute in adversity. Jonathan Trumbull was the Governor of Connecticut, than whom no more vigilant and painstaking an administrator ever raised a regiment or levied a wartax; and he thus expressed himself to the Commander-in-Chief of the army which he was labouring night and day to feed and to reinforce. "It is nothing with God to help, whether with many, or with those that have no power. He hath so ordered things in the administration of the affairs of the world as to encourage the use of means, and yet so as to keep men in continual dependence upon Him for the efficacy and success of them." [1]

That was no waste of ink, even in an official correspondence. The faith which actuated, and the spirit which possessed, not a few among her leading men became of ever increasing advantage to America when misfortune darkened down upon her hopes. Those men had seldom exulted unduly over their successes; and they did not murmur or quail beneath disaster, inasmuch as, to their view, it came straight from One who never chastised unjustly or without design. When the colonists were victorious, His was the glory; and when they were brought within sight of destruction, it was a speaking testimony from Heaven against a sinful nation.[2] That was the creed of religious Americans, who were the leaven of the people, whatever proportion they might bear to the entire mass. It was held alike among the rich and the humble; and it was a creed especially well suited

---

[1] Governor Trumbull to Washington; August 31, 1776.

[2] The *American Archives* contain a fine letter of September 1776, referring to the evacuation of New York by Washington's army. "Trouble," said the writer, "does not spring out of the dust, nor rise from the ground. It is God who has blunted the weapons of our warfare, and fashioned the counsels of our wise men to foolishness."

for fighting men.   There was many a soldier who honestly strove to mend his ways, and make himself a better Christian, in order that he might contribute towards averting the Divine wrath from his cause; who spent his leisure, not in criticising his superior officers, but in searching his own heart and examining his own conduct; and who went into battle with a quiet conviction that his life was in God's keeping.

Such an one was Amos Farnsworth, who came of a homely, a thriving, and, (it is almost needless to add,) a very numerous Massachusetts family.   He did not spell his own name correctly on the title-page of his diary; but that diary is nevertheless a record worth the attention of all such as care to understand the inner springs of the American Revolution.   Soon after the young man joined the army before Boston, he anxiously and solemnly devoted himself to God's service, and prayed earnestly that he might be strengthened to keep his resolution.   On Sunday, the eleventh of June, he listened to a sermon on the duty of resting all our care on Him who cares for us: and, before the week was out, his faith was put to the test; for on the following Friday, (he writes,) "Our Regiment paraded, and about Sunset we was drawn up and heard Prayers, and about dusk marched for Bunker's Hill, under command of our own Colonel Prescott."   Next day Farnsworth did not leave the redoubt until it was filling fast with British infantry; and, before he had retreated fifty yards, he was struck by two bullets, one of which shattered his right arm.   They sent him back to the care of his "honoured father"; and after eight weeks of suffering, on the first day that he could make shift to form the letters of an entry in his journal, he rejoined the regiment in such a condition that the surgeons insisted on his undergoing a severe and painful operation.

He belonged to a class of men who entered on the war gravely and ruefully, but who meant to see it through. Their path had been made very plain before them by the Declaration of Independence.   That event, (to use their own words,) had called them out of darkness into a marvellous light; for they were as those who in time past were not a People, but who now were determined so to bear themselves, under their passing trials and perils, that a People for all future time they should remain.   Of such material was composed that handful of Washington's followers, the last remnant of a great host, who, when they found themselves, — starving indeed and exhausted, but safe, and for the moment unassailable, — behind the broad and rapid Delaware, deliberately re-crossed the river, and went once more into the lion's mouth.   Sandwich and Rigby called these poor people cowards : and undoubtedly they feared God, a weakness from which the Bedfords were exempt.   But they were not afraid of the midnight torrent, swirling with ice-blocks; and, when they reached the further shore, they were not afraid of the Hessians.   Hating war, — shocked by the coarseness, the vice, and the self-seeking from which camps are never free, — they continued under arms until peace was secured ; and then they went home, purposing thenceforth to do their share as citizens towards making the country, which they had saved, worthy of the signal favours accorded to it by Providence.[1]

[1] Some extracts from Amos Farnsworth's Diary for 1775–6 are given in the Second Appendix, at the end of this volume.

CHAPTER XVIII

CROWN POINT. GENERAL HOWE ON STATEN ISLAND. AN INTERLUDE IN WAR

DURING all summer and autumn, in that year of 1776, the gaze of the American continent was, from time to time, directed with anxiety towards the quarter whence Sir Guy Carleton and his army were expected. The command of the Northern department had been entrusted to General Philip Schuyler; a leading personage among a group of Dutch families, endowed with vast landed possessions in the province of New York, and closely connected among each other by the ties of marriage. Schuyler's wife was a Van Rensselaer, whose ancestor had been the Patroon, (or, in more familiar terms, the Hereditary Superior,) of a manor extending over six hundred square miles; within the boundaries of which he nominated the administrative and judicial officers, held a Court Leet and a Court Baron, received a tenth part of the revenues, and was responsible for conducting civil government and for maintaining order.[1] Before 1775 that immense district, which constituted the Van Rensselaer property, had been divided among the heirs, male and female; but the value of each share

---

[1] Mr. Floyd de Lancey, in a careful essay, has drawn a distinction between the Freehold Manors of America and the Feudal Manors of mediæval Europe; but the resemblance between the two systems was stronger than modern opinion would tolerate. In 1830 the New York Legislature put an end to what was exceptional in the territorial institutions of the State, and declared in so many words that "all feudal tenures of every description, with all their incidents, are abolished." Mr. de Lancey's paper was a contribution to the valuable, and very bulky, work, entitled *History of Westchester County;* edited, and largely written, by J. Thomas Scharf, A.M., LL.D.

had grown rapidly, and the proceeds of the several estates had become enormous, in kind, if not in money.
The sons were very great people, and the husbands of
the daughters also. Schuyler, who himself had succeeded to several large fortunes, had a noble town-house
in the suburbs of the provincial capital, and a country
seat beneath whose roof he fondly hoped that his declining years would be passed. But the future of that
mansion was less secure than the owner had anticipated;
although it was situated in a peaceful valley on the head
waters of the Hudson, in the pleasant hamlet of Saratoga.[1]

Schuyler, as a youth, had behaved with courage in the
French war. He had a great name among the Indians,
whom he knew how to regale and to amuse, and whose
self-respect he flattered by treating with their chief men
on equal terms when they approached him in the character of negotiators. During the Revolutionary war his
popularity with the tribes did much to counteract the
influence of the Johnsons, — the famous Tory and Loyalist house of Tryon County on the Mohawk river.
Schuyler sate, whenever he chose, in the Provincial
Assembly, where he was resolute against the Stamp
Act; and in June 1776 Congress appointed him one of
the first four Major Generals. None of the four displayed high merit; and the great New York land-owner
had his points of superiority over each of the other
three. A man of honour and ability, he showed himself
more unselfish and trustworthy than General Charles
Lee; and he was much younger than General Putnam,
and very much younger than General Ward. But the
profuse and continuous hospitality which he dispensed
in town and country had told a tale upon his constitution.[2] In the previous autumn he had accompanied the

[1] *The Life of Catherine Schuyler*, by Mary Gay Humphreys, throws
much light on the character and motives of General Schuyler; although
that attractive volume does not professedly bear upon the disagreeable
historical controversies which have clustered around his reputation.

[2] At the funeral of Mrs. Cornelia Van Cortlandt, the General's mother,
140 gallons of wine and two barrels of ale were consumed by the mourners.

expedition to Canada in person, as far as St. John's on the Sorel river, until gout and rheumatism brought him back from the front. He returned to the camp from time to time, when his health permitted; but he never was successful in the field. He remained for the most part in Albany, providing and forwarding men and military stores, and loyally guiding the main operations of the Northern war in a direction conformable to the general plans of Washington.

When Schuyler was at the base of operations, the charge of the active army devolved upon General Horatio Gates. Of him it is sufficient to say that, although his name is linked with the most celebrated American triumph of the Revolutionary war, the historians of a patriotic and, (where signal public services are in question,) a lavishly grateful nation, say much to his discredit, and very little indeed in his praise.[1] The future conqueror of Saratoga, except in his appetite for fame and preferment, was a very ordinary man; and, when he took over Sullivan's beaten army, he had to deal with extraordinary difficulties. Crown Point, in June and July 1776, was not a camp, but a lazar-house. A visitor from Connecticut related that he never looked into a bed or a hut in which he did not find a dead or dying man. "Everything about this army," (so Gates

---

A visitor from Maryland acknowledged the Schuyler Madeira to be sounder than any that was drunk in his own colony; and a French Marquis, who had no provincial jealousy to qualify his relish of it, was still more emphatic in his commendation. But gout comes from other causes than strong liquor, as our own sober generation sadly recognises. Mrs. Grant of Laggan relates how the tea-table at Madam Schuyler's was covered with "all sorts of cake unknown to us; cold pastry; and great quantities of sweetmeats and preserved fruits of all kinds. In all manner of confectionery these people excelled. Having great fruit in abundance, which cost them nothing, and getting sugar home at an easy rate in return for their exports to the West Indies, the quantities of these articles used in families, otherwise plain and frugal, was astonishing."

[1] Senator Henry Cabot Lodge speaks of Gates as slow and ineffective in battle, but sufficiently active in looking after his own advancement; Bancroft calls him shallow, vain, and timorous, and of small administrative ability; and Mr. John Fiske shortly describes his career as one of intrigue and imbecility.

truly reported,) "is infected by the pestilence; the clothes, the blankets, the air, the ground they walk upon." During an early stage of the retreat from Canada, Sullivan had written to Washington in ominous terms. "The raging of the small-pox," he said, "deprives us of whole regiments in the course of a few days. Of the remaining regiments from fifty to sixty in each are taken down in a day, and we have nothing to give them but salt pork, flour, and the poisonous waters of this lake."[1] Sullivan enclosed a return of soldiers, absent from duty, which was only forty-eight hours old; with the remark that, in the short time which had elapsed since the enumeration was made out, a quarter part of those given as effectives had been prostrated by the camp disorder. Of Colonel Paterson's battalion, (he observed,) there was no return at all. That officer had but five men fit for duty; and those had been ordered southwards to join the rest of their comrades who were all sick at Crown Point. Sullivan, as is known from other sources, did not unduly darken the colour of that gloomy story. Colonel Paterson had marched out of New York, on the twenty-first of April, at the head of six hundred healthy well-appointed troops. In December, Schuyler sent him back to the assistance of Washington, in Washington's utmost need; and, when he arrived among the bivouacs of the Southern army, he had only two hundred rank and file present with the colours.[2]

That was the state of things under Sullivan in June. In July Gates represented to Washington that it would be to the last degree improper to order reinforcements

[1] Sullivan's allusion to the poisonous character of the lake is explained in a narrative left by one of his Generals, who speaks of a white scum on the face of the water in the morning, which was driven by the ripples against the shore, and which, in the middle of the day, had become putrefied by the sun, and very offensive to the smell. *Memoirs of Brigadier John Lacey*, published by the Historical Society of Pennsylvania, in July 1901.

[2] Note to Washington's letter of July 19, 1776, in the Edition of Mr. Jared Sparks. *American Archives* for June and July 1776. *The Life of Major General John Paterson*, by Thomas Egleston.

to Crown Point or Ticonderoga, until obliged by the
most pressing emergency, as it would only be heaping
one hospital upon another; — if indeed hospitals those
could be named which contained no accommodation for
invalids, and no medicines whatsoever. "No emetic or
cathartic, no mercurial or antimonial remedy. It would
melt a heart of stone to hear the moans and distresses
of the sick and dying." So the doctors averred; but
they did not fold their hands in despair; and, since they
could not physic the sick, they tried at any rate to keep
the well fit for duty. They served out to the soldiers
rum, infused with four pounds of gentian root, and two
pounds of orange peel, to a hogshead; and, where these
ingredients might not be procured, the Regimental Surgeons were directed to use as a substitute snakeroot,
dogwood, and centaury. In either case the men were
none the worse for the flavouring matter, and presum-
ably somewhat the happier for the rum. Though their
medicine chests were empty, American physicians, already in the van of their profession, did not love to be
idle: and their industry took a shape which, in the view
of a commanding officer whose object was to keep his
ranks full, was more than questionable. Inoculation for
the small-pox, rendered fashionable in Europe sixty
years before by the example and teaching of Lady
Mary Wortley Montagu, had become an article of medical faith, and a very popular social institution, in the
colonies. The clergy preached against it as rash interference with the designs of Providence; but it com-
mended itself to parents, to family physicians, and, what
was more to the purpose still, (since America in that
respect was already America,) to the young people
themselves. They selected a spacious and pleasant
house with an enclosed garden, made up a cheerful
party, and were all inoculated together. They reckoned
upon only two or three days in bed with the illness;
and then, during six weeks of quarantine and conva-
lescence, they gossiped, and lounged, and made each
other merry, and drank tea at all hours, — little thinking

that the time was close at hand when, except by stealth, they would not venture to drink it at all. The custom, it was confessed, "could not be regarded as an unmixed blessing; for the patients were sometimes very ill, and a few died. Still, when successful, it gave complete immunity, and saved innumerable lives."

There is a time for all things; and the time to choose for inoculating an army is not the moment when the hostile columns are breaking through its line of outposts; but no mere military considerations were powerful enough to deter the American doctors from obeying the voice of their professional conscience. They fell to work, at first without orders from the general, and afterwards in direct defiance of his prohibitions. There might be no drugs wherewith to treat the small-pox; but the vehicle for communicating it from one individual to another was only too readily procurable. The medical staff answered all objectors by the doctrine that the disease "was very mortal to those who took it in the natural way." But, in the first place, the poor fellows who were the subjects of their attentions were already half dead with exhaustion and starvation, and had not the vitality to endure even the beneficent workings of an artificial malady; and the soldiers who had not been inoculated caught the infection, by hundreds a day, from those who had undergone the operation. On May the twenty-seventh the army, which then was still commanded by General Thomas, was described as broken and disheartened, half of it being under inoculation and other diseases. Thomas already had small-pox upon him, "having taken it in the natural way." But he passed his days in the saddle, and his evenings at the writing-table, until the second of June arrived; and then he died, and his country has not forgotten him.

With that melancholy and conspicuous example to point their warnings, the men of science carried with them the opinion of the army, in every rank below the highest. Where a surgeon hesitated to disregard those express orders, which were repeatedly issued from head-quarters, the soldiers made shift to inoculate themselves and each other. Precaution was in some cases a mere excuse for poltroonery. Certain officers of the force which had been ordered north under Sullivan, on the pretext that they were going where small-pox was prevalent, withdrew themselves from their duties; paid a complaisant practitioner to do them the required service, and write them out the necessary certificate; and then passed their time among the pleasures of the city. In one single corps a lieutenant colonel, a captain, and a doctor organised an inoculation frolic of their own, and were not to be found when the battalion started. Three other field-officers left their regiments on the march, and went back in search of an apothecary whose poverty, or whose Toryism, would consent to their wishes. Even at this distance of time it is satisfactory to relate that the whole party were tracked to their haunt in New York, placed under arrest, and sent north to be court-martialled. The patience of commanding officers was in the end exhausted. "A villain of a surgeon," General Gates wrote in August, "is inoculating the militia as fast as they arrive. Such a slave to private gain, who would sacrifice this army for the sake of a few dollars to himself, deserves condign punishment. As fine an army as ever marched into Canada has this year been entirely ruined by the small-pox." At last it came to an indignant colonel denouncing his regimental doctor as a damned puppy of a quack who had carried on the abominable practice to the utter destruction of his battalion.[1]

Such words, and worse yet, were beginning to be frequently uttered throughout all the cantonments which lay between Lake George and Lake Champlain.

[1] The passion for inoculation in the New England regiments was intensified by recollections of the great epidemic of 1764. A very interesting letter from Mr. James Gordon, written in the spring of that year, has been published by the Massachusetts Historical Society. Whether or not it accurately records the facts and statistics, it faithfully represents the belief prevailing in the colony with regard to them. We are told that, of the first twelve people seized with small-pox, ten perished; that the Pro-

Dreadful reports of the strange oaths which were fashionable in those regions brought sorrow and consternation into many a New England household.   Young militiamen received from their parents earnest remonstrances against "the most foolish and unaccountable of vices," and solemn reminders that the business of religion ought to be the daily concern in the life of a soldier.[1]   The Reverend William Gordon, the chronicler of the war, who did not bestow the inestimable honour of his presence lightly, or without conditions, promised Gates a visit as soon as he could be assured that there was a marked improvement in the language employed at Ticonderoga.   "Let not," he said, "any future historian have to remark that the best troops in the world were most given to cursing and swearing." He described himself as plotting to set off in September for both camps, and as expecting a cordial reception from General Gates and General Washington.   If the good man's presence at the head-quarters of either commander depended upon all the adjectives used in their immediate neighbourhood being fit for the ears of a clergyman, it was likely to be long deferred.   Washington, on the third of August, addressed to the troops round New York a general order regretting that profane cursing and swearing, which theretofore had been little known in an American army, was growing into fashion; and warning them that it was idle to hope for a blessing on their arms from Heaven if they insulted it by such impiety and folly, and, (so that true Virginian gentleman did not shrink from declaring,) by such detestable and despicable vulgarity.[2]

vincial Assembly adjourned to Cambridge ; that a special Act was passed to enable the Courts of Law to sit elsewhere than in Boston ; and that everyone who could afford to travel left the city.   At length hospitals were opened, and three thousand persons inoculated, of whom only three or four died ; and by that policy the plague was stayed.

[1] Letter from Governor Trumbull to his son in the Northern army; September 1776.

[2] There was one military station where Mr. Gordon might have escaped being scandalised ; that is to say, if he had got there before the British

If the Northern army swore terribly, it was with as much excuse as ever army had, whether in Flanders or anywhere else. The American soldiers in Canada suffered on the one hand from the miserable poverty of a recently organised and a struggling government; and, on the other, from administrative defects and corruptions which had survived from the days of the old system. "Every kind of abuse," (wrote Sullivan in May 1776,) "is practised that men long versed in villainy could devise. I found at Stillwater a number of barrels of pork that the waggoners had tapped, and drawn off the pickle to lighten their teams. This pork must inevitably be ruined before it can reach Canada. The waggoners learned this piece of skill in the last war." The supplies of clothing, provisions, and warlike stores had been exhausted; and consignments of those articles, which at long intervals reached their destination, were mostly of the wrong sort. When General Thomas, with death close upon him, was trying to rally his defeated regiments, and induce them once more to face the enemy, a ton of lead, fifty quires of paper, and fifteen pounds of thread were still required to bring the ammunition for small-arms up to four and twenty rounds a man. Later in the campaign some hogsheads of paper arrived; but the material was too thick for musket cartridges, and too thin for cannon. Congress had nominated Dr. Franklin, and two others from among its prominent members, to inspect the condition, and regulate the operations, of the Canada army. As the artillery department of that army had not credit to hire a cart, the Commissioners brought on three barrels of powder in their chaise; and at one village on their route they purchased thirty loaves from a baker's shop

took it, as take it they did, from its blameless garrison. " Business goes on slow at Montgomery since you left it. Nothing has been done except to the small battery on the South side of the hill. If Colonel Humphry can git his officers together to sing Salms, and tell people how well he can govern men without Swearing at them, he is content." Peter Tappin to General Clinton ; August 19, 1776.

to feed a company of famished infantry. "We cannot," (so these gentlemen reported to Congress,) "find words to describe our miserable situation; — soldiers without discipline, and reduced to live from hand to mouth, depending on the scanty and precarious supplies of a few half-starved cattle, and trifling quantities of flour, which have hitherto been picked up in different parts of the country. Your military chest contains eleven hundred paper dollars. You are indebted to your troops treble that sum, and to the inhabitants above eighteen hundred dollars." That was plain speaking, and it produced some effect; for Congress transmitted for the use of the Northern army sixteen hundred pounds in specie, together with copies of "a spirited Resolution in favour of national independence." But fine words, — and very fine words it must be admitted that they were, — are a poor substitute for bread, and fresh meat, and broad-cloth, and shoe-leather. After the Republic was established, its soldiers were fed, clad, and shod no better than when their legal status was still that of unauthorised rebels against the British Crown. So late as October 1776, a Patriot on his travels wrote as follows from Saratoga: "The regiment is now within a few miles of this place, marching with cheerfulness, but a great part of the men barefooted and bare-legged. There is not a single shoe or stocking to be had in this part of the world, or I would ride a hundred miles through the woods to purchase them with my own money. I shall empty my portmanteau of the stockings I have for my own use on this journey; but this is a drop of water in the ocean."

Under these distressing circumstances it is not matter of wonder that the General responsible for the safety of the Northern department should have taken measures to refresh and re-fashion his battered army at a point as far as possible removed from hostile observation and interruption. The retirement to Crown Point had been viewed by Washington with doubt, and even with disapprobation.[1] In May he had urged Thomas to maintain a stand on the lower reaches of the Sorel river, inasmuch as the tract of country within his lines would remain faithful and useful to the American cause; whereas all the districts which might be abandoned would fall, perhaps not unwillingly, into the power of Carleton. These gloomy anticipations were fulfilled; and there was worse in prospect. For a hundred and fifty miles south from the sources of the Connecticut river, throughout the whole of New Hampshire and of what is now Vermont, the farming population slept at night with their most valuable furniture packed ready for an instant move. They had lent their stores of ammunition for the use of the Continental army; and Congress was besieged by expresses begging and praying for powder, without which the whole of that fertile region would have to be evacuated, and the very townships of Massachusetts would, as a consequence, be laid open to the ravages of Indians and French Canadians in the Royal pay.[2]

The withdrawal of the army to the south end of Lake Champlain was a grave calamity for the Republican Government; and, in July, Gates announced that he must make a further move backward to the north end of Lake George, and place his head-quarters in security behind the fortifications of Ticonderoga. This resolution was not carried into effect until it had been unanimously sanctioned by a council of generals, amongst whom was Benedict Arnold; and there is, to say the least, a strong presumption that no military step, to which Arnold gave his assent, can have erred in the direction of pusillanimity, or even of excessive caution. The decision, however, found plenty of critics. A remonstrance was drawn up in the Northern camp, and signed by over twenty Colonels and Majors. Washing-

---

[1] The operations detailed in this chapter may be followed on the map at the end of the volume.

[2] Letter from Exeter in New Hampshire, of June 29, to James Warren, President of the Massachusetts Congress.

ton, in terms which for him were blunt, assured Gates that nothing short of a dislike to encourage inferior officers in the practice of animadverting upon the action of their superiors, and a belief that the works at Crown Point had already been demolished, prevented him from insisting upon the re-occupation of that post. His own council of generals, (he said,) had advised him to override what they regarded as a disastrous and altogether unnecessary measure. Gates combated the arguments of the Commander-in-Chief with powerful reasons, put forward earnestly, but most respectfully.[1] None the less he keenly resented the interference of the New York generals, who did not confine themselves to giving their advice when called upon by Washington, but enforced it in unceremonious private letters addressed to their colleagues at Ticonderoga. Putnam, in particular, wrote his mind very plainly, and was answered by Gates with a spice of fraternal raillery which suggests a lively impression of the relations existing between the citizen-soldiers of the early Revolution.[2]

For the next fifteen months Benedict Arnold was a shining figure in the stormy foreground of the war. When the rest of Canada was abandoned by the Americans, he had held on to Montreal until the place was threatened by an overpowering English force. " Then he made a masterly retreat to St. John's. After seeing all the men embark, and the last boat leave the shore, he, with a single attendant, mounted his horse and rode back to reconnoitre the British. Coming in sight of the

[1] Washington to Gates; July 19, 1776. Gates to Washington; July 29.
[2] " Dear Put, Every fond mother dotes on her booby, be his imperfections ever so glaring. Crown Point was not indeed your own immediate offspring; but you had a hand in rearing the baby. You cut all the logs which are now as rotten as dirt. Why should you not be fond of Crown Point? If I live to be as old as you, I shall be as fond of Ticonderoga. What have *you* done, and what you *not* done? Have you blown up Staten Island? Have you burned the enemy's fleet? Have you sent the two brothers Howe to Hartford Jail? I shall preserve your letter for a winter's evening's subject, when we meet again. Remember me affectionately, as you ought; and believe me, veteran, your sincere well-wisher, Horatio Gates." Crown Point, August 3, 1776.

advancing columns he satisfied himself of their numbers and character. He wheeled his horse just in time to escape, and galloping back to the shore of the lake, and stripping his horse of saddle and bridle, the animal was shot to prevent his falling into the hands of the enemy. With his own hands he pushed his boat from the shore, and, leaping into it, he was the last man to leave Canada." [1] Arnold had displayed marked ability and valour during the whole period that Sullivan was manœuvring on the St. Lawrence; but it had not been within his power to avert defeat. His commanding faculties were deprived of free play so long as he was under the orders of a self-sufficing, and rather pretentious, general; and his rare military perception informed him that the attempt on Canada had failed, and that the forward position of the army was untenable. In June 1776, (to use the words of John Adams,) Arnold was wholly in the dismals.[2] But when the retreat had attained its utmost limit, and the Americans turned to bay, the brilliant officer was himself again, and fixed the attention of both the contending nations upon his audacious, resourceful, and masterful personality. He had a fever on him; and his wound, to which he had never given the chance of being healed, was very painful. Arnold did not consider his own health; and, where he suspected shirking, he required very strong proof of illness in others. He checked the practice of surreptitious inoculation by putting the sick on half-rations — a device which was quite in Franklin's style; but he spared no pains, nor was he scrupulous about the methods which he employed, in order to provide abundant, and even appetising, food for the soldiers who were doing their duty.[3]

[1] *The Life of Benedict Arnold,* by Isaac N. Arnold. The impartiality of this book is indicated by the motto on the title-page: "He will give the Devil his due."

[2] John Adams to Samuel Chase; Philadelphia, June 24, 1776.

[3] Complaint was made, in a letter to Arnold, that his people had dug up two fields of young potatoes, and had swept bare an acre of peas, and five or six acres of corn. The case was all the harder because the injured party had recently sent to Arnold's quarters a present of nearly fourscore salmon.

Gates, who had some self-knowledge, allowed full
scope to his formidable subordinate.   Whatever depart
ment Arnold took in hand was at once made alive by
his energy and inventiveness.   An opportunity now befell him for utilising the experience which he had
acquired on the high seas as a merchant captain.   "Our
little fleet," Gates wrote from Ticonderoga, "is equipping under the direction of General Arnold, with all the
industry which his activity and good example can inspire.
As fast as they are fitted they are sent to Crown Point.
Three hundred men and officers have been drafted from
the corps here to man the vessels; one half seamen, the
other to act as marines.   As soon as all the vessels and
gondolas are equipped, General Arnold has offered to
go to Crown Point, and take the command of them.
This is exceedingly pleasing to me; as he has a perfect
knowledge of maritime affairs, and is, besides, a most
deserving and gallant officer."   These naval preparations, (the General went on to state,) were of the last
importance; for should the enemy establish a superiority over the American flotilla on Lake Champlain, the
great water-way was theirs, let who would possess
Crown Point.[1]

That superiority was already a fact, undeniable, and
in all likelihood irremediable; and so Arnold well knew,
for he was admirably served by those on whom he depended for information.   The country in possession of
the Royal army swarmed with his spies, carrying their
credentials between the soles of their shoes, together
with a promise to pay each of them two hundred and
fifty dollars if he returned alive.   The American commander was perfectly aware that he had on board his
fleet only one gun for every two of Carleton's; and that,
compared with the larger British vessels, his own were
toy-boats.   But the object at which he aimed was to
present such a threatening appearance as would impose
upon his adversary, and delay the English advance until
the season for concerted action between Howe and

[1] Gates to Washington; July 29, 1776.

Carleton, for that year at all events, was past and gone. And at the bottom of his heart, like other men of his stamp, he cherished a secret hope that by desperate and aggressive action, — by putting in his last ship, and risking the lives of all his crews, — he might violate fortune; and might snatch a victory which in his cooler moments, if he ever had them, he himself would recognise as beyond the remotest bounds of possibility.

Arnold attacked his task in a spirit of joyous confidence, which any show of opposition in any quarter at once converted into overbearing insolence. His letters, during the summer of 1776, read like the correspondence of a generalissimo. He was surprised, (he declared,) at the strange infatuation and economy of Congress, whose parsimony and negligence would ruin all at last. His written requisitions for men and materials were flying about through all the continent, addressed sometimes to public authorities, and sometimes to private employers and capitalists, but always couched in a strain which did not brook refusal. On the first of July a contract was signed securing to him shipwrights at the rate of thirty-five dollars a month, a ration and a half of victuals, and one half-pint of rum a day; and he spared no trouble or expense to engage leading workmen who might act, (for that phrase was already current,) as "bosses." A fortnight later Arnold asked for five hundred blocks, and seventy anchors and hawsers. Then came "a Memorandum of Articles which have been repeatedly wrote for, and which we are in extremest want of;" cordage for eighty galleys; seventeen or eighteen hundred cannon-balls; old useless iron that would do for canister-shot; a hundred seamen who were no land-lubbers; and, (to wind up all,) snowshoes for a winter campaign on the chance of the Americans beating Carleton, and pursuing him home to Canada. What lay in Arnold's own power was very thoroughly done. Everything was foreseen, and almost every requisite for a naval expedition was provided, except a chaplain. The colonial ministers of religion were never very willing to

embark on ship-board; and, if any motive could overcome their reluctance, it would hardly be the temptation
of sailing on a forlorn hope with Benedict Arnold.[1] His
final care was to get a medical officer for the flag-ship.
" I don't think it prudent," (he wrote,) "to go without
a surgeon. The surgeon's mate of Colonel St. Clair's
regiment has a good box of medicines, and will incline
to go with the fleet. I wish he could be sent here, or
some one who will answer to kill a man *secundum artem*.
Nothing but a surgeon prevents our proceeding." [2] Colonel St. Clair's doctor declined to come; and in the end
Arnold borrowed a case of instruments, and sailed without him. It was his own affair. Until a battle was
fought, he himself was the only wounded man on board
the squadron. After a battle the chances were ten to
one that all the Americans, who did not feed the fishes
of Lake Champlain, might have their hurts treated by a
surgeon of the Royal Navy in the cock-pit of an English
war-ship.

Arnold's amphibious proceedings brought him into
many quarrels both on sea and land; from all of which,
at this period of his career, he emerged a victor. The
first person with whom he came into collision was, as
might easily have been foreseen, the naval officer in
charge of the American squadron. Commodore Wyn-
koop made a stout fight against the degradation of having to take his orders from an infantry general. " I
brought him to reason;" Arnold wrote. "I have given
him to understand that, if he did not incline to remain
in the service, he would not be compelled to it." There

[1] " Sir, I received yours yesterday, and am very much obliged to you
for your advice. As to your complaints of the morals of the people belonging to the Navy, I am now to let you know that I did not enter into
the Navy as a divine, and that I am not qualified to give directions in that
matter. The Congress whom I serve have made provision for a chaplain;
but to my mortification I have not been able to get a single man to act
in that character, although I have applied to many. If none can be procured, I cannot but condole with you on the depravity of the times."
Commodore Hopkins to the Pastor of the First Congregational Church at
Newport; October 1776.
[2] Arnold to Gates; August 23, 1776.

certainly could be no mistake about the meaning of the letter which conveyed this warning.[1] Arnold handled his pen something too much as if it were a bludgeon; but he saw the point in controversy as clearly as he discerned the key of a position in battle, and went for it as straight. The outraged Commodore appealed in vain to Gates, and from Gates to Schuyler. He was packed off down the river to Albany; and his place as second in command was made over to a brigadier, who, like so many American soldiers, was a practised seaman. "As General Waterbury and General Arnold," (thus Gates reported,) "are on the best terms, no dispute about command will retard the public service;" which was well for the public service, and very well indeed for General Waterbury. Arnold's next antagonists were Colonel Hazen, a personage of mark and merit, whom he accused of wilful disobedience; and Colonel John Brown, whom he charged with having pilfered from captured British stores. These disputes were carried before a court-martial of officers, who were treated by Arnold in their collective capacity exactly as he would have behaved to any individual among them who had been rash enough to cross him. But, where a man is indispensable, the forbearance of those above him, while the crisis lasts, had best be quite unlimited. "The warmth of General Arnold's temper," (so his superior officer wrote from Ticonderoga,) "might possibly lead him a little further than is marked by the precise line of decorum to be observed towards a court-martial. Seeing and knowing all the circumstances, I am convinced that, if there was a fault on one side, there was too much acrimony on the other. I was obliged to act dictatorially, and dissolve the Court-martial the instant they demanded General

[1] "You must surely be out of your senses to say no order must be obeyed but yours. Do you imagine that Congress has given you a superior command over the Commander-in-Chief? If you do, give me leave to say that you are much mistaken; and, if you do not suffer my orders to be instantly complied with, I shall be under the disagreeable necessity of convincing you of your error by immediately arresting you." Arnold's letter of August 18, 1776.

Arnold to be put in arrest. The United States must not be deprived of that excellent officer's service at this precise moment."[1] General Schuyler was of the same mind, and predicted that Arnold would always be the subject of complaint from his subordinates, because his impartiality and candour would not allow him to see impropriety of behaviour with impunity. The letter in which that opinion was expressed called forth the following response from Gates. "I am astonished at the calumnies that go to Congress against General Arnold. To be a man of honour, in an exalted station, will ever excite envy in the mean and undeserving. I am confident the Congress will view whatever is whispered against General Arnold as the fouled stream of that poisonous fountain, detraction."[2]

These generous tributes to a great man of action, whose fame was then unsullied, will always be read by Americans with sorrowful interest. Arnold still wished for nothing better than to be the servant of his country, if only he were allowed to serve her uncontrolled, and with rank and station which fairly represented his by no means extravagant opinion of his own value. For the present he had no ambition ungratified. He was very popular with the rank and file of the army, and counted many warm partisans among the officers. Abundant supplies were forwarded northwards, from many quarters, in response to his eager and ubiquitous importunities. Everywhere within the circle of his personal influence courage revived, attended by hopes which he knew how to inspire, but was too perspicacious unreservedly to entertain. The colonel, who had been left in military command at Crown Point, bore delighted testimony to the improved condition of the fleet. "It is now," he wrote, "truly respectable. It goes down the lake to-morrow under General Arnold. I make no doubt it will prevent the enemy from coming up this year, unless some extraordinary disaster should happen to

[1] Letter from Gates in the last week of August 1776.
[2] Correspondence of Generals Schuyler and Gates in September 1776.

it." [1] All through August letters came south from Ticonderoga, narrating how much the Americans had to eat,
and how little they now feared the British. The garrison, by the fifth of August, already mustered thirty-
five hundred effective men, and militia were marching
in fast. Ten days afterwards the multifarious elements
of the army had shaken down into their places; and the
troops were already in fair discipline and in high spirits,
"for they had large quantities of fresh beef." Again a
month, and Gates wrote to Governor Trumbull that
fever and ague existed at Ticonderoga; but his comments showed plainly that the season of prostration,
or even of depression, had passed away. "The same
climate," the General said, "that affects us, distresses
our enemies; but with this difference, that they have
not half the comforts which our troops enjoy. The
provisions delivered here are excellent, and plenty reigns
in the camp. The two hundred sheep sent by your Excellency are a seasonable supply. About a hundred
thousand feet of boards have been distributed to the
troops, so there has been little distress for want of tents."
Meanwhile Arnold had gone on ship-board, leaving all
those comforts behind him. The gratitude felt towards
him by the soldiers on shore evinced itself in their regrets
that he must henceforward live on salt provisions, which
were bad for his wound; and the sympathy of landsmen was increased by the knowledge that, the day
after he sailed, he had come in for a heavy gale. But
a storm on inland waters seemed a trifle to an old
West Indian skipper, whose cargo had sometimes been
of such a nature that, when Revenue cruisers were
in the offing, he had rather courted than feared foul
weather.

On the last day of June, 1776, Washington's Adjutant
General, at the request of his chief, wrote thus to the
President of the New Jersey Convention : " No doubt
General Howe is arrived at the Hook with a very large

[1] Colonel Hartley's letter of August 21, 1776.

force. It would be too dangerous a secret to trust to a letter how inadequate our army is to encounter it. I am therefore to enjoin the Honourable Body, over which you preside, to exert their utmost efforts at this critical juncture when, in all human probability, the fate of our country, our lives, liberty, and property depend upon the spirit and activity that will be shown in a very short time." The place referred to in this communication was Sandy Hook, not ill described by a contemporary historian as a point of land at the entrance into that confluence of sounds, creeks, and bays which is formed by the peninsula, at the southern extremity of which the city of New York stood; by Staten Island and Long Island; by the North and Raritan rivers; and by the continent on either side of that network of estuaries.[1] Howe arrived at the rendezvous long before his time. He had been desperately uncomfortable at Halifax, — that nook of penury and cold, as it was styled by Edmund Burke,[2] — where the barren soil could with difficulty support the native population, and the lack of room in the town was such that all the private soldiers had been kept on ship-board during the whole of their stay. Howe was to have waited there for the Hessians, and for the English regiments which had been despatched from home ports; and now, in his impatience, he sailed without them. He picked up on his way, and brought with him, such of the Highlanders as had not been intercepted by American privateers; but he reached Sandy Hook a month earlier than the day that Clinton and Cornwallis started from Charleston; and he outstripped by a fortnight Lord Howe's fleet, which, for operations of the nature that the brothers had in view, was not less important than his own army.

The British troops were put ashore on Staten Island,

---

[1] *Annual Register* for 1776; chapter v. of the " History of Europe." The places named in this account of the New York and New Jersey campaign may be found in a map at the end of the volume, adapted from several plans in the Atlas belonging to Marshall's *Life of Washington*.

[2] Burke to Rockingham; May 4, 1776.

which was free of access, inasmuch as it had not been included in Washington's scheme of defence. They were received with an ovation; for a number of local Tories got together to celebrate the occasion by a bonfire, which they fed with forty pounds' worth of Continental paper-money, "damning the Congress, and saying they would have nothing more to do with it." [1] Loyalists flocked in from the main-land as soon as news of the disembarkation was noised abroad. Sixty men, of whom some carried muskets, came over from the Jerseys, and announced that five hundred more would follow. They expressed themselves as very anxious for the arrival of the Admiral with offers of peace; but they declared it as their opinion that quiet would never be restored until the rebels had been soundly beaten. Howe had found Tryon, the Governor of New York, expecting him at Sandy Hook on board a vessel, from the deck of which, during a twelvemonth past, he had done his best to administer his province for the advantage of the Crown. [2] Tryon now gave the English Commander-in Chief very accurate intelligence with regard to the numbers and disposition of the Republican forces. The Governor of New York had every reason to hate the Revolution. It had put a stop to a course of proceedings enormously lucrative to himself; of a sort which was customary then, but in which no administrator of a British colony would now venture to engage without certain ruin to his career. [3] Tryon was reckoned the ablest of the Royal deputies in America; and he certainly was a crafty and, (whenever he got the chance,)

[1] Letter from Staten Island; July 8, 1776.

[2] Despatch of General Howe; published in the *Gentleman's Magazine* for August 1776.

[3] "The Tryons came late in June. They were taken to the Schuyler country-place after some gala-making at Albany. Saratoga was looking its loveliest. Here Mrs. Tryon stayed while the Governor and his host were off on one of the land-purchasing expeditions which none of the colonial governors were known to neglect. Vast purchases were made. Governor Tryon acted as agent for a number of foreign noblemen. His fees alone amounted to 22,000 *l.* 'A good summer's work,' Philip Schuyler wrote." *Memoirs of Catherine Schuyler;* chapter viii.

a very cruel vindicator of what he regarded as the Royal interests. No one else in King George's employment, from first to last, did so much injury to the cause of the master whom he served.

In 1779, when Tryon's rancour as an ex-Governor had had three years to cool, he obtained command of an expedition, made a descent upon the New England coasts, and laid town and country waste; not in the hope of subduing, but for the avowed object of punishing, the people of Connecticut. Wherever Tryon's soldiers landed, they never re-embarked without leaving misery and desolation behind them. They plundered New Haven. They plundered Fairfield, and then set it on fire. Two Episcopal churches, and four belonging to other denominations, perished in the flames. From Fairfield they went on to Norwalk, and burned the little sea-port, with every building appropriated to Divine worship. The story of these proceedings was told, with damning fidelity and impartiality, by Mr. Justice Jones, — an eminent Judge of New York Province, firm and devoted in his loyalty to the Crown. "Upon the sacking of the town of New Haven in Connecticut by General Tryon in June 1779, Yale College, situate at that place, was plundered of a library consisting of many thousand books which had been collecting for very near a hundred years, with many curious and valuable manuscripts; besides a selection of well-chosen books, a present to that seminary from the late Dean Berkeley, afterwards Bishop of Cloyne, in Ireland, and known by the name of The Dean's Library. In the same month, upon plundering and burning the town of Norwalk, in the same colony, under the orders of the same General, a most elegant, large, beautiful, and well-collected library, an heirloom which had for safety been removed to Norwalk, was pillaged, carried to New York, and disposed of by the thieves in the same manner as those plundered in New York had been before disposed of. All this was done with impunity, publicity, and openly. No punishment was ever inflicted upon the plunderers." [1]   Sir Henry Clinton, then Commander-in-Chief in America, was deeply offended at the Royal troops having been employed for such a purpose.   But he was debarred from animadverting on subordinate offenders, or from protesting officially against Tryon's action, when once he had entrusted the honour of the British army to one who had been so indifferent a guardian of his own.

Staten Island, which was somewhat larger than Bute, easily held the Royal army; but the Jersey Whigs had been provident enough to transport all the sheep and cattle across the channel.   The market afforded the British soldiers nothing besides pickled pork, not so different from their own salt pork that they cared to pay sevenpence a pound for it; and there were no vegetables even for generals.   Long-boats and launches, manned from the crews of the Royal frigates which had convoyed the troop-ships from Halifax, scoured the coasts of New York Bay, and ascended the North River for many miles above the city.   But George Clinton, the American officer entrusted with the care of the New York Highlands, had posted strong parties at all the landing-places, and had warned the farmers to drive their flocks and herds up-country of an evening; so that the British foragers took very little, and that little mostly from their friends.   Their largest capture consisted in live-stock, belonging to a partisan of the Royal cause who accompanied them as guide; and they pillaged and burned a house high up the stream, in the neighbourhood of Fort Montgomery, where Clinton was quartered.   "Commander Wallace," (so that General reported,) "headed the party who committed this little robbery.   His share of the plunder was a handkerchief full of salad, and a pig so poor that a crow would scarcely deign to eat it.   Another officer got a pot of

---

[1] *History of New York Province during the Revolutionary War*, by the Honourable Thomas Jones, Justice of the Supreme Court of the Province; Vol. I. chapter 7.   Judge Jones manfully declared that to rob and destroy defenceless, unfortified towns " was not a method of conciliating the deluded."

jelly, and six bottles of castor oil. We thought the owner so poor as not to need protection; and he was a noted Tory as well." [1]

The region which became the scene of the approaching campaign was of singular conformation, and presented, to the General responsible for repelling an invader, problems, both political and military, which may fairly be said to have been incapable of satisfactory solution. The city of New York, then containing twenty-two thousand inhabitants, and covering with its streets and houses about six hundred acres, lay at the southern end of Manhattan Island, which was an island only in the same sense as the Isle of Thanet. It was in fact a peninsula some fourteen miles long, and nowhere more than two miles broad. The North, or Hudson, River, as wide as Manhattan Island itself, skirted it on the west; and it was watered along the other flank by the Haerlem River, and by a creek which went by the name of the East River. This creek, a mile across, separated the promontory where the city stood from Long Island; which extended almost due east for near a hundred and twenty miles into the Atlantic Ocean. It was a tract of land equal in superficial extent to Somersetshire, and parts of it were as fertile and attractive as a pleasant English county. The resemblance is acknowledged and cherished by New Yorkers who have such an excess of leisure as to be able to spare one morning in the week for recreation. Long Island, with its grass-clad hills, and its autumn woods for a background in the landscape, has long been their favourite country for fox hunting. That institution is nowhere more expensively organised, and more replete with the excitement of danger; for an endless succession of high timber fences reminds the sportsman rather of the Roman Campagna than of a Warwickshire or Leicestershire pasture. Fox hunting is no novelty in that

[1] *Public Papers of George Clinton;* Published by the State of New York, 1899. Letter from the same officer, of July 1776, in the *American Archives.*

district. Years before the Revolution broke out a provincial satirist, in bad verse, had expressed wonder
that it should require so many dogs and men to kill an
animal, which itself made no great matter of killing a
score of fowls in a night. The foxes on Long Island
did not starve, for the hen-roosts were exceptionally
well stocked. The soil on the coast was rich, and the
farmers prosperous; possessing, as they did, famous
orchards, cornland of good quality, and flocks and herds
in abundance. After the island had been occupied by
the British, an American foraging party carried off three
thousand sheep, and four hundred horned cattle, as the
produce of a single raid. In the summer of 1776, however, the Revolutionary Government hesitated to treat
Long Island like Staten Island by confiscating, and
removing, the live-stock. That policy, applied on such
a vast scale, would have been barbarous, and indeed
impracticable; for the inhabitants, very generally, were
faithful, and by no means passive, adherents of the
Crown. Their attitude had been so threatening that,
in January, Congress had meditated sending a powerful
force to keep them in awe; and, shortly before Howe
appeared at Sandy Point, a number of them took arms
for the King, and retired to forests and morasses where
the Continental soldiers, whom Washington sent in
pursuit of them, were unable, and probably not very
desirous, to follow.[1]

"Long Island," (a leading patriot declared,) "has the
greatest proportion of Tories, both of its own growth,
and of adventitious ones, of any part of this colony."
The island belonged to the province of New York; and
the political condition of that province had a material
influence upon the military operations which were now
imminent. A correspondent of a Whig newspaper in
London, writing from New York in January 1776, computed that the colony contained about two hundred
thousand people, and that forty thousand of them were
able to bear arms. Two thousand of these, at the most,

[1] Washington's letters of January 23, May 21, and June 28, 1776.

might be counted as lukewarm, or actively opposed to the Revolution; which left thirty-eight thousand fighting men heartily devoted to the American cause. So ran the story as dressed up for the readers of a party journal; but New York was in fact a stronghold of the Crown, and contained more Loyalists than any other among the thirteen provinces. "The inhabitants," said an officer of the Continental army, "promise us three thousand of City militia; but we do not believe we shall see half so many. If the strength of the Whigs be a match for the Tories, it is as much as we shall ever experience in our favour."[1]   That was the case with the city; and it was the same in smaller towns, and throughout the more thickly settled agricultural districts in the southeast of the colony. Halfway through July a partisan of the Revolution stated that in the county where he lived, which was less Tory than most, one hundred militiamen out of four hundred had already been disarmed on account of their Royalist proclivities; and he unsparingly condemned the folly of bringing out persons to oppose an invading army which they were daily seeking opportunities to join.[2]   Join it they did, in great numbers, and of all sorts; from the de Lanceys, a family which furnished Great Britain with two generations of capable military officers, down to citizens of a somewhat poor type who loved their own skins better than any political cause, and who accordingly attached themselves to the party which had the least need of their services as soldiers.[3]

Loyalism, all the province of New York over, was fashionable in every rank; and those who go counter to

[1] Colonel Jedediah Huntington to Governor Trumbull; Camp at New York, June 6, 1776.

[2] Egbert Benson to the New York Convention; July 1776.

[3] "I have examined the prisoners," (General Greene reported on one occasion,) "and find them ignorant cowardly fellows. Two are tailors, and the other two common labourers. They candidly confess that they set off for Staten Island, not with any intention of joining the enemy, but to get out of the way of fighting here. It was reported that they were to go into the Northern Army, and that almost all who went there died, or were killed. The prospect was so shocking to their grandmothers and aunts

fashion, where politics are at fever-heat, are apt to find their position very disagreeable in good society, and quite unendurable in humbler and rougher circles. A farmer complained to the Committee of Safety that, when attending a cattle-mart, he had been much abused and ill-treated because he was a Whig. His cockade was snatched from his hat, and trodden on; his companion, a Dutchman who was a staunch Republican, had his hair pulled on account of his opinions; and the crowd grew still more mischievous when a loyal tavern-keeper had served out some fresh lime punch, of which the Whigs got none. The schoolmaster at Rye, on the coast opposite Long Island, had lived there in peace for fourteen years, saving money, and keeping on good terms with his neighbours, until he aroused their antipathies by arguing in favour of the Revolution. On the pretext that he had lent money to a person who kept a disorderly tavern, he was committed to prison; and, while he lay there, the townsfolk broke open his house, and robbed him of twenty pounds without any explanation, and of three hundred more on the pretence of taking bail.[1] The poor man admitted, in a most significant sentence, that "he alone was a real friend to America out of all the foolish and simple town of Rye." The children and the ladies, as always, were uncompromising politicians. An early, if not the first, protest against the assertion of national independence was made by some schoolboys who unfurled the Royal colours on a day appointed by Congress for solemn fasting and humiliation. The Governor of New Jersey informed

that they persuaded them to run away. Never did I see fellows more frightened. They wept like a parcel of children. They don't appear acquainted with any public matter. They have been Toryish, I fancy not from principle, but from its being the prevailing sentiment in the county."

[1] The schoolmaster named, as the chief instigators, "that arch-Tory and enemy to his country Timothy Wetmore, who has and does yet keep up the spirit of Toryism in Rye, he being their Grand Moloch whom they adore and worship; and a vile woman whose house is frequented only by persons who discourse about the hanging of leading gentlemen who stand gloriously for their country."

Washington that six or seven women had come over to that province from New York. "Though they appear to be Whigs, they have a number of stories to tell which discourage the weaker part of our inhabitants. The sex are mistresses of infinite craft and subtlety, and I never read of a great politician who did not employ petticoats to accomplish his designs. Certain it is that the greatest politician on record, (I mean the Devil,) applied himself to a female agent to involve mankind in sin and ruin."

Most of the rich people in New York, (and the rich were many,) declared themselves more or less openly against the Revolution. Enough among the leading citizens to form a fair-sized viceregal court lived with Tryon on his ship in the harbour. Others remained in their town mansions, taking care that his behests were obeyed as if he were still at Government House; [1] sending information, and assurances of fidelity, to General Howe; and never losing an opportunity of giving their bad word to the Republic. One ingenious aristocrat put about a theory that Washington was for ever marching and counter-marching his troops through the city, like the manager of a second-rate theatre, in order to make a great show of a few men; which was all the more objectionable, (it was added,) because the privates of the Continental army were so unlike soldiers, and the officers bore so distant a resemblance to gentlemen, that no person of taste would care to see them pass his door twice. Another promised that the King's standard should float on the public buildings of New York before the King's birthday, even if he himself had to hoist it with his own hands; whispered it about that matters would mend when a dozen persons whom he could name in the town of Albany had been hanged; "and further endeavoured by artful insinuations to depreciate the Continental currency." More practical members of the same party

---

[1] "The city seems to be entirely under the government of Tryon, and the captain of the man-of-war." Washington to Joseph Reed; January 31, 1776.

took a shorter path towards a similar end, and counter-feited the notes issued by the State Conventions of Massachusetts and Connecticut. The individuals, who had been placed on a suspected list as enemies of America, were of many occupations, and every diversity of outward appearance; — a licensed victualler, with no sign-board, four doors from the corner of Broadway; a fat man in a blue coat; a short thick man in a white coat; a silversmith who had lately been ridden on a rail; two young gentlemen, who shut themselves up at home, and refused to train; a son that threatened his father with the gallows if he would not sign a paper against a Congress or a Committee; a shoemaker living next to the sign of the Buck, who talked too freely to his journeyman, questioning the right of Congress to raise soldiers, and wishing, with very strong asseverations, that all the townsmen of New York were as big Tories as the Mayor. That constituted an exacting standard of Loyalism; for the Mayor was a partisan who shrank from nothing. Very confidential messages had long been passing between his parlour in the city, and Governor Tryon's cabin on board the Royal cruiser in the Bay. Arrangements were made to blow up the powder magazines, and to kidnap Washington and his principal officers. One of the General's own bodyguards had been suborned to do the blackest part of the business; and the man was said to have accomplices among his companions. It would have required a numerous, and a very determined, gang of traitors to carry off George Washington alive and against his will; but all who were in the secret perfectly well understood what the seizing and securing the person, whether of a king in his palace, or of a Commander-in-Chief in the midst of his army, always meant, and always will mean. That hackneyed euphemism for assassination never saves the neck of an obscure hireling who has the courage of his wickedness; although it may salve the conscience, and possibly screen the reputation, of more high-placed conspirators. The plot was detected; the Mayor was thrown into gaol; the guilty soldier was tried by court-martial, and executed in a field near the Bowery; and Washington, who seldom let slip an opportunity of instilling a moral lesson into his younger comrades, earnestly cautioned the troops "to avoid lewd women, who, by the confession of this poor criminal, first led him into practices which ended in an untimely and ignominious death." [1]

So deeply and equally was opinion divided all through this tract of country which Washington had undertaken to maintain in obedience to the Revolutionary Government, and to protect against the attack of an army larger and better than his own. During an interview at Philadelphia with the Committee, appointed by Congress to gather his view on the military necessities of the nation, he had emphatically declared that success was all but impossible unless the Americans were to the English in a proportion of two to one. And now, for the combined purpose of holding in check a disaffected population within his lines, and of keeping the British outside them, he had at his disposal a force which, as compared with the enemy, stood in the proportion of only two to three. Nor could he shut his eyes to a contingency, exceedingly likely to occur, under which the circumference of those lines would be enlarged to an extent altogether beyond his means for defending them. If Admiral Howe's ships could silence, or slip past, the outer batteries, they might ascend the East River on the left, and the North River on the right, of the American position; General Howe might, in that case, land on the peninsula of Manhattan at any spot which he preferred along thirty miles of open coast; and, if once General Howe disembarked his troops in rear of the city, New York must fall without a blow. Nor was that all. The case, in the end, would not be less grave even if Lord Howe failed to force a passage up the rivers, and was obliged to confine himself to the Bay. To defend New York it

---

[1] The material of the last three paragraphs is derived from many sources; but principally from the *American Archives* of the year 1776, from Washington's Letters, and from Sabine's *Loyalists of the American Revolution.*

was absolutely necessary to hold the heights of Brooklyn opposite the city, which commanded New York within easy artillery fire, just as Bunker's Hill commanded Boston;[1] and the heights of Brooklyn were on Long Island, whither General Howe might transport all his troops at pleasure. There he would find a magnificent base of operations; abundant provisions; inexhaustible forage; and farmers so much attached to the Crown that they would almost have been prepared to feed his men and horses for nothing, and were still more ready to sell him their produce at war prices. To dispute the possession of Long Island against Howe's whole army, Washington could only afford to spare a portion of the American force; and that portion, whether greater or smaller, if once beaten was almost certainly lost; for Brooklyn was separated from New York by a deep navigable channel of salt water. Should battle be joined on Long Island, the American generals might be never so skilful; but the most consummate tactics on their part, (if such indeed were forthcoming,) could do little to obviate the defects of a hopeless strategical situation.

With this prospect before them, some Americans held that the most prudent, as well as the most truly courageous, policy would be to destroy the supplies in Long Island; to sacrifice New York; and to withdraw the Revolutionary army, in unbroken strength, to a carefully selected position in the interior of the country. That opinion, however, was held by very few; and those few were under no temptation to proclaim it. Nine out of ten members of Congress, and ninety-nine out of a hundred among the partisans who had elected them, were for fighting at all hazards, and as far to the front as possible. The strategy of withdrawal appeared positively despicable to an average Whig politician at Phila-

---

[1] Those are the words employed by Mr. Charles Francis Adams, the younger, in his article on the Battle of Long Island. Military criticisms by Mr. Adams are those of a born historian, who has served through a great war, and has had plenty of time since to think over the lessons which his old campaigns taught him.

delphia, especially to one who hailed from a district within the region which was the seat of war. " Is New York to be evacuated, as well as Long Island, without fighting? Or will our army, like the Romans of old, attack the enemy wherever they find them, knowing that death is to be chosen rather than life upon the terms our enemies will suffer us to hold it?" Those expressions were employed by a New York representative, whose desperate patriotism was confessedly stimulated by the reflection that delegates from a State, which had been conquered by the British, could not hope any longer to be repaid their expenses at Philadelphia.[1]

During this period of his career Washington considered himself as the servant of Congress, bound "implicitly to obey their orders with a scrupulous exactness,"[2] even at the risk of his military reputation. He did not hold out to his employers any definite assurance of victory; nor on the other hand did he dissuade them from imposing on his acceptance a plan of campaign based on the retention of New York city. He confined himself to promising them his utmost exertions under every disadvantage. Though the appeal, (he owned,) might not terminate so happily as could be wished, yet he trusted that any advantage the enemy might gain would cost them dear. This much he said; and, from that time forward, he held his peace. He never, either then or thereafter, pleaded that he had acted under compulsion, or endeavoured to shift upon others his share of responsibility for the misfortunes which befell the army. His silence in the face of criticism was complete and lifelong. Some of Washington's admirers have done their best to make out a case for him by arguing

---

[1] Letter from a member of Congress for New York ; August 10, 1776.

[2] Those were Washington's words ; and that was the interpretation put upon his conduct by Charles Lee, who wrote thus to Gates: " The Congress seems to stumble at every step ; I do not mean one or two of the cattle, but the whole stable. I have been very free in delivering my opinion to 'em. General Washington is much to blame in not menacing 'em with resignation, unless they refrain from unhinging the army with their absurd interference."

that, if he had not detained the British all through the autumn within a few miles of the sea-coast, Howe would have pushed on to Albany, taken Gates in the rear, crushed him up against Carleton, and so have finished the war before ever the year ended; but nothing of all this was uttered, or written, by Washington. The world does not know, and never will know, whether he followed his own unbiassed judgement of what was the least ruinous expedient in an almost impossible situation; or whether he conformed reluctantly to the will of his official superiors; or whether, (for he was a man like others,) he could not bear to disappoint the belief of his countrymen that the General who had re-conquered Boston would succeed in retaining New York. In any case it may safely be affirmed that, if Washington aimed at preserving the city, he was trying for an impossibility; and that, if his object was to prevent the British from reaching Albany, he should have waited for them further up the Hudson, on ground carefully reconnoitred and prepared, and with an army which had not been diminished and demoralised by a series of unsuccessful engagements. The fact remains that in August 1776 he placed, and kept, his troops in a position where they were certain to be defeated, and where, when defeated, they would most probably be surrounded and destroyed.

It soon became evident that all hope of confining the British to a frontal attack upon the southern extremity of the New York peninsula would have to be abandoned. Lord Howe had sailed from Spithead before the middle of May; although tidings of his arrival in America did not reach England until the end of September. The Opposition journalists in London were furious at what they suspected to be a wilful suppression of important news, and complained that nothing more was published about Howe's movements than if he were a mandarin, commanding a fleet of junks in the service of the Emperor of China. They calculated the millions of pounds that had been spent since the year opened, and compared them with the very minute amount of satisfaction and amusement which, as a reader of the newspapers, the taxpayer had obtained for his money.[1]   But in truth the fault lay with the east wind, which had delayed the American packet; and the continued silence of the London Gazette was not chargeable to the Government censor, nor to any sloth on the part of the British admiral.   Lord Howe had been prompt enough.   He touched at Halifax on the first of July; and, on the twelfth, Washington informed Congress that a ship of war, flying St. George's flag at her foretop-mast-head, had that morning appeared at Sandy Hook, and had been received with a general salute from all the Royal vessels which lay in the harbour.

On his way to the south Lord Howe met the Boston squadron, retiring to Halifax with one shot-hole in the upper works of the flag-ship; and the Commodore explained that he was shifting his quarters from Nantasket Road because he had been annoyed by batteries.   Lord Howe quietly observed that in the last war he, for his part, sought batteries instead of avoiding them.[2]   It was a habit which he never lost.   In the afternoon of his arrival off Staten Island two men-of-war, with a favourable breeze and on a flowing tide, carrying breastworks of sand-bags on deck as a protection against rifle-bullets, ran past the American works.   They took their station five-and-thirty miles above New York, in Haverstraw Bay, where the Hudson River was more than a league across. There they remained, as little damaged as if they were lying opposite Gravesend after a peaceful journey up the Thames from the Nore, and, (to all appearance,)

---

[1] On September 20, 1776, the London *Evening Post* thus addressed the Ministry: "Lord Howe sailed from St. Helens on the 12th May last, with a considerable fleet.   This is 139 days ago, or to-morrow will be 20 weeks, and you have never given any account whatsoever about his Lordship or his fleet, either good, bad, or indifferent.   Notwithstanding this dead silence, you have had this year the fingering of fifteen millions of the people's money, without a shilling of it being left, or without a single act being done by either the land, or sea, department but what are disgraceful to this unhappy kingdom."

[2] The *Last Journals* of Horace Walpole.

in quite as secure a berth. Their awnings were spread against the summer sun; and their boats ranged to and fro on the current, taking the soundings, and watching an opportunity for plunder. To those who looked into the future it was evident that the city of New York was as good as taken; and the comfort of farmers in the provincial districts was already destroyed. Three regiments of local militia were called out to man the forts; and smaller detachments bivouacked at frequent intervals along the banks. The service was of such a nature that night was no less toilsome, and more anxious, than the day. There was brief and broken sleep for the minutemen, with nothing to occupy their waking thoughts except a mental picture of the most noble crop, which had ripened within their life-time, rotting on the stalks.[1] Their leaders also had a sacrifice to make, the greatness of which it would not be easy to appraise in money. General George Clinton could not spare the time for a journey to Philadelphia in order to affix his name, as a New York delegate, to the Declaration of Independence; and the case of Colonel Robert Livingston was harder still, for he had been one of the five members who drafted the document which he was now too busy to sign.

There was a project much nearer Lord Howe's heart than that of exchanging cannon-shots with those whom he regarded as his injured, rather than his misguided and erring, fellow-countrymen. Old quartermasters, who had sailed with him all the world over, professed to know when a general action was impending by "Black Dick" being seen to smile; but the admiral, at no time of his life, was ever so keen to fight Frenchmen as he

---

[1] "The Men turn out of their Harvest Fields to defend their Country with surprizing Alacrity. The absence of so many of them, however, at this Time, when their Grain is perishing for want of the Sickle, will greatly distress the Country. I wish a less number might answer the Purpose." Clinton to Washington; July 15, 1776.

The Americans after a while extemporised a small squadron of armed galleys, and a couple of fire-ships, which at length made Haverstraw Bay a hot anchorage for Englishmen. The two men-of-war dropped down the river, and rejoined their fleet on the 18th August, having remained for the space of five weeks in the heart of the enemy's country.

now was eager to make friends of the colonists. He
had inherited the title of a gallant brother, more beloved
by Americans, not indeed than Lord Chatham, but than
any Englishman of eminence who had ever set his foot
on American soil. He himself had been prime mover in
the last attempt made, before Benjamin Franklin took
his departure from Europe, to draw the mother-country
and her revolted provinces once more together.   Lord
Howe's advent as a pacificator, and a supposed plenipotentiary, was heralded by the sanguine anticipations of
all partisans of peace whom he left behind him in
London.   The Lord Mayor and Common Council, sitting
in the Guildhall, had wished him well in his character of
negotiator, and had prayed the Government to publish
a specification of the powers which he carried with him,
in order that the King's benevolent intentions might not
be misrepresented by demagogues in the colonies who
desired to keep the quarrel open.   Private persons wrote
eagerly and often, urging their correspondents in
America to trust the British Government, and to make
much of its emissary. " Do, my dear friend," (so one
such letter ran,) " let me persuade you that Lord Howe
goes to America as a mediator, and not a destroyer.   He
has declared he had rather meet you, and that immediately on his arrival, in the wide field of argument, than
in the chosen ground of battle." [1]   In America there was
every disposition to treat Lord Howe with respect, and
a widespread belief that the offers which he brought
were of a nature to be acceptable.   Pamphleteers of the
Revolutionary party, if they cared to retain their readers,
were obliged to speak gently both of him and of his
mission.   The most uncivil of all these writers felt himself bound to promise that the colonists would be as
courteous at the Council Board as they were valiant in
the field; and that, if agreement proved impossible, the
British Commissioners should be bowed out genteelly,

[1] Dennis de Berdt in London to Joseph Reed of Philadelphia ; May 3,
1776. Mr. Reed was a trusted and valued informant of Lord Dartmouth, —
as long as the colonist cared to write letters, or the peer ventured to receive them.

and not dismissed after the fashion in which Hanun the son of Nahash treated the messengers of David.[1]

As a first step towards the accomplishment of his amicable purpose, Lord Howe endeavoured to place himself in communication with the American whose co-operation he was especially anxious to secure. A letter for " George Washington Esquire " was sent to New York, under a flag of truce, and was returned unopened, never having got further than the guard-boat which lay off the landing-place at Castle Garden. A few days afterwards Colonel Paterson, the Adjutant General of the Royal army, obtained an interview with Washington, and handed to him an envelope bearing the same superscription.[2] Colonel Paterson, in obedience to his instructions, addressed the American Commander-in-Chief as His Excellency, and assured him that Lord Howe and his brother did not mean to derogate from the respect or rank of General George Washington, and held his person and character in the highest esteem. Washington, (so a story goes,) looked at the letter, and remarked that it must be for a planter of the name, residing in the State of Virginia, with whom he was acquainted, and to whom he would deliver it, with the seal unbroken, after the war was over. That part of the anecdote rests upon French tradition, and was probably manufactured on the banks of the Seine for the gratification of Parisian supper-tables. Washington's own account of the affair was marked by his customary gravity and precision. He reported to Congress that, while he would not sacrifice essentials to punctilio, he had in this instance deemed it his duty towards his country to insist upon a

[1] *A Watchman;* Philadelphia, June 13, 1776. Other passages in the same production show the patriotism of the author to have been of a very pronounced type. " If I forget thee, Oh Lexington, let my right hand forget his cunning! Yea, let my right finger forget how to pull the trigger! " That was his style when he was writing solely to please himself.

[2] The actual address on this second letter was "George Washington Esquire, &c. &c. &c." Washington was earnestly entreated to believe that the magic symbols, which followed his name, implied every title of honour that he might desire to read into them.

mark of respect which, as an individual, he would will ingly have waived. Congress, in return, complimented him for having acted with dignity becoming his station, and enjoined all other officers to follow his example, and receive no messages from the enemy but such as were directed to them in the characters they respectively sustained. The principle involved is clearly laid down in a despatch which Washington, on a previous and somewhat similar occasion, had written to General Gage, as the commander of the British garrison in Boston. " You affect, Sir, to despise all rank not derived from the same source as your own. I cannot conceive one more honourable than that which flows from the uncorrupted choice of a brave and free people, the purest source and original fountain of all power." That was news to such as Gage ; but the Howes were both of them born Whigs, who did not need to be indoctrinated with an obvious political truth, — as well as men of sense, who made a point of calling people by the names which they called themselves. It was noticed that Lord Howe, when conversing with Americans, spoke of the colonies as " States " ; and General Howe informed the Ministry at home that, if necessity arose for conducting negotiations about the exchange of prisoners and the treatment of wounded, he intended, since once the question had been started, always to give an American general his full military title.

Lord Howe, in his cabin at sea, had composed a circular letter to the Royal governors of the colonies, accompanied by a Declaration setting forth the nature of his authority as Commissioner from the King, together with the terms of reconciliation which the Cabinet had sanctioned. These documents were transmitted to Washington, who duly forwarded them to Congress. It at once became evident why the ministerial offers had been kept a secret from the London Corporation, and from all other communities which were guided by reason and good feeling ; for those offers amounted to nothing more than a bare promise of pardon and favour to all who should return to allegiance and assist in restoring public tranquillity. Congress forthwith printed the papers in full, with the object, (so their Resolution was worded,) that the good people of the United States might know the conditions of peace with the expectation of which the insidious Court of Great Britain had endeavoured to amuse and disarm them, and that the few who had founded hopes on the justice or moderation of their late King might now at length be convinced that their valour alone could save their liberty.[1] George Washington took his share of the Royal clemency as a direct insult which he could not away with. His attitude recalls to a reader of Beaumont and Fletcher the dialogue between a calumniated subject, and an estranged sovereign, in the stately drama of "The Maid's Tragedy."

> *Melantius.*   Where I am clear,
> I will not take forgiveness of the gods,
> Much less of you.
> *King.*   Nay, if you stand so stiff,
> I shall call back my mercy.
> *Melantius.*   I want smoothness
> To thank a man for pardoning of a crime
> I never knew.

The American Commander-in-Chief, in a printed letter, described Howe and his brother as nothing more than a couple of agents dispensing pardons to repentant sinners; and he openly warned his soldiers not to heed a report, set about by designing persons, that the British admiral had brought with him propositions of peace. His own duty, (he told the army,) obliged him to declare that no propositions had been made; but on the contrary, from the best intelligence which he could procure, the Americans might expect to be attacked as soon as the wind and tide should prove favourable. He hoped, therefore, that every man's mind and arms would be

---

[1] Resolution of Friday, July 19, 1776. On the 23rd July a Member of Congress wrote to Charles Lee from Philadephia : "The Tories are quiet, but very surly. Lord Howe's proclamation leaves them not a single filament of their cobweb doctrine of reconciliation."

prepared for action, in order to show the whole world that freemen contending on their own land were superior to any mercenaries on earth.[1]

John Adams accused Lord Howe of pursuing a Machiavellian policy;[2] but the admiral was a straightforward sailor, who resembled the celebrated Italian statesman in one point only. Lord Howe's patriotism embraced all his countrymen, in whatever part of the world their fortune had fixed them; and he was now striving to restore amity and concord between two great sections of the British people as strenuously as ever Machiavelli had laboured, in his own very peculiar fashion, for the unity of Italy. Even after the armies had met, and the English had gained a victory, Lord Howe persevered in his attempt to settle the dispute by pacific methods. He adopted as an intermediary the first American general who was taken prisoner in battle. That general was the good-hearted, but loose-tongued and feather-headed, Sullivan; — an instrument well suited to an honourable but visionary undertaking. Sullivan presented himself before Congress with no credentials; carrying no written proposals from the British Commissioners; and provided with nothing more definite than certain hazy recollections which he had brought away from a conversation with Lord Howe. No notes of that conversation were in existence, for the very sufficient reason that none had been taken; nor had a minute embodying the conclusions, at which the two parties arrived, been agreed upon between them.

From such offhand diplomacy nothing but confusion and scandal could come. Sullivan's appearance struck dismay into every patriot acute enough to perceive that the only practical consequence of listening to those shadowy overtures must be to throw upon Congress the unpopularity of prolonging the war. "Oh the decoy-duck!" exclaimed John Adams. "Would that the first bullet from the enemy had passed through his brain!"

[1] Washington to Gates; July 19, 1776. General Order of August 20.
[2] John Adams to Mrs. Adams; September 8, 1776.

Lord Howe would scarcely have been better pleased than Adams if he had been present when Sullivan told his story. That impulsive orator began by confiding to all the members of Congress, and any other citizen who cared to listen in the gallery, that the British admiral maintained the extreme colonial opinion, and denied the right of Parliament to tax America. He then proceeded to deliver what he called his verbal message; and, (since his hearers were very much better men of business than himself,) he was requested to put it on paper. On paper the message was vague and illusory, — insinuating a conception of Lord Howe's powers, and of the views held by the British Ministry, so hopeful as to be positively dishonest; but it was the dishonesty of well-intentioned, inaccurate men, who contrived to deceive themselves. Howe, in his zeal for peace, had promised more than he could perform; and Sullivan had persuaded himself to remember a great deal more than Howe had said. The most substantial part of the communication was to the effect that the British Commissioner was forbidden to recognise the authority, or even the official existence, of Congress; but that he would most gladly have a conference with some of the members whom he would consider, for the present, only as private gentlemen. Congress, as became it, resolved that it could not with propriety send any members to confer with his Lordship in their private characters; but that, ever desirous of establishing peace on reasonable terms, it would despatch a committee of its body to learn whether, under the powers which he possessed, he could treat with persons appointed to act on behalf of America. That resolution was passed on the fifth of September; and next day Edward Rutledge of South Carolina, John Adams, and Benjamin Franklin were selected by ballot to serve on the Committee.

To a lover of peace it might have seemed that a more promising choice than that of Franklin could hardly have been made. Up to the very moment that his trunks were packed for leaving England he had been engaged with Lord Howe in an honourable conspiracy to stop the war. The earliest letter that the admiral wrote to an American, after he arrived in American waters, was a greeting to his worthy friend, Benjamin Franklin; and in that letter Lord Howe represented himself as inspired by the hope that he might gratify the King's paternal solicitude by promoting the establishment of a lasting union between Great Britain and the colonies. But already the colonist, to whom these amiable words were addressed, had no mind to resuscitate the paternal and filial relation in what he henceforward regarded as international, and not as colonial, politics. He was no longer the same Benjamin Franklin with whom the Whig nobleman had conversed in whispers over Miss Howe's chess-table. An American colonel, on a visit to the British flag-ship with a message from Washington, happened to be in attendance when Franklin's reply came to hand. According to the account given by this officer, Lord Howe's countenance, as he read onward, frequently exhibited marks of astonishment; and, when he had mastered the contents of the letter, he lamented that his old friend had expressed himself very warmly. Warm, indeed, the effusion was. Americans, (so Franklin wrote,) could not by any possibility even dream of submission to a Government which had burned their defenceless towns in the midst of winter; had excited savages to massacre their farmers, and slaves to murder their planters; and was even now bringing over legions of German hirelings to deluge their settlements with blood. "Long did I endeavour, with unfeigned and unwearied zeal, to preserve from breaking that fine and noble China Vase, the British empire. Your Lordship may possibly remember the tears of joy which wet my cheek when, at your good sister's in London, you once gave me expectations that a reconciliation might soon take place. I had the misfortune to find those expectations disappointed, and to be treated as the cause of the mischief I was labouring to prevent. My consolation was that I retained the friendship of many wise and good men in that country; and, among the rest, some share in the regard of Lord Howe."[1]

Franklin and his brother Commissioners accepted the charge which Congress imposed on them; although they had no hope, and little desire, that any very tangible result would ensue. There was yet more cause for despair than they knew of. Lord Howe's powers extended no further than the offer of a pardon; and from all hope of pardon the Privy Council had expressly excepted John Adams by name. That formidable fact was unknown to Adams. He was not aware that, to the mind's eye of the British admiral, he would appear at the conference with a halter round his neck; and yet for reasons, public and not personal, he repaired to that conference most unwillingly. Adams had been entirely unconvinced by the arguments put forward by Congressmen who were in favour of the negotiation. "Some," he wrote, "think it will occasion a delay of military operations; which we much want. I am not of that mind. Some think it will clearly throw the odium of continuing this war on his Lordship and his master. I wish it may. Others think it will silence the Tories and establish the timid Whigs. I wish this also, but do not expect it. All these arguments, and twenty others as mighty, would not have convinced me of the necessity, propriety, or utility, if Congress had not determined on it. I was against it from first to last. All sides agreed in sending me. You will hear more of this embassy. It will be famous enough."[2]

---

[1] Lord Howe to Franklin; on board the Eagle, June 20, 1776. Franklin to Lord Howe; Philadelphia, July 20, 1776. Colonel Palfrey to President Hancock; July 31, 1776.

It is curious to observe the names of the transports which brought the British army across the ocean; the Felicity, the Three Sisters, the Amity's Admonition, and the Good Intent. The First Grenadiers sailed in the Friendship, and the Sixty-fourth regiment in the Father's Goodwill. It is difficult to believe that these vessels were not specially re-christened for the voyage, and that Admiral Lord Howe had nothing to do with it.

[2] John Adams to James Warren; Philadelphia, September 8, 1776.

Franklin, who had been far from well, was once again in excellent case. When acting as commissioner to the Northern army he had felt his age for the first time; and towards the end of May he came back from Canada an invalid. At one point on the route he did not expect to return alive, and addressed to his friends at home a communication which, for a valedictory epistle, was singularly cheerful;[1] but before August he had cured himself by temperance, and by setting in practice those quaintly expressed theories of health which his observation had taught him, some scores of years before they became the truisms of medical practice. There was better travelling-ground between Philadelphia and the British head-quarters in New York Bay, than among those wild and inhospitable regions which separated Albany from St. John's and Montreal; and yet, as they drew near the scene of active hostilities, the three Committeemen found their journey not without its hardships. "The taverns," wrote Adams, "were so full that we could with difficulty obtain entertainment. At Brunswick but one bed could be procured for Dr. Franklin and me, in a chamber little larger than the bed, without a chimney, and with one small window. The window was open, and I shut it close. 'Oh,' says Franklin, 'don't shut the window. We shall be suffocated!' I answered, I was afraid of the evening air. Dr. Franklin replied: 'Open the window, and come to bed, and I will convince you. I believe you are not acquainted with my theory of colds.' Opening the window, and leaping into bed, I said I had read his letters to Dr. Cooper; but the theory was so little consistent with my experience that I thought it a paradox. However, I had so much curiosity to hear his reasons that I would run the risk of a cold." The Doctor then

---

[1] "I am here on my way to Canada, detained by the present state of the Lakes, in which the unthawed ice obstructs navigation. I begin to apprehend that I have undertaken a fatigue that, at my time of life, may prove too much for me. So I sit down to write to a few friends by way of farewell." Franklin to Josiah Quincy; Saratoga, April 15, 1776.

began to harangue on the theme that catarrhs were usually produced by over-eating and stuffy rooms, and in the course of a few minutes sent himself and his bedfellow fast asleep.[1]

They both were in somewhat of a holiday humour. To these terribly overworked men the excursion presented the character of an agreeable jaunt. Except when they were travelling on public business, their unpaid and unassisted toil, — for at Philadelphia they had neither salary nor secretary, — seemed likely to allow them no rest on that side the grave; or rather, in the event of their country being conquered, on that side the gibbet. They reached Amboy, at the mouth of the Raritan, on the eleventh September, and were rowed to Staten Island by the admiral's own boat's crew. Lord Howe, deeply disapproving, was privy to the fell intentions which his Government harboured towards one, at least, of the American Commissioners; and he accordingly had sent across the water an English officer, with an intimation that he might be retained in the American camp as a hostage for their safety. Adams and his colleagues exchanged a few words in private, and then requested this gentleman to return in their company to the British side of the channel. "We told the officer," (so Adams wrote,) "that, if he held himself under our direction, he must go back with us. He bowed assent, and we all embarked in his Lordship's barge. As we

---

[1] During his last three years in London, Franklin, as if he had nothing else to think about, paid great attention to "the causes of colds or rheums." Much useful advice, and still more amusement, may be gathered from his letters to Doctor Samuel Cooper, to Benjamin Rush, and to Monsieur Dubourg ; as well as from his *Preparatory Notes and Hints for writing a Paper concerning what is called Catching Cold.*

John Adams never forgot the night at New Brunswick. He heard the news of Franklin's death, when at last it came, the less inconsolably on learning that the Doctor had fallen a sacrifice to his own theory; "having caught the violent cold, which finally choked him, by sitting for some hours at a window with the cold air blowing in upon him." Whichever of the two was right on this particular medical question, Adams undoubtedly succeeded, (and it was not the least of his achievements,) in living for a good many more years than Franklin.

approached the shore, his Lordship came down to the water's edge to receive us, and, looking at the officer, he said, 'Gentlemen, you make me a very high compliment, and you may depend upon it, I will consider it as the most sacred of things.' We walked up to the house between lines of grenadiers, looking fierce as ten furies, and making all the grimaces, and gestures, and motions of their muskets which, (I suppose,) military etiquette requires, but which we neither understood nor regarded." The house had been inhabited by soldiers, and was as dirty as a stable; but Lord Howe had prepared a large handsome room with a carpet of moss and green sprigs, which made it " not only wholesome, but romantically elegant; " and there was a table spread with good bread, good claret, cold ham, tongues, and mutton.

John Adams, if man ever did, knew the difference between play and work; and he now wrote about trifles because the nature of his embassy forbade him to expect that he would find anything of solid political importance to record. The serious part of the business was over in a single interview. Lord Howe assured the three Congressmen that, before accepting the office of Commissioner, he had stipulated for power to confer with any persons whom he should think proper. He had distinctly forewarned the British Government, (so he stated,) of his intention to meet in a friendly way precisely those whom the Cabinet called rebels, because they were the men best acquainted with colonial grievances. This piece of information, set off by a few courteous flourishes, was the beginning and the end of what the Admiral had to say. The Americans, in return, represented to his Lordship that, since he left London, Independence had been declared at Philadelphia with the full approbation of all the colonies; that those colonies now considered themselves as States, and were settling, or had already settled, their forms of government accordingly; and that it was not within the competence of Congress to agree on their behalf that they should revert to a condition of dependence upon the British Crown. Lord Howe replied that, such being the case, the situation was new, and that his instructions did not inform him how to meet the altered circumstances. He admitted with regret that no accommodation could take place, and announced the conference at an end.[1]

There are occasions when it is not easy to reconcile politeness with sincerity; and the American envoys made no pretence of being credulous or pliable. A moment arrived, in the course of the parley, which seemed to call for an exchange of compliments. The Admiral was by nature reserved and saturnine;[2] but there was one topic which lay very near his heart, and on which he was always ready to discourse. He accordingly now became profuse in expressions of gratitude to the State of Massachusetts for erecting a monument in Westminster Abbey to his elder brother, who had been killed at Ticonderoga in the French war. He esteemed, (he said,) that honour above all things in the world; he felt for America as for a brother; and, if America was overwhelmed, he should lament its ruin like a brother's loss. Franklin bowed and smiled, and, with a collected countenance, and some affectation of simplicity, answered that he and his colleagues would do their utmost endeavours to save his Lordship from that mortification. Somewhat earlier in the colloquy

[1] Besides the report made to Congress by the delegates, a clear account of the meeting with Lord Howe is given in letters from John Adams to Samuel. Samuel Adams, now Secretary to the Massachusetts Assembly, liked the notion of a conference as little as any one. "Your Secretary," John Adams wrote to President Warren, "will rip about this measure; and well he may." But Samuel Adams, though hot, and even red-hot, against political opponents, was not captious in his judgements about his friends. He admitted the difficulties of the American commissioners, and heartily praised their conduct. Their sentiments and language, he said, were becoming the character they bore; they managed with great dexterity; they maintained the dignity of Congress; and the independence of America stood thenceforward on a better footing than before. So he told John Adams, in a letter of September 30, 1776.

[2] Walpole called the Howes "those brave, silent brothers." *Last Journals;* February 1775.

the English Commissioner had defined his position by observing that he was not authorised to regard the gentlemen, with whom he had the honour to find himself, as members of Congress, but only as private persons and British subjects. Adams answered quickly that he was ready to assume any personality which would be agreeable to his Lordship except that of a British subject; and the Admiral thereupon turned to Franklin and Rutledge, and remarked that Mr. Adams was a decided character. Decided characters are apt to get their own way. Some years afterwards, when the Bostonian was a minister plenipotentiary at the Court of St. James's, Lord Howe showed that he had not forgotten the give and take of that historical conversation on Staten Island. "At the ball on the Queen's birthnight," (John Adams wrote,) "I was at a loss for the seats assigned to the foreign ambassadors and their ladies. Fortunately meeting Lord Howe at the door, I asked his Lordship where were the ambassadors' seats. His Lordship, with his usual politeness, and an unusual smile of good humour, pointed to the seats and said, 'Aye; now we must turn you away among the foreigners.'"

CHAPTER XIX

LONG ISLAND. NEW YORK AND HAERLEM [1]

THE farce of negotiation had not been finally played out before public attention was diverted to the stern realities of war. General Howe took no part in this last attempt at a diplomatic settlement. The junior British Commissioner was already occupied over sharper and more practical methods for reducing the colonies to their allegiance. By the first of August his reinforcements began to make their appearance; and they were pouring in, at frequent intervals, during the three weeks that followed. The earliest to report themselves at head-quarters before New York were Clinton and Cornwallis from Carolina. Then came the fresh regiments from England, and two complete divisions of German auxiliaries. Sir Peter Parker's unlucky squadron soon followed, carrying some more Royal governors who had been ejected from their provinces, together with a small collection of loyal Virginian militia, exhibiting every shade of colour, and known in Whig circles by the designation of Lord Dunmore's Own Ethiopians. [2] From Governors downwards, all were very tired of being on ship-board. Even the Footguards, who always had the pick of everything, and certainly did not sail on the worst-found vessels, complained that their food had been bad, and the water putrid. [3] The

[1] This spelling was adopted by the early colonists, and was in general use during the Revolutionary War. The American town is written as "Haerlem" in Marshall's *Life of Washington*, Philadelphia, 1807; and the city in Holland is so spelt in Dr. Watson's *Philip the Second*, published in 1779.

[2] A computation of Howe's army, made by an American patriot in August 1776, includes "Lord Dunmore's scrubby fleet, with negroes, Tories, &c. — 150 men."

[3] Letter in a London newspaper of October 1, 1776; British Museum.

Highlanders, for their part, professed to have no intention of ever tempting the sea again, and had brought their churns and ploughs with them, in the expectation of settling down on the confiscated lands of the rebel farmers.[1] Except that Staten Island did not pitch and roll, the army for the present was not more luxuriously circumstanced than during the voyage. The quarters were very close for such a multitude, and there were no provisions besides the remains of the abominable stores with which the contractors had sparingly stocked the transports. The situation, moreover, had become one of moral, as well as material, discomfort. Those battalions, which Howe brought with him from Halifax, had already outstayed their welcome as far as the islanders were concerned; and the Hessians, on their arrival, found no welcome at all. For the Royal troops had already adopted towards the civil population, irrespective of political opinion, a behaviour which, taking the war as a whole, did as much as anything else to render impossible either the reconciliation, or the re-conquest, of the colonies. " They have eaten all the cattle, and are now killing and barrelling up all the horses they meet with. The Tories on the island are very ill-treated lately, so that the inhabitants, who at first were so pleasant, would now be willing to poison them. They take everything they choose, and no one has anything he can call his own." That was the condition of Staten Island towards the end of August. The inhabitants were eager to be rid of the soldiers; and the soldiers were keen to go. All eyes were turned across the narrow channel towards the verdant shore of Long Island, where between four and five score thousand beeves were still grazing unslaughtered, and whither the King's servants were pressingly invited by a loyal people who had not yet learned by experience what a military occupation meant.

If Livy had been the chronicler of that campaign, he would have had a story to tell after his own heart; for the omens were appalling. A dreadful thunder-

[1] Letter from Staten Island; August 1776.

storm broke over Washington's camp. "Three officers were struck dead instantly; the points of their swords for several inches were melted, with a few silver dollars they had in their pockets." [1] Any competent soothsayer would have interpreted the portent as an indication that the weapons of the Republic would be shattered in war, and that its treasury would cease to pay in specie. The regimental officers, however, and the common men of the American army were in no desponding mood. The weather was fearfully hot; but they took their duties coolly. One general reported to Washington that he was obliged to chase the soldiers from tree to tree, to prevent their lounging. A commander with reasonable foresight must have reflected that, if it was so difficult to drive them back to their drill from beneath the shade of the branches, it would be a still harder matter to get them from behind the shelter of the trunks on a day of battle. Minute-men and Continentals alike, they enjoyed the plenty which abounded, and the fun which was constantly on foot, within the city; and contrasted their own jovial life with the short commons, and irksome inactivity, prevailing in the hostile cantonments on Staten Island. They were vastly amused by the exulting shouts with which the hungry British greeted the arrival of a canoe laden with cabbages, and hailed the unaccustomed spectacle of a live bullock being hoisted on land from on board a barge. The wilder spirits made a pastime of rowing themselves across the channel in order to give Howe's people a false alarm. It was a great diversion, (they declared,) to see the red-coats throwing away their powder, and wasting bullets on the trees. The young militiamen did well to snatch the delights of the passing hour; for there were many grim months in store for them.

The jubilant confidence, which overflowed among the lower ranks in the American army, was not shared by older and wiser citizens. Men of that class were resolute, but grave and anxious. "Sir," (so one of them

[1] Letter in the *American Archives* of August 22, 1776.

wrote to another,) "this will be the trying year. **If**
possible they must be hindered from getting any foot-
hold this season.   If that can be done, I think the day
will be our own, and we shall be for ever delivered from
tyranny."[1]   A trying year it was, and there were more
such to follow; but people, who have an immense and
perilous task in front of them, sometimes obey a wholesome instinct when they school themselves to look
no further than a twelvemonth ahead.   As the crisis
approached, Washington, who discerned the danger
more clearly than he saw the way to meet it, was per-
turbed far beyond his wont; but he did not dishearten
those around him by giving direct expression to his
apprehensions.   Evidence of his inward trouble must
be sought in the exceptional character of the steps
which he adopted, and in the intensity of his appeals
to the patriotism of others.   On the twelfth of August
six-and-thirty British vessels entered the Bay, where
near twice that number already were lying ; and next
morning Washington packed up all his documents
which bore upon politics, and sent them to Philadelphia, in charge of a trustworthy field-officer, to be
deposited in the custody of Congress.   Four days afterwards he desired the State authorities to take measures
for the removal of non-combatants.   "When I consider," he wrote, "that the city of New York will in all
human probability very soon be the scene of a bloody
conflict, I cannot but view the great numbers of
women, children, and infirm persons remaining in it,
with the most melancholy concern.   When the men-of-
war passed up the river, the shrieks and cries of these
poor creatures, running every way with their children,
were truly distressing, and I fear they will have an
unhappy effect on the ears and minds of our young and
inexperienced soldiery."[2]   His own receipt for preparing the young and inexperienced to face danger

[1] Josiah Bartlett to John Langdon of Philadelphia.
[2] Washington to the President of Congress, August 13, 1776 ; to the
New York Convention, August 17.

and difficulty was to tell them the truth calmly, but forcibly and without disguise. "The hour," so he informed them, "is fast approaching on which the honour and success of this army, and the safety of our bleeding country, will depend. Remember, officers and soldiers, that you are freemen, fighting for the blessings of liberty; that slavery will be your portion, and that of your posterity, if you do not acquit yourselves like men."

That was one of a series of proclamations enforcing with ever increasing earnestness, and reiterating in the minutest particulars, the duties of officer and soldier on the eve of a battle, and in the heat of action. It is entered in the Order-book of the twenty-third August; and by that time Howe was already in Long Island. At nine in the morning of the twenty-second, fifteen thousand men, and forty guns, were disembarked within the curve of Gravesend Bay, six or seven miles to the south of Brooklyn. English and Highlanders were the first on shore; and then Count Von Donop's Jägers and Grenadiers were ferried across in large flat-boats, with muskets sloped and in column of march; preserving the well-considered pomp of German discipline on that salt water which few of them had ever smelt until they attained manhood. The British lines were soon thronged by country-people wearing badges of loyalty; cattle and sheep were driven in from the morasses and thickets; supplies of every description reappeared from their hiding-places in great abundance; and, very shortly afterwards, two more brigades of Hessians, under General von Heister, came over to Gravesend Bay, and raised the numbers of the invaders, present on Long Island, to twenty thousand rank and file. The American Commander-in-Chief, misinformed by his scouts, under-rated the host that General Howe had taken with him, and over-estimated the detachment which was left behind on Staten Island, and which was therefore disposable for a direct assault upon the city of New York. The incurable faultiness of the situation, in which Washington had allowed himself to be placed, was now painfully visible. He was under the necessity of keeping the halves of his own inferior force separated from each other by an arm of the sea, which the British fleet might at any moment render impassable for his rafts and barges ; while Howe, by the aid of that fleet, could throw the whole of his superior strength on any point along the extensive coast-line which encircled the American position. Washington informed President Hancock that he had been unable to send more than six additional battalions to the camp on Long Island, because the British fleet might move up with the remainder of their army, and make an attack on New York at the next flood-tide. The troops, (he said,) went off in high good humour ; and those on the spot discovered great cheerfulness, and an excellent temper.[1] The colonists had need of all the gaiety which they could muster ; for the American garrison of Long Island, even after it had been reinforced, did not exceed eight thousand men.

The views of both the opposed generals were coloured, and their tactics governed, by recollections of Bunker's Hill. Howe moved cautiously, and in overwhelming force, with the intention of first driving the Americans within the lines of Brooklyn, and then besieging those lines deliberately and systematically, as if they were the ramparts of a fortified town. Washington, on the other hand, was not without an expectation that the enemy, — remembering their victory of the preceding year, and forgetting the price which it had cost them, — would march against his breastworks in uncovered line of battle ; and that his own people would have the opportunity of fighting under circumstances which made them the equals of any soldiers in the world. The British army would then be exposed to the probability of a sanguinary repulse, which would go far to disgust the British nation with the war and its authors. Daniel Webster has related how, when

[1] Washington to the President of Congress ; New York, August 23, 1776.

the first tidings of Bunker's Hill reached Philadelphia, Colonel Washington made careful enquiry about the behaviour of the New England militia. On hearing that they had reserved their fire until the advancing column was within eight rods, and then had delivered it with fearful effect, he pronounced that in that case the liberties of the country were safe.[1] And now, hoping against hope, General Washington made arrangements for securing that the scene on the heights above Charlestown should be repeated at Brooklyn on a larger scale; and with this difference, that the intrenchments would remain in American hands after the slaughter was over. The Order-book testifies to the pains which he expended over his preparations for this result. Brigadiers were directed to measure out a certain space in front of each several redoubt, and to make sure that the enemy had stepped within the fatal limit before ever an American musket was discharged. Piles of brushwood were to be laid along the line of demarcation, so as to render it distinct and familiar to the marksmen behind the bulwark. The captains were to see that bullets fitted the bore, that flints were properly fixed, and that cartridges were dealt out in equal parcels, with each man's name written legibly on his bundle; and privates were especially enjoined to be attentive and silent, lest they should miss or mistake the order to fire, when at last that order came. Whether or not the race is to the swift, Washington had long ago been taught, both by triumph and defeat, that in the days of fire-arms the fight is always to the cool.

Nothing could be better planned than Washington's scheme of battle; but with troops like his, at this early stage of the war, he should himself have been on the

---

[1] Daniel Webster spoke twice on Bunker's Hill; — first in 1825, when Lafayette laid the corner-stone of the Monument, and again in 1843, when the Monument was finished. It was on the latter occasion that the story quoted in the text was told to a crowd of a hundred thousand persons, including eleven veterans who had fought in the battle.

spot to see that his conceptions were carried into effect. He could not, however, any more than his army, be in two places at once. The proper post for a Commander-in-Chief, whose personal courage was above dispute, — and whose responsibilities extended over all the forces of the State, and over a theatre of war which covered six thousand square leagues, — was in his opinion at New York. He therefore maintained his head-quarters, where he had planted them, on the mainland, and in a great city whence it was easy to establish communications with all parts of the continent. As the plot thickened, however, he went over daily to the scene of action; where, even in his absence, it cannot be said that there was any scarcity of officers. Indeed, the Americans on Long Island suffered from being over-generalled. Their story, during that eventful week, reads like one of those campaigns in ancient Greece where a different commander, in a group of several, directed the operations on each day in turn. Until a very short time before the storm of war burst upon the island, Nathanael Greene had been in charge; and a better substitute for George Washington it would have been hard to find. Knox, the American general of artillery, whose praise was well worth having, has described Greene's soldiership as intuitive. " He came to us the rawest and the most untutored being I ever met with: but in less than twelve months he was equal, in military knowledge, to any General Officer in the army, and very superior to most of them." [1]

Those twelve months had now elapsed; but they had been a period of strain, hardship, and exposure to many, and to Greene even more than others. On the fifteenth of August he reported himself in bed with a raging fever; although he hoped, by the assistance of Providence, to be on horseback again before the enemy landed. But either he had broken down more completely than he thought, or the British came sooner than he expected; for Washington found it necessary

[1] Garden's *Revolutionary Anecdotes;* Vol. I., page 65.

to inform Congress that General Greene had been extremely ill, and still "continued bad"; and that he had therefore been obliged to appoint Major General Sullivan to command on the island. So Washington wrote on the twenty-third of August; and within forty-eight hours Sullivan had been superseded by Israel Putnam. Though now a full Major General of the Continental army, Putnam was the same shrewd, genial, New England uncle as ever; perfectly ready to die for his country, but regarding life as a great joke so long as it lasted. A few days back he had been engaged in assisting the State authorities to remove women and children from the city of New York to a place of security. In the course of that operation he despatched to a friend at a distance what he apparently meant for an official letter. General Putnam sent him, (so the communication was worded,) his daughter. If he did not like her, he might send her back again; and she would be taken good care of, and provided with a Whig husband.[1] The veteran was only too well fitted for infusing an extra dose of hopefulness and enthusiasm into soldiers who, just then, would have been none the worse for a little self-distrust; but he did not possess either the training, or the temperament, indispensable for the leader of a regular army. A day after he assumed command, he had to endure something very like a severe scolding. It was with no small concern, (Washington wrote,) that he had listened to a scattering, unmeaning fusillade from the American lines. That unsoldierlike and disorderly practice wasted ammunition; frightened away any British or Germans who might be in the mind to desert; and removed all probability of distinguishing between a real, and a false, alarm. Good tactics consisted in keeping the main force alert, and in hand, behind the intrenchments; in sending forward strong, well-led skirmishing parties for the purpose of harassing the adversary; in laying traps

[1] General Putnam to Major Moncrieffe. *Historical Manuscripts;* Fourteenth Report, Appendix, Part x.

and ambuscades for his foragers; and, above all, in accustoming the young troops to fatigue and danger, and supplying them with the honestly earned, and therefore valuable, self-confidence which arises from an experience of success.

That system of tactics, in the process of time, Washington made, as it were, his own; — the true Fabian policy, on which his fame as a captain largely, and indeed mainly, rests. But Putnam did not catch the idea when it was first presented; and the British left him very little time to think it out. The old champion of the Indian border construed his instructions into a permission to have a battle royal in any position, and against any odds. Washington spent the whole of the twenty-sixth of August on Long Island, and made his dispositions with the object of securing that the advance of the British should be slow and arduous, and that the defenders of Brooklyn should not be attacked unawares. A range of densely wooded heights lay all along the front of the American position, distant from it about two miles at the nearest point. Towards the British left, in the neighbourhood of the sea, that range was traversed by a highway from Gravesend Bay. Four miles to the east two waggon roads, in close proximity to each other, climbed from the hamlet of Flatbush, over steep and broken ground, into the centre of the American lines. And again three miles in the same direction, far away on Putnam's left, a fourth road crossed the ridge, and conducted the traveller into an excellent causeway leading to Brooklyn, through Bedford, from the village of Jamaica.[1] Washington stationed infantry in each of the three defiles on his own right and centre; and historians affirm that he gave orders to watch the Jamaica road, and that those orders were neglected. So it has been affirmed, but not by him; for in this matter, as in all others, those who wish to hear what George Washington has to say in his own

[1] All these roads are clearly marked on the map at the end of the volume.

defence must wait until the day of Judgement. At nightfall, when he went back to New York from Long Island, the American Commander-in-Chief left the western approaches to Brooklyn covered by twenty-five hundred men. The rest of his troops slept on their arms within the fortifications, having been carefully drilled and indoctrinated to meet an assault which, after the precautions he had taken, could not come upon them as a surprise.

At nine o'clock that evening Howe began to move. He did not despise his adversary; and indeed, until close upon the very end of that protracted campaign, he never erred except from superabundant and untimely caution. His main body, accompanied by a very powerful artillery,[1] advanced on the extreme right from the village of Flatland. Clinton, who led the van, halted two hours before daybreak at the foot of the pass, half a mile short of the junction with the Jamaica road. Behind him stood Lord Cornwallis and Lord Percy; while the long column was closed by the forty-ninth regiment, escorting a battery of heavy guns. General von Heister held the three brigades of Germans, deployed in a line nearly a mile in length, within cannon-shot of the two central passes. General Grant, meanwhile, with two brigades of English, and the Forty-second Highlanders, marched forward by the coast road. There was no weak man among the commanders, who had all served in famous wars; and the affair went like clock-work. At midnight Grant assailed the American pickets, with a tremendous noise, and an ostentatious display of energy so regulated as not to carry him an inch further northward than his orders warranted. Howe's purpose was twofold; — to distract the attention of the American general from the peril which threatened his left flank; and to induce him, by the temptation of beating Grant, to send a large portion of his army so far to the front that it could almost certainly be enveloped and destroyed.

[1] According to Lord Howe's despatch, there were twenty-eight pieces of artillery with the right-hand column.

The snare was deftly baited; and it caught Putnam. At three in the morning of the twenty-seventh of August he heard that his outposts on the coast road had been driven in; and he thereupon directed Lord Stirling, with the first troops on whom he could lay his hand, "to advance beyond the lines and repulse the enemy." Shortly afterwards Putnam was informed that cavalry and infantry were in motion just south of the Jamaica highway. The neglect to provide themselves with mounted scouts was now disastrous to the Americans. Half a troop of light dragoons, under the charge of a brisk partisan, would have supplied Putnam with specific information of a character to sober even that boisterous warrior. No commander in his senses would have knowingly and deliberately commenced a general action when he himself had not a left wing, and when the enemy's right wing was more than twice the size of that part of his own army which was present in the battle. But the news from the eastward, in the shape in which it reached Putnam, failed to alarm him. He did not recall Stirling; he did not think it worth his while to advertise Washington; and the only step he took was that of sending Sullivan, with a minute reinforcement, to assume the command of the weak New England regiments which faced an enormously superior number of Germans on the central roads. The Americans were scattered through the woods, as sheep that had too many shepherds. They were, in all, somewhere between four and five thousand, and they had six pieces of cannon as against forty. Man to man, their chance would have been a poor one; and, when contending in a proportion of one to four, they had no chance whatever.

The sun, (as Americans remembered it after the events on which it shone became matter of history,) rose with a red and angry glare. Clinton, who headed the British advance on the right, had no one to oppose him. He reached the meeting of the two highways, wheeled to the westward, and pushed vigorously along the Jamaica road. Between eight and nine in the morning he was at Bedford, in great force; and he at once assailed Sullivan's Americans in flank and rear. Against their front the Hessians advanced two deep, with colours flying, and to the music of drums and hautboys, as if they were marching across the Friedrichs Platz at Cassel on the Landgrave's birthday. They did not fire a shot, but pressed steadily forward until they could employ their bayonets. Sullivan did neither worse nor better than any ordinary, or perhaps any extraordinary, officer would do in such a hopeless predicament. He cannot be blamed for the plight in which he found himself; for it was the business of the general in charge of the whole army, who had placed him where he stood, to provide against his being surrounded. Intercepted between Clinton and von Heister, the Americans made no resistance worth the name. Sullivan kept together some of his people, and showed fight for a while; but the show must have been a poor one, for only two Hessians were killed. When the case was desperate he told his remaining soldiers, or as many as could hear him, to shift for themselves; and the greater part of their comrades had already anticipated his orders. One regiment, at least, had been withdrawn by its colonel soon enough for safety, and rather too soon for glory; the men of other battalions broke their formation, and hid themselves in the bushes or maize fields until they could regain the American lines under cover of night; but Sullivan himself had stayed too long under fire, and he was taken prisoner, together with some hundreds of his followers.

On the English left, General Grant attacked at daybreak; first with artillery; and then, (as an approaching tumult from the northeast showed that the enemy opposite to him were well within the net,) he sent forward his skirmishers, and, after a due interval, thrust the main body of his infantry into close action. The Americans in that quarter displayed no backwardness to meet him. Lord Stirling had brought from camp an excellent Delaware battalion, and another which was recruited from the families of men of property in and about Baltimore. These were the young Marylanders who had paid so little deference to the homely New England generals, and who now were well content to serve under one who passed for a British nobleman, and who possessed qualities which did not derogate from the title. The ranks of both regiments were full, their uniforms smart, their weapons the best that money could purchase, and their courage high. Stirling himself, then and afterwards, was a hearty fighter; but he had much to learn, or rather to unlearn, for he was not yet emancipated from a pedantic reverence for the drill-book. Colonel Reed, the American Adjutant General, commented on his action as follows in a spirit of respectful criticism. "My Lord, who loved discipline, made a mistake which probably affected us a great deal. He would not suffer his regiments to break, but kept them in lines and on open ground. The enemy, on the other hand, possessed themselves of the woods and fences. His personal bravery was conspicuous." In these battles, where the numbers engaged were exceedingly small as compared with the issues which were staked upon the event, the personal bravery of a commander went for very much indeed; and Grant and Stirling made themselves felt all along their respective lines of battle. Encouraged by their example, both parties so comported themselves that each paid the other an unstudied and unintended compliment by greatly overrating the force of their adversaries. The English subsequently confessed that objects seen through the medium of smoke and fire are always magnified, and that their own people reckoned the Provincials at three times the real figure; and Washington's Adjutant General claimed that the Americans on the right wing, whatever they lost, had preserved their honour, since the enemy were as ten to one.

So much tenacity was shown on both sides that there was no need of exaggeration. The British men-of-war had attempted to advance by sea on a course parallel to Grant's line of march; but wind, and afterwards tide, were against them, and they could not beat up the Bay. The struggle on land was so severe that the English at one time had expended their ammunition, and were halted near the edge of the forest. Admiral Howe, powerless on his own element, and glad to be of what use he could, rowed on shore with a supply of ammunition, and sent his boat's crew up the hill laden with sacks of cartridges. It was a fierce and even combat; but the decision was being worked out elsewhere. Stirling, before ever he knew, was involved in an entanglement from which neither valour nor conduct could extricate him without immense loss. Two miles to his rear ran Gowanus Creek, a sea-water inlet bordered on north and south by a broad and deep marsh. The only passage across the obstacle was a bridge commanded by the buildings of a mill, the machinery of which was impelled by the tide that flowed up and down the estuary. That bridge had been burned by a Connecticut colonel, who had made a premature retreat from his station in the centre, and who, (so long as his own command escaped intact,) cared little what might befall the hindmost. And now Lord Cornwallis, passing round the rear of Clinton, marched a regiment of Highlanders, and another of Grenadiers, to the neighbourhood of the ruined bridge, and strongly occupied a defile which would have been almost impassable even if it had been left undefended.

When Stirling became aware that his communications were cut he issued the word to retire, and his troops withdrew in perfect order. He might well have been excused if he had given up all for lost; but he was fully determined that something considerable should be saved. He could rely upon his soldiers to second his intentions; because on this, as on similar occasions throughout the war, men of English blood in both the contending armies evinced great unwillingness to surrender. Stirling directed the main body of his people to struggle through the mire and the water as best they could; while he himself, with one wing of the

Maryland regiment, remained behind to confront Cornwallis. Seven of the retreating Americans were drowned; but the rest got safe across, and carried with them a score of British prisoners. Stirling kept up a long and very spirited struggle; but he was encircled on every quarter. Cornwallis had not been slow to accept his challenge; Grant had followed him up from the southward; while Clinton and the Hessians, having finished their own business in the centre, marched promptly in the direction of the firing. The five companies from Baltimore were wiped off the rolls. The ground was thickly strewn with their buff and scarlet; and the survivors, all but nine, were captured. Stirling gave up his sword to General von Heister; whose presence on the spot testified both to the admirable skill with which Howe had brought his right wing to bear on all the critical stages of the battle in succession, and to the heroism of those young Marylanders who had held their ground until the entire hostile army was assembled to overwhelm them.

The loss of Americans in killed and wounded was variously estimated, and has never been ascertained. Washington reported it at a very few hundreds; though he gave no details, and admitted that he had not been able to obtain a precise account. General Howe computed that more than two thousand of the enemy had been killed, wounded, drowned, and suffocated in the marsh; but in the same paragraph of his despatch he put their number engaged at ten thousand, which was more than double the real amount. Howe was a poor hand at figures. During the earlier part of his career he had been accustomed to charge straight at the enemy without stopping to count them; and, as a general in chief command, he counted them wrong. Not a dozen Americans were drowned in the creek; and the country-bred militiamen picked their way through the bog without being suffocated.[1]   It is hard to be-

[1] Colonel Haslet, who commanded the Delawares, and brought them back across the creek, saw only one man drowned.

lieve that, exclusive of prisoners, they can have lost anywhere near a thousand. According to Howe's own statement, less than seventy of their wounded were left behind on the field; and yet those of them who had been badly hurt must all have been there. A great Anglo-Indian proconsul, who had witnessed as much war as most civilians, was in the habit of remarking that he had never been present at an affair where the victors were not firmly persuaded that their opponents had carried off the greater part of their dead and dying.[1] That was asserted, and believed, on many occasions by both parties in the Revolutionary War; but the Americans who retired from the fight on Long Island had enough to do in carrying off themselves.

All which can be said for certain is that more Provincials would have been hit if more of the British had shot straight. Our people had behaved to perfection. Howe's plan was worthy of Frederic the Great; and the execution of it, — in accuracy, punctuality, and dash, — could not easily have been bettered by Frederic's army. It had been a performance, on a smaller scale, almost as artistic to a military eye as the manœuvres by which the King of Prussia rolled up the Austrian line at Leuthen; and yet some of Stirling's officers, who kept their heads in the *mêlée*, observed that the fire of the British was less deadly than their discipline was exact, and their onset determined.[2] Three hundred of Howe's own troops

---

[1] Lord Lawrence told the author this, more than once; and no one who knew the worth of words ever forgot what he had even once heard Lord Lawrence say.

[2] "The Major, Captain Ramsey, and Lieutenant Plunket were foremost, and within forty yards of the enemy's muzzles. The enemy were chiefly under cover of an orchard, save a few that showed themselves and pretended to give up, clubbing their firelocks till we came within that distance, when they immediately presented and blazed in our faces. They entirely overshot us, and killed some men away behind in our rear. I was so near that I could not miss. I discharged my rifle seven times that day as deliberately as I ever did at a mark, and with as little perturbation." That passage occurs in an American letter of the thirty-first of August. Colonel Attlee, who was with Stirling at Long Island, wrote that, if Grant's soldiers had been marksmen, they must have cut off the greater part of his detachment.

were killed or wounded, and a handful captured. Stirling and Sullivan, between them, had six guns in action, and lost them all. The British took prisoners near eleven hundred of the enemy, including three generals,[1] and, (as was to be expected when an American army had met with a disaster,) an exceptionally large proportion of colonels.

Washington came over to Long Island too late to prevent the battle, but in time to mitigate the severity of its consequences. When Howe directed a strong column against the Brooklyn lines, — on the chance of carrying them by a rush amidst the confusion and dismay which at such a moment might beset the garrison, — he found the American Commander-in-Chief already there, with three fresh regiments from across the water; and, after a few rounds had been discharged, the British retired. At another period of the morning Washington was on the west front of the fortifications, sending troops to protect and assist the remains of his right wing during their passage through Gowanus Creek, and witnessing the self-sacrifice of the Marylanders with emotion the outward signs of which he is described as having been unable to repress. He had need of all his self-command; for there was little comfort to be drawn from the sights around him, or from the prospect which was before him. His militiamen, who required the encouragement of an early success in order even to begin their conversion into real soldiers, had been flung into action against a regular army so numerous, and so admirably handled, that it would have been able to give a good account of twice, or perhaps even three times, their number of European veterans. They had no food except biscuits, and some meat which they could not cook; for on the morrow the weather broke. Rain fell continuously; the men in the trenches were up to their waists

---

[1] Besides Sullivan and Stirling, General Woodhull was captured at Jamaica after the action, and died of wounds received under circumstances not very clearly recorded. In Howe's report, which has been followed by some English historians, he is misnamed " General Odell."

in water; their cartridges were sodden, and most of
their fire-arms useless. For in those days of flint-locks
the effect of very heavy rain was to put military science
four centuries back, by reducing good musketeers to the
condition of indifferent spearmen;[1] and the Americans
were in worse case still, because some of their regiments
were not even provided with bayonets. Several battalions had left their blankets far away in the woods, at
the bivouacs which they occupied on the night preceding the battle. Nine thousand disheartened soldiers, the
last hope of their country, were penned up with the sea
behind them, and a triumphant enemy in front; shelter-
less and famished on a square mile of open ground
swept by a fierce and cold northeasterly gale.

That disagreeable circumstance was the salvation of
the Republic. Towards the close of August, in those
regions, the prevailing wind was from the southwest;
and, whenever it once more blew from that usual quarter, all would be over with the American army, and, in
all probability, with the American cause as well. During the engagement on Long Island one of Lord Howe's
vessels, which had contrived to get within range of the
battery at Redhook, speedily dismounted the guns and
wrecked the earthworks. Such had been the execution
done by a single man-of-war, and that none of the largest. Washington could have no illusions as to what

---

[1] Till percussion caps came into use, no improvement in the weapon
could obviate this drawback. At the battle of Dresden, in August 1813,
Murat's cuirassiers cut down and captured great masses of Austrian infantry whose muskets would not go off on account of the wet; and on the
previous day Blucher's cavalry, largely from the same cause, had ruined
Marshal Macdonald's army on the Katzbach.

The British soldiers in America, — fine fellows that they were, — prayed
for the sort of weather which would enable them to come to close quarters
with their adversary. An English officer, who was in Burgoyne's expedition, wrote thus of the army when on the way to Saratoga. "The heavy
rain afforded another consolation to the men during the march, which
was, in case the enemy had attacked us, that the fate of the day would
have rested solely upon the bayonet. This idea prevailed so strongly in
the minds of the men that, notwithstanding they were acquainted with the
superiority of the enemy, an attack seemed to be the wish of every
soldier."

would be his fate when the whole British fleet lay in the East River, shelling New York; searching every corner of his position on Long Island with thirty-two pound cannon-balls; and rendering the provisioning and reinforcement of his troops hopeless, and their retreat impracticable. Even before the English Admiral could bring his guns to bear, the situation of the beleaguered Provincials was to a high degree precarious. There was a belief in both camps that, if Howe's infantry had been led to the assault, they would have walked over the intrenchments behind which the beaten army was now gathered.[1] If that supposition was correct, the minute-men, who defended the redoubt upon Bunker's Hill, saved the American lines on Long Island. Their courage, and the precision of their fire, in the battle of the preceding year, had made such an impression upon Howe's memory that on this occasion he declined to repeat the experiment of a general assault across open ground. His sappers drew the first parallel at a distance of six hundred yards from the hostile ramparts, and his engineers proceeded to mark out sites for breaching batteries. His methods were slow, but as certain in their operation as the laws of nature. When once the wind changed, and the leading British frigates had passed within Governor Island and taken Brooklyn in the rear, the independence of the United States would have been indefinitely postponed; and, whenever they became a nation, their capital would have been called by another name.

But the end was not yet; and, if it did not come now, it might come never. Washington allowed himself forty-

---

[1] "Could we have trusted our spies' account," (an English officer wrote,) "a terrible slaughter might have been made. But the General appears to have been very wary." That opinion was held by some intelligent Americans inside the lines. "On the morning after our first night's watch, Colonel Shee took me aside, and asked me what I thought of our situation. I could not but say that I thought it a very discouraging one. He viewed it in the same light, and added that, if we were not soon withdrawn from it, we should inevitably be cut to pieces." *Pennsylvanian Memoirs;* chapter vi.

eight hours within which to make his preparations; and of those hours he spent none in sleep, nor wasted any in tentative and misdirected efforts. His first care was to cheer up the disconsolate people around him. He sent to King's Bridge, sixteen miles above New York, for two Pennsylvanian regiments, which, (to use his own expression,) had been trained with more than common attention. In the forenoon of the twenty-eighth of August they marched up from the landing-place, gaily and expensively dressed, with heads erect and shoulders squared, and a bayonet at the end of every barrel; while the spectators, proud to be the comrades of such a gallant company, were overheard saying that those were "the lads who might do something." With them arrived Colonel Glover's regiment of Massachusetts fishermen who, — although they had been deprived of their livelihood under that Statute against the passing of which Charles Fox vainly protested,[1] — were soon to make it evident that nautical skill and hardihood could not be extinguished by Act of Parliament. Throughout the morning the sky was gloomy, and with the afternoon rain came; but all that day, and all the next, the American General, ordinarily so frugal of powder, encouraged those of his riflemen, who could keep their priming-pans dry, to exchange shots with the enemy's firing parties. The crackle of musketry, which ran along the parapet, held the besiegers in respect, and did something to restore and maintain the confidence of the Provincials. Taking into his secret one or two officers of high rank and tried discretion, Washington transmitted orders to New York, and up the estuaries on either flank of the Manhattan peninsula; and the precautions which he observed were so stringent that not even his aides-de-camp knew his purpose. General Heath, who commanded at King's Bridge, — and the Assistant Quarter Master General, who was stationed in the city, — were commissioned to impress every kind

[1] An Act for Restraining the Trade and Commerce of the New England Colonies. *The American Revolution;* chapter vii.

of water-craft which had either oars or sails, and which could be kept afloat, and to have them all in the mouth of the East River by dark on the evening of the twenty-ninth. Then, and not till then, Washington assembled what was as near to a Council of War as a commander who had self-respect, and an opinion of his own, would permit himself to convene. When his generals had heard all that he had to tell them, they unanimously resolved to withdraw the army, and they put on paper a catalogue of most convincing reasons in favour of that course. The evacuation of Long Island, (so they stated,) was unavoidable, because the woods which covered the position had been occupied by the British; because the soldiers had no roof over their heads, and the rain had spoiled their ammunition; because the lines were weak in places, and the garrison was insufficient to guard them; because the enemy were bringing round ships to cut off their retreat; — in short, and in fact, because, if they were ever to get away at all, it was the utmost they could do to get away now.

Washington had to solve the problem of preparing his army for a rearward march without giving any intimation of his actual project. At dark on the twenty-ninth of August his colonels were ordered to get their regiments under arms for a night attack upon the enemy; and good, rather than harm, would have resulted if that tale had been carried across to the British outposts. Secrets, as the Commander-in-Chief more than suspected, were ill-kept in those easy-going ranks; and soldiers, who had money to leave, were soon engaged in explaining to each other what, in case of accident, they wished to be their testamentary dispositions. When the troops had fallen in, to the surprise of all concerned the embarkation commenced. The wind was adverse. The sailing-vessels made very little way, and the rowing-boats were few, and in constant danger of being swamped; but the mariners from Gloucester and Marblehead had navigated stormier seas; and not a few of them, it is to be feared, had often plied their oars, even in time of peace, under circumstances which imperatively demanded both expedition and secrecy. Before midnight the northeast gale, after having raged for three days, died away ; a breeze sprang up from the right quarter ; and, while air enough was stirring to fill the canvas, the surface of the channel became so smooth that the very smallest pinnace could be loaded to the gunwale. There was some crowding and hustling in the neighbourhood of the ferry. A throng of militiamen, conscious that the bayonets of a regular army might at any moment be at their backs, could not be expected to wait their turn as placidly and courteously as a string of fashionable ladies and gentlemen filing up the gangway of the Calais packet.[1] Those Americans, however, who were told off for special duties obeyed their orders with composure. General Mifflin undertook to hold the intrenchments with some picked regiments, until the less disciplined portion of the force was in safety ; and he kept with him the Pennsylvanians, the Delawares, and all that remained of the Marylanders. These troops, in consequence of a mistake which never was explained, were withdrawn prematurely from the front, and marched down in the direction of the boats. They were met by Washington in person ; and at his bidding they wheeled round into the darkness, and were back at their posts before their absence had been discovered by the enemy. The pick-axes and shovels of the British working parties were distinctly audible in the American lines ; but the besiegers either did not notice any suspicious sounds, or failed to detect their meaning.

Heaven, to all appearance, was bent on helping that side which tried the hardest to help itself. As day

---

[1] Washington himself acknowledged that " matters were in much confusion at the ferry ; " — confusion which seemed worse confounded to observers not in sympathy with the American cause. The crowd was so great, according to a Tory authority, that it was impossible to get within a quarter of a mile of the stairs. The rebels in the rear were mounting on the shoulders, and clambering over the heads, of those before them.

approached, a thick fog enshrouded the two camps, the village of Brooklyn, and the East River up to the very quays of New York, but not a yard beyond; for the city itself was in sunshine. About six in the morning Washington, — who, weary of the saddle, had been standing on the water-steps while his rear-guard took their places on the thwarts, — was the last man to step on board; and the mist cleared in time for watchers on the northern point of Long Island to see his boat, and two others, still only half-way through their journey to the shore of refuge. Seldom had a retreating army made a cleaner sweep of its own property. Howe captured three stragglers who had stayed behind to plunder. There fell into his hands likewise a train of waggons; and a few ancient cannon of the description which insurgents eagerly seize upon at the outbreak of a revolution, but of which, when serious fighting has begun, the artillerymen who work them are only too thankful to be quit. When the English at last bethought themselves of going to see why there was no noise or movement behind the hostile breastworks, they found that everything of military value had been removed, — field-guns and horses; ordnance stores; and even the biscuits which had not been, and the raw pork which could not be, eaten. The provisions, indeed, were no great loss; but privates in the Provincial army exultingly declared that the British soldiers, however hard they might look, would be unable to discover a single drink of rum.

The renown of this historical achievement owes nothing to the vanity of its author. Washington contented himself with informing Congress that the retreat had been effected with no loss of men or ammunition, and in as good order as could reasonably have been anticipated. He and all his aides-de-camp, (as he begged the president to believe,) were too weary to write at any great length.[1] Still less was to be learned from

---

[1] " The extreme fatigue," he said, " which myself and family have undergone rendered me, and them, entirely unfit to take pen in hand. Since

the report which Howe drew up for the information of the Ministry in England. When his despatch appeared in print, the battle of Long Island was related, as it had been fought, in three long and serried columns; while the withdrawal to the mainland of the American army occupied barely the half of one brief and colourless paragraph.[1] In that century war news was kept in store at head-quarters until a large batch had been collected; the events of several weeks were compressed into a single letter; and it was easy for a general in command, when at last the packet sailed, to compound a narrative of his successes and failures in such judicious proportions as would gratify and reassure his countrymen at home. Horace Walpole, the least credulous of readers, acknowledged rather sulkily that it was a splendid Gazette. The frantic presumption, (he said,) which the tidings had aroused in Court circles, seriously endangered the relations between Great Britain and France.[2]

On the Continent of Europe the friends of Congress were dejected, and those of England "in a frenzy of joy;"[3] but public opinion in America, which was nearer the spot, very soon disentangled the various elements of the story, and recognised that the escape of the Provincial army was not second in importance to the conflict by which it had been preceded. The Committee of Secret Correspondence at Philadelphia informed their agent in Paris that both Whigs and Tories agreed in their admiration of General Washington's performance.[4] Greene, who knew every inch of the ground, — whose military

Monday, scarcely any of us have been out of the lines till our passage across the East River was effected yesterday morning; and, for forty-eight hours preceding that, I had hardly been off my horse, and never closed my eyes."

[1] *Gentleman's Magazine* for October 1776. The volumes of the Magazine, used for this history, belonged to one who knew the truth about Long Island; for they contain the book-plate of Marquis Cornwallis. The set was purchased by Macaulay, so that the well-thumbed pages have never passed out of Whig hands.

[2] Walpole's letters of October 13 and 31, 1776.

[3] Wharton's *Diplomatic Correspondence;* Vol. II., page 185.

[4] Wharton; Vol. II., page 158.

judgement was excellent, and whose favourite study had always been military history, — pronounced that, considering the difficulties, the retreat from Long Island was the best effected retreat he ever read or heard of. The relief and gratitude of the Revolutionary party were expressed in a contemporary effusion which has been preserved among the national records. To transport, (so this document ran,) across a wide channel of salt water a great multitude of troops, with all their baggage, military stores, and cannon, from out of the enemy's mouth, in a short summer night, — " without even those who were retreating knowing anything of the matter till just before they were embarked, — required the conduct, the vigilance, the generalship of a Washington ; and, if Fame does not clarion his praise for it, she is not impartial." [1]   Fame, in the United States of America, seldom falls short of her duty ; and it may be doubted whether any great national deliverance, since the passage of the Red Sea, has ever been more loudly acclaimed, or more adequately celebrated, than the master-stroke of energy, dexterity, and caution by which Washington rescued his army and his country.

According to an old Turkish proverb, — which refers to an illusion not confined to Turkish anglers, — every fish that escapes appears larger than it really is. It was believed by English staff-officers that Washington had got away with fifteen thousand men, and that at least twice that number of Americans were now assembled on the Manhattan peninsula. This belief seems to have influenced Howe's strategy, or rather his absence of strategy, during the golden hours and weeks which immediately followed his success on Long Island ; but that is all matter of conjecture, for posterity has not been admitted to his counsels. Three years subsequently, when he had returned to England a failure, — after he once more took his seat at Westminster, and before the constituents, who complained of his having deceived

[1] *American Archives;* September 1776.

them, got an opportunity of displacing him,[1] — he enjoyed the melancholy privilege of defending his generalship in Parliament. On the twenty-second of April,
1779, in a long speech delivered to a Committee of the
whole House, he fought his battles over again; and,
(which was a harder task,) he gave his reasons for having more than once abstained from fighting when victory was all but certain. He dwelt in voluminous detail
on the successive military problems which he had to encounter between the autumn of 1775, when he took over
the command from Gage, and the spring of 1778, when
he was replaced by Sir Henry Clinton; but he slurred
over the cardinal question of his inaction during the first
fortnight of September 1776 in one meagre, and far from
convincing, sentence.[2] It is equally difficult to explain
satisfactorily why Howe was so long about landing on
New York Island, and why Washington was so slow in
evacuating the city. As an error, — palpable, and from
a tactical point of view quite indefensible, — one mistake
may be set against the other; but the American commander had an excuse which was wanting to his opponent. Howe was bound to advise with no one except a
brother who was as little likely to be a clog on spirited
and aggressive action as any naval colleague that British
general ever had; whereas, on a decision so grave and
irreversible as the abandonment of an important city,
Washington esteemed himself to be under the obligation of consulting, and, (in the last resort,) of obeying,
Congress.

The consent of that body to the evacuation of New York
was obtained with much trouble, and by stages. On the
third of September, Congress had only got so far as to

---

[1] *American Revolution;* chapter viii.

[2] " The necessary preparations, and erecting batteries to facilitate the
landing upon the Island of New York, and battering the enemy's works
at Horen's Hook, occupied us till the fifteenth of September, when the
possession of New York was effected." The batteries under cover of
which the British ultimately landed on the island of New York were the
broadsides of their men-of-war; and the fleet might have been opposite
Kip's Bay by the first of September just as easily as a fortnight later on.

determine that, in the hypothetical case of the town proving to be untenable, it should not be destroyed, even
though its unburned houses would provide commodious
winter quarters for the British. Washington summoned
a council of war, which voted in favour of keeping five
thousand men in the city, and of establishing their main
force in a strong position some miles to the northward.
New York was quite sure to be taken, and its garrison
with it ; and therefore, so long as Congress was inclined
to maintain the place at all hazards, it was a less evil to
lose a quarter, than the whole, of the American army.
That is the utmost that can be said for the course which
the generals of that army agreed to adopt.

There were soldiers, and civilians too, who remon-
strated vigorously against a half measure which in their
eyes was the less respectable because it seemed inspired
by a desire to avoid the imputation of pusillanimity.
Charles Lee declared that, so far from clinging perti-
naciously to the islands, he would give Mr. Howe the
fee-simple of the whole group. Jay expressed his apprehension that the hope of saving a few acres of territory would plunge the country into inextricable difficulties.
Colonel Rufus Putnam, in his official report as Chief Engineer, represented to Washington that, so long as the
troops were extended from New York to King's Bridge,
the enemy would always be able to attack with superior
force; that, if the Southern army were caught in the
toils, and forced to surrender, nothing could prevent
Howe from reaching Albany ; and that, when Albany
had fallen, the Northern army must forthwith quit Ticonderoga on pain of being annihilated. " I know," Putnam
wrote, " that this doctrine gives up New York to destruction, and exposes many other towns to be ravaged. But
what are ten or twenty towns to the grand object ? "
Nathanael Greene contributed to the controversy a
paper of very drastic strategical advice, enforced by
apt historical instances, on which the leisure of con-
valescence tempted him to expatiate. He reminded
Washington that Francis the First, when his dominions

were invaded by the Emperor of Germany, laid whole provinces waste, and by that policy starved and ruined Charles's army, and defeated him without a battle. And yet, in the sixteenth century, Provence and Champagne had been French, and loyal to the French King ; whereas two thirds of the property in New York belonged to Tories, who would receive no more than their deserts if the city and the suburbs were levelled with the ground.[1]

Washington did not at once repulse the suggestion ; but New York was never condemned by him to the fate of Moscow. The dictates of humanity, combined with the highest principles of statesmanship, forbade him deliberately to set on fire a great city, the home of twenty thousand people, even though his own party was in a minority among them. Nor had the grave and immediate danger which threatened his army been as yet fully borne in on his convictions. The advice which he addressed to Philadelphia was less clear-cut and emphatic than the crisis demanded ;[2] and at last the civil authorities were beforehand with him in resolving to face the inevitable. On the tenth of September, President Hancock informed General Washington that it was by no means the sense of Congress that the army, or any part of it, should remain in the city a moment longer than he should think it proper for the public service. Such

---

[1] Regimental officers who could not, like Greene and Putnam, make known their sentiments at head-quarters, talked freely among themselves about the danger of lingering at New York. " There cannot," wrote a Pennsylvanian captain, " remain a doubt that this city should have been evacuated as soon as possible after the quitting of Long Island. This was as obvious to me then as it is now; and I had backed my opinion with the bet of a beaver hat that there would be no attempt to defend it."

[2] " That the enemy mean to winter in New York there can be no doubt. That, with such an armament, they can drive us out is equally clear. The Congress having resolved that it should not be destroyed, nothing seems to remain but to determine the time of their taking possession. It is our interest and wish to prolong it as much as possible, provided the delay does not affect our future measures." That is an extract from a letter of Washington to the President of Congress, dated as late as the eighth of September. It most certainly cannot be read as an urgent appeal for permission to hurry on the evacuation of the city.

an admission, — emanating from a quarter where a sentiment, or rather a passion, adverse to the policy of retirement had notoriously prevailed, — was equivalent to
a command. Something had already been done towards
removing the enormous collection of stores which filled
New York; and every effort was now devoted to acceler-
ate the process. The land transport was deficient; but
cargoes of heavy goods were despatched by boat up the
Hudson River; an operation which the British Admiral,
with a negligence which was foreign to him, did nothing
to interrupt. Even thus the work went slowly; and
meanwhile the army was so distributed as to present
an attractive opportunity for an enterprising enemy.
Washington's head-quarters, and his best troops, were
stationed on the heights of Haerlem, behind strong lines
which ran right across from sea to sea exactly half-way
up the peninsula. General Putnam remained in the city
with some infantry, and a few companies of artillery,
to preserve order in the streets, and to superintend the
depletion of the magazines; while five brigades of militia
were posted at intervals along the eastern shore, ready
in case the British made a forward movement before the
city was finally abandoned.

Time was no longer wasted; but far too much had
been lost already. After Washington's thoughts were
once fairly set upon departure, he did not enjoy an easy
moment; and the acuteness of his anxiety was an unanswerable condemnation both of his own temerity in
prolonging the retention of New York, and of Howe's
apathy in delaying to grasp the prize which so long had
been dangled before him. "I fully expected," Washington wrote on the fourteenth of September, "that an
attack somewhere would be made last night; and happy
shall I be if my apprehensions of one to-night, or in a
day or two, are not confirmed by the event." Ever
since the month commenced, the British had been encamped on the northwest angle of Long Island, in
and about the villages of Newtown and Flushing, and
on the high ground which, from across the channel,

overlooked the centre of the American position. It was not, however, until Friday the thirteenth that any considerable naval force was transferred to the quarter where its action could materially assist the army. On that afternoon two ships of forty guns, and two of twenty-eight guns, penetrated the East River, and anchored above the city; on the evening of the next day they were reinforced by some of their consorts; and at eleven o'clock on the morning of the fifteenth of September a heavy cannonade was opened upon the American troops who lined the earthworks at Kip's Bay, where Thirty-fourth Street now comes down to the water. At the same time four long columns of barges, laden with British light infantry and German Grenadiers, emerged from Newtown inlet. Their movements were directed by Commodore Hotham; an excellent officer, whenever he had a still better officer to command him. Hotham gave the signal; and the flotilla spread itself into line, and swept forward to the hostile shore. It was an imposing spectacle. The amazing fire from the shipping, the soldiers in scarlet clambering up the steep rocks, and the river covered with boats full of armed men pressing eagerly to the shore, were described as forming one of the grandest and most sublime stage-effects that had ever been exhibited.[1]

Such was the scene as painted by a British officer, for the admiration of his home circle; but those spectators who occupied the front places opposite very soon had enough of the show. The New England militiamen who lined the coast were too intelligent to be deceived as to the nature of the service demanded of them, and too little disciplined to perform that service heartily if it did not commend itself to their liking and approval. They had been posted where they stood, as every man of them was aware, in order to secure the

[1] Captain William G. Evelyn, of the British Light Infantry, to his aunt, Mrs. Boscowen, England: given in the Appendix to Mr. Henry Johnston's important treatise on the Battle of Haerlem Heights.

retreat of the American army; and they at once proceeded, by the most direct method, to secure the retreat
of that part of the army in whose safety they were
specially interested.   The troops who were behind the
intrenchments ran away; and two brigades, which had
been told off to support them, retired in confusion along
the Haerlem road.   Washington, who had galloped up
to the sound of the cannon, shouted for the officers to
get their people off the highway, and place them behind
the walls, and among the fields of Indian corn, which
flanked it on either side; but, on the appearance of
sixty or seventy red-coats, (as Washington counted
them,) the whole assemblage broke and fled.[1]   Howe's
great chance had come.   The garrison of New York,
— as well as three brigades of infantry which had been
stationed along the bank of the East River, south of the
point where the British landed, — might all be had for
the taking.   An advance guard of the Hessians, with
little trouble, and no loss to themselves, secured three
hundred prisoners; and not one of the retreating battalions would ever have reached the American lines in
military order, and with half its full numbers, if Howe
had promptly pushed his troops athwart the peninsula,
which here was less than three thousand yards wide.
He had several hours to spare, while Putnam was rid-
ing furiously about the town, collecting the various portions of his command, and starting them for Haerlem
Heights.   Not till four of the afternoon did the British
commence a stately progress northward along the route
which, in modern New York, goes by the name of Fifth
Avenue; while, on a parallel road, separated from them
only by the breadth of the present Central Park, the
long column of sweltering American militiamen toiled
over the ground now covered by those less fashionable
thoroughfares that more nearly skirt the Hudson River.
Putnam brought off safely all his regiments, and even
some of his field-pieces.   Between fifty and sixty can-

[1] Washington to the President of Congress; September 16, 1776.
American Archives; October 25.

non, mounted or dismounted, and a vast quantity of shells and roundshot, remained in the city as a prize for the victors. In both armies together, less than a score of warriors bit the dust; and among the Americans very few had so much as bitten a cartridge. Their troops, (said one of their generals,) never fired a gun; but as soon as the British began to land, they ran as if the devil was in them.[1]

It was a day of small carnage, but of many legends.[2] According to a very popular American anecdote, the British Commander-in-Chief never got further westward than the country-seat of a New York merchant, which stood on a pleasant eminence half-way across the peninsula. The owner of the house happened to be a Quaker; and, as such, he was almost as a matter of course rich, and a Tory. His lady, however, — the mother of Lindley Murray the grammarian, — held Revolutionary principles, and was so handsome and attractive that she might air them with impunity in any company whatsoever. She enjoys the credit of having kept Howe and his generals drinking her husband's Madeira, and listening to a merry argument on politics between Governor Tryon and herself, until the day was so far advanced that no time remained for arranging to inter-

---

[1] General Cæsar Rodney to Messrs. Reed and Mackean; September 18, 1776.

[2] New York was taken on a Sunday. David How, (whose diary has been quoted frequently in earlier chapters of the *History of the American Revolution,*) arrived in camp from Boston on the twenty-sixth of August, and at once fell into the busy, queer way of life which he always pursued on active service. He had already been under cannon-fire; had done a good stroke of work on the Haerlem intrenchments; and had purchased a jacket and a pair of breeches for fifteen shillings from one of his comrades. As soon as he settled down in his new quarters, How was careful to note the Sundays, and, (whenever he could get to meeting,) the text. On the fifteenth of September he was too much occupied for church going; but he gives a discreet, and remarkably indulgent, account of the motives which prompted the American retreat. " Our people thought best to leave the lower part of the Town so that the shipping might not play on us. Our army all marched to the upper part of the Town this after Noon." This expression of "The Town" is here apparently used for the whole township which covered the island of Manhattan.

cept Putnam.   There are other stories, not less widely
current, which represent Washington as having altogether lost his self-restraint when his troops disbanded
themselves for headlong flight.   Which, if any, of his
words and actions were truthfully reported it is at this
time impossible to distinguish; but nothing is more certain than that, during some minutes of bitter agony, he
showed himself indifferent to the preservation of a life
which belonged to his country, and was not his own to
throw away.   When all allowance has been made for
exaggeration, the semi-mythical narratives of that Sunday morning and afternoon have their value as embodying the indelible impression left on the public mind of
America by Howe's untimely inactivity, and by Washington's disappointment and despair.[1]

That despair endured through the night, but was
dispelled ere the morrow closed.   "We are now encamped," (Washington wrote at sunrise on the sixteenth
of September,) "on the Heights of Haerlem, where I
should hope the enemy would meet with a defeat in
case of an attack, if the generality of our troops should
behave with tolerable bravery.   But experience, to my
extreme affliction, has convinced me that this is rather
to be wished for than expected.   However, I trust there
are many who will act like men, and show themselves
worthy of the blessings of freedom.   I have sent out
some reconnoitring parties to gain intelligence."   The
post had only just gone off with the General's letter
when news was brought that the British were advancing.
Washington's scouts had come into collision with Howe's
outposts, and had retired after a sharp and close exchange of musketry.   The American army turned out at
the noise of the firing, and covered Haerlem Heights
with a triple line of infantry divisions.   At length the

---

[1] General Greene's sober phrases relate as much of the truth as is worth
knowing.   "Fellows's and Parsons's whole brigade ran away from about
fifty men, and left his Excellency on the ground within eighty yards of the
enemy, so vexed at the infamous conduct of the troops that he sought
death rather than life."

English van-guard came into view, — splendid troops, overflowing with contempt for a foe whom they had thrice within one month chased and scattered ; and whom, now that he had taken refuge in his intrenchments, their buglers tauntingly saluted with the hunting-call which announced that a fox had gone to ground. Washington saw his opportunity, and sent out a detachment which, cleverly pushed forward and then in turn withdrawn, tempted his impetuous adversaries down into the valley that lay in front of the American lines. In the meantime two hundred riflemen and rangers, the flower of the Virginian and New England sharpshooters, fetched a circuit to the eastward with the intention of encompassing, and cutting off, the English skirmishers. The Southerners were commanded by Major Leitch, and the Northerners by Captain Thomas Knowlton, whose youthful promise has won him a place in the affectionate memory of his countrymen. By some mistake their attack commenced too soon, in flank, and not in rear, of the force which was opposed to them ; but, when once begun, it was pushed home. The English fell back, fighting stiffly, and making the pursuit a very dangerous form of sport to those who followed them. They retreated no further than the spot where they found their reinforcements, which consisted of two battalions of light companies, and the Forty-second Highlanders, with the welcome addition of a couple of field-pieces. Then they took their stand along a slope crowned by a field of buckwheat, not far from the village of Bloomingdale, on ground which is now overlooked by the bold and imposing dome of President Grant's mausoleum.

It is a pity that old Ulysses was not there to see ; for it was the sort of fight which he liked to watch, and knew well how to set going. The American supports came thronging up, accompanied by many superior officers whose special functions should have kept them elsewhere ; but the recollections of yesterday were rankling in their breasts, and they were determined that on this occasion the result should be such as would do the army credit. The Bloomingdale road, on that forenoon, was a very bad neighbourhood for shirkers. General George Clinton had left his pistols behind him in camp, or otherwise he would, (so he declared,) have shot "a puppy of an officer" whom he caught skulking off in the heat of the action. Colonel Reed, the Adjutant General, when he had extricated himself from under his dying horse, had a private battle of his own with a runaway made desperate by terror.[1] A vast majority of the men, however, needed no driving; and they were superbly led. Knowlton was slain on the field. Leitch had three balls through him, and died a fortnight after. Nor did the Provincials fire in the air. Nineteen holes were counted in a single rail of the fence behind which the British infantry had been posted. On both sides the loss was heavy for the numbers who had been engaged. The English list of casualties was the larger; but more of the Americans were killed outright; for our light infantry were marksmen selected from all the regiments, and shot like so many backwoodsmen.[2] The conflict ended towards three in the afternoon, a couple of miles to the south of Haerlem Heights. Howe had ordered up several more English battalions, and von Donop's brigade of Hessians; and on their approach the firing ceased, and the combatants retired to their respective

[1] "I suppose many persons will think it was rash and imprudent for officers of our rank to go into such an action. General Putnam, General Greene, Mr. Tilghman, and many of the General's family were in it; but it was really done to animate the troops, who were quite dispirited, and would not go into danger unless their officers led the way." That is an extract from a letter written by the Adjutant General to his wife. One of the fugitives pointed his musket at Colonel Reed, and pulled the trigger. The Colonel thereupon seized a piece from a soldier, and snapped it at his assailant; but both guns missed fire. "He has been tried," (Reed said,) "and is now under sentence of death; but I believe I must beg him off, as, after I could not get the gun off, I wounded him in the head, and cut off his thumb with my hanger." And so the man lived; and, for all that history knows, he may have figured as a mutilated soldier of the Revolution on Fourth of July platforms in the nineteenth century.

[2] "The troops fought well on both sides, and gave great proofs of their marksmanship." *General Heath's Memoirs;* September 16, 1776.

quarters. That is the account given in Washington's despatch; and his story is confirmed by a young officer in a famous English regiment, who lived to conquer Mysore at the head of the largest British army that had ever marched to victory in India. "We were trotted about three miles, (without a halt to draw breath,) to support a battalion of light infantry which had imprudently advanced so far as to be in great danger of being cut off. This must have happened, but for our haste. The instant the front of our columns appeared, the enemy began to retire to their works, and our light infantry to camp. On our return we were exposed to the fire of the Americans. A man in my company had his hat shot through, nearly in the direction of my wound, but the ball merely raised the skin." So wrote Captain Harris, of the Fifth Fusiliers, whose head had been broken by a bullet at Bunker's Hill. He had now come back from hospital, in fine spirits and with a very solid appetite,[1] to serve another turn in that rude apprenticeship which in his case was the path to lofty fortunes.

Howe claimed the affair as a success; but his best officers thought differently. Sir Henry Clinton, long afterwards, recorded his view in a note on the margin of Stedman's History. "The ungovernable impetuosity," (he wrote,) "of the light troops drew us into this scrape." Colonol von Donop, a very gallant man, and no boaster, reported that, if it had not been for the opportune arrival of his Jägers, the Highlanders and the British Light Infantry would perhaps have been

[1] "We placed our picquets; borrowed a sheep; killed, cooked, and ate some of it; and then went to sleep on a gate which we took the liberty of throwing off its hinges. The sixteenth of September, before we started in the morning, our dinner, consisting of a goose and a piece of mutton, had been put on the fire. Our domestic deposited the above-named delicacies on a chaise, and followed us with it to our ground. When the fight was over, he again hung the goose to the fire, but the poor bird had been scarcely half done when we were ordered to return to our station. There again we commenced cooking, and, though without dish, or plate, or knife, did ample justice to our fare, which we washed down with bad rum and water, and then composed ourselves to rest on our friendly gate." Captain George Harris to his uncle; September 1776.

captured. Von Donop's estimate of the serious char-acter of the engagement at Haerlem was shared by the professional grumblers of the army, who were not so modest, and most of them not so brave, as the veteran German. One of these gentry took into his confidence some American prisoners confined on a hulk which was stationed in the Bay. On Sunday, (we are told,) he came on board, abusing the Yankees for runaway cowards, who would not stand their ground long enough to give a British officer a chance of getting honour and promotion. He was in the Monday's action also, and returned in the evening cursing the war, and saying that, after all, the Americans would fight, and that it would be impossible to conquer them.[1] Washington, in measured and tranquil language, imparted the relief and satisfaction, which filled his own mind, to the pleased and repentant army. "The behaviour of yesterday," (so ran his General Order of September the seventeenth,) " was such a contrast to that of some troops the day before as must show what can be done where officers and soldiers exert themselves." And so it comes about that Haerlem, — though not among the decisive, and still less the gigantic, battles of the world, — has always been fondly regarded by American writers as a turning-point in the uphill progress of their national military efficiency.

The spread of New York City has obliterated all rustic features of the locality ; for the district over which the contest swayed to and fro now lies between One Hundred and Fifth Street to the south, and One Hundred and Thirty-first Street to the northward. Patriotic antiquaries must find what consolation they may in the reflection that the hollow lane, into which the British skirmishers rashly descended, and the bush-grown ledges where Knowlton fell, are now worth a great many more dollars a square yard than the sacred soil of Thermopylæ or Bannockburn. A very different fate,

---

[1] Extract from the MS. *Literary Diary and Journal of Occurrences* kept by Dr. Stiles, in possession of Yale University, as given in Mr. Johnston's *Battle of Haerlem Heights*.

from the point of the picturesque, has befallen another
Haerlem, from which the American village originally
derived its name. On the narrow north front of that
old Dutch city lie the bastion of the Cross and the bastion of St. John, where over the space of six full months
a terrible conflict raged between the burgesses and their
wives on the one hand, and the son and the soldiers of
Alva on the other. Those bastions now form the ter-
race-walks of a little pleasure ground, sloping down to
an ornamental canal which formerly was the town moat.
It is a scene to be visited in early summer. Then, out
of the sweet green foliage, just across the water, in a
bend of the winding pool, there rises a graceful tower
attached to an ancient almshouse. All the front part of
the building, which the Dutch cannon ruined, was re-
constructed in the seventeenth century; but a closer
examination discovers, to the rear of the group of dwellings, a small outhouse which, in the gable of its high-
pitched roof, displays a date some ten years anterior to
the siege of 1573, and which looks its age. Behind those
very walls the veterans from Spain and Italy were over
and over again mustered, in preparation for furious and
fruitless assaults on the crumbling breach and the starving garrison. Nowhere, perhaps, are associations so
thrilling, and so authentic, gathered around so fair a
spot as that which the long death-grapple between martial discipline, and homely valour, made horrible for a
space of time, and ennobled for ever.

CHAPTER XX

DURING the rest of the summer Howe lingered at New
York, opposite the American lines, which were elab-
orately fortified, and manned by six times as many
troops as were sufficient to defend them.   He easily
found a justification for not attempting to carry that
impregnable position by direct assault.   In 1779, when
he was addressing the House of Commons in his own
defence, he laid it down as the most essential duty of a
general never wantonly to expose His Majesty's troops
in a case where the required end could be attained with
little bloodshed.   As for Haerlem Heights, (he truly
urged,) the loss of a thousand or fifteen hundred Royal
soldiers would have been an excessive price to pay for
the capture of intrenchments which the Americans
could not have held, even for a very few days, after
the British had once begun to break ground towards
their own right flank by proceeding to occupy the
neighbouring peninsula of Westchester.   The reasons,
however, which Howe gave for allowing those very few
days to extend themselves into not a few weeks were
miserably inadequate.   He pleaded ignorance of the
mainland which lay to the eastward.   The country,
(he said,) was ill adapted for reconnoitring-parties of
infantry; he was badly provided with cavalry, for most
of his horse-transports were still on their passage out
from England; and little or nothing could be learned
from the inhabitants, who were totally unable to supply
a military description of the districts in which they
resided.   Nor was this the only, or the most serious,

point on which Howe's expectations of assistance from the American Loyalists had been falsified; for he confessed that, to his infinite chagrin, the colonists were not so well disposed to enlist in the service of the Crown as, before leaving England, he had been taught to anticipate.[1]

Some years after this date, — when the most sanguine among the English Ministers had given up all hopes of conquering the North in the North itself, and when the war had been transferred to the Southern provinces, — inhabitants of those provinces freely rallied to the British standards. In the course of the long and dubious struggle for the possession of Georgia and the Carolinas, the Royal cause was aided, and sometimes sadly discredited, by bands of numerous, devoted, and much too truculent partisans. But taking into account the whole of the Southern levies, — and including all the King's Rangers, and Queen's Rangers, and Royal Fencibles, and Royal Guides and Pioneers, and Loyal American Legionaries, and Prince of Wales's Volunteers, throughout the entire continent, — the sum total of colonists who took arms for the Crown, between 1775 and 1783, did not exceed twenty-five thousand. During those years the State of Massachusetts alone furnished thrice that number of recruits to the armies of the Republic.[2]

A very interesting description of rural Loyalists

---

[1] Sir William Howe's speech of April 22, 1779, in the *Parliamentary History of England;* Vol. XX., pages 679, 680. When examined before Parliament in the May of the same year, Lord Cornwallis stated that a knowledge of America, for military purposes, was extremely difficult to be obtained from the inhabitants. Little or no information, (he said,) could be got by reconnoitring, as the country was everywhere hilly, and covered with wood ; intersected by ravines, creeks, and marshes ; and presenting at every quarter of a mile a post fitted for ambuscades.

[2] Chapters iv. and viii. of the Historical Essay prefixed to Sabine's *American Loyalists.* Mr. Sabine is a just-minded and well-informed writer ; and his feeling towards the Loyalists of the Revolution was such that he might safely be trusted not to under-rate the sacrifices which they made to their opinions. A return of the numbers of men, contributed by each several State to the Continental Army, was prepared by General Knox after the war had ended, and was recently reprinted by order of Congress, at the suggestion of Senator Cabot Lodge. According to this return Massachusetts, from first to last, furnished 78,471 soldiers.

in the province of New York is given by Mr. Henry
Dawson, a writer of our own generation, whose sympathies, if not hostile to the Revolution, are at all events
very strongly against the Revolutionists.   The farmers
of Westchester County, in Mr. Dawson's view, were
universally conservatives; but "their simple domestic
habits, and controlling love of home," rendered them
averse to fight for their political creed.   Their fidelity
to the Royal cause, (so he tells us,) was inspired by
recollections of the quiet times which they had enjoyed
under the Royal Government; when good feeling between
neighbours, regard among friends, and affection in
families, had not yet been banished from their corner
of the earth; before ever the strife of faction prevailed
through the land, and the people "hunted every man
his brother with a net."[1]   Tories were Tories because
they loved and regretted the old peaceful days; and, if
they could not get back peace as a community, they
were determined to have as small a share of war as possible in their character of individuals.   Few, of their own
choice, joined the Royal army; and those among them
whom Whig persecution drove from their homes, and
constrained to take refuge in the English ranks, became
reluctant and exceedingly unprofessional soldiers.   The
innocent letters which they wrote to their parents from
camp fully explain what Sir William Howe, and Lord
Cornwallis, meant when they told the House of Commons
that very little military information of value could be
extracted from the country folk of New York and New
Jersey.   It may readily be believed that the Selectman
of a loyal district, with the best will in the world to
assist King George's officers, could not throw much
light upon the strength, and probable destination, of an
American column which had marched once across his
township, when his sons in the cantonments on Long
Island failed to guess, within fifty thousand men, the
numbers of the British and Hessians in the midst of

[1] Paper by Mr. Henry B. Dawson, inserted in the *History of Westchester
County*, New York.

whom they lived, and whose battalions they might count, like so many pawns on a chess-board, as often as the army was paraded.[1]

Howe remained in front of Washington's position for four livelong weeks after the fight at Haerlem, slowly and painfully erecting earthworks which the American spadesmen would have thrown up in the course of as many days and nights; writing testy despatches to the War Office in London; and chaffering with the American Government about the relative value of the prisoners whom he had lost and the prisoners whom he had captured. A bargain was at length concluded. Lord Stirling was exchanged for a Royal governor, and Sullivan for an English brigadier named Prescott, whom Montgomery had taken at Montreal. Howe sent over for Washington's inspection a bullet fixed on the end of a nail, which had been found in a deserted American encampment, and expressed himself as well assured that the contrivance had not come to the knowledge of the American commander; and Washington replied that no pains should be spared in order to prevent so wicked and infamous a practice being adopted in his army. It was a very interesting correspondence, but the price of postage was excessively high; inasmuch as every additional fortnight that Howe loitered on Manhattan Island cost the British Treasury more than the whole annual revenue derived from the British Post Office. On the night of the twentieth of September a conflagration broke out in New York City, and consumed more than a tenth part of the

[1] "Honoured Mother, and Brothers, and Sister, it hath pleased God of his Bountiful goodness, among the rest of abilities Bestowed upon me, to give me a small use of the Pen, the Noblest of Arts, that I may convey the Ideas of my mind Though at ever so great a Distance. It hath been my Misfortune to Seek on this Island a place of Refuge from wicked and ungodly men. Eli is well; and likewise I are well. Caleb and Nathan are well likewise. Our army Consists now of Eighty Thousand, Besides Rangers, and 200 Transports is expected every day laden with men. Unless the rebels lay down their arms, and accept of Mercy, they will be destroyed and cut off." Letter from Newtown, Long Island; Sept. 28, 1776.

four thousand tenements before the troops and sailors could get the flames under. In the panic and wrath consequent upon such an event, at such a moment, each of the adversaries accused the other of having deliberately set the town on fire. The British and German soldiers, being the stronger party of the two, acted upon their own theory of the case, and executed summary and indiscriminate vengeance upon individuals whom they suspected. "The gentleman," wrote Washington, "who brought the letter from General Howe, told Colonel Reed that several of our countrymen had been punished with various deaths, some by hanging, others by burning." Governor Tryon, judging another by himself, did not scruple to affirm that Washington had devised the plot; had selected and instructed the actual incendiaries; and had sent all the bells of the churches out of town, under pretence of casting them into cannon, in order to prevent the alarm of fire being given from the steeples.[1] An exhaustive collection and collation of evidence has proved that the calamity was accidental.[2] Whatever might have been its origin, the affair was an object-lesson of real importance; for the soldiers of the Government by whose orders Falmouth and Norfolk were laid in ashes had it very forcibly brought home to their convictions that it was a crime to destroy a town.[2]

At length Howe once more set his troops in motion; and the movement, though tardy, was strongly and

---

[1] Governor Tryon to Lord George Germaine ; New York, Sept. 24, 1776.

[2] The Librarian of the New York Historical Society has been good enough to place in my hands a paper drawn up by his late brother, Mr. William Kelby, who preceded him in his present office. This compilation, printed in 1866 in the *Manual* of the Corporation of the City of New York, contains extracts relating to the Great Fire taken from histories written near the time, from official despatches, from authoritative newspaper reports, and from contemporary private letters. There was talk of a thousand, or even fifteen hundred, buildings having perished ; but the most precise computation, which classed the houses destroyed according to the districts, placed them at four hundred and ninety-three. A great multitude of persons were arrested and examined ; but no evidence was found against them, and they, one and all, were set at liberty. In a city under military government, and in a case where severity to the utmost limit of justice was a public duty, such lenity would never have been displayed

thoughtfully planned; as was the case with all his operations throughout the campaign until the period arrived when success had relaxed the springs of caution. His scheme was to leave, behind his intrenchments on Manhattan Island, a force adequate to protect New York from attack during the next few days; and within a few days the danger would be over. He himself purposed to shift eastwards, and place his main army in the peninsula of Westchester, on the flank and rear of the Americans, directly between them and their base of supply in Connecticut. British warships, meanwhile, were to ascend the North River, and cut off Washington from a retreat into the province of New Jersey. With promptitude, conduct, and a reasonable share of good fortune, Howe had every hope of capturing the best and largest part of the American forces. The project, in the earlier stages, was ably and luckily executed. Lord Percy, with three brigades, took charge of the fortifications which covered the city. At dawn on the twelfth of October, 1776, eighty vessels, of all sorts and sizes, heavily laden with British troops, passed between Montresor's Island and the northern shore of Long Island, and stood up the Sound; and they were followed in the afternoon of the same day by another fleet of from forty to fifty sail. The whole force was disembarked at Frog's Point, in the extreme southeast corner of the Westchester peninsula.[1] The withdrawal of the army from the vicinity of the American camp,

if there had been any serious belief in the minds of the authorities that the fire was intentional.

Nothing is known of the antecedents of those who were put to death on the night of the conflagration, except in one case only. " There were very few inhabitants in the city at that time; and many of those were afraid to venture out at night in the streets, fearing of being taken up as suspicious persons. An instance to my knowledge occurred. A Mr. White, a decent citizen and house-carpenter, rather too violent a loyalist, who latterly had addicted himself to liquor, was on the night of the fire hanged on a tavern sign-post at the corner of Cherry and Roosevelt streets." That passage occurs in Mr. David Trim's narrative.

[1] These places are all indicated, and the general features of the campaign portrayed, in the map at the end of this volume.

and its removal to a new scene of action, were concealed from hostile eyes by a thick fog which enshrouded land and sea.   That circumstance, however,
neither disturbed nor impeded the naval operations; so
perfect were Lord Howe's arrangements, and so admirable the skill of our sailors, and the discipline of
our soldiers, amid a maze of tortuous channels and
rapid and uncertain currents.   General Howe spent
six days in the immediate neighbourhood of the spot
where he had landed; while the ships went and came,
laden with his military stores and provisions, as well as
with the horses and waggons required for their convey-
ance on the journey up-country.   That interval of time
may have been well employed; but, when the advance
at last began, the forward movement of the British
was dilatory beyond all explanation or conception.   It
was not until the twenty-fifth of October that their
columns encamped on Bronx River; a league, and more,
to the south of the White Plains.   The sun had set
and risen more than forty times since General Howe
broke up his summer cantonments on Staten Island.
In seven weeks, — with an irresistible army, and a fleet
which there was nothing to resist, — he had traversed,
from point to point, a distance of exactly thirty miles.

Thus far into the bowels of the land had he marched,
but, (unlike the Earl of Richmond in Shakespeare's
drama,) not without impediment.   When Washington
had assured himself that the war was transferred to the
mainland which lay to the east of him, he passed his
army over King's Bridge, and edged it gradually northwards along the right bank of the Bronx River.   His
progress was slow and painful; for almost all his provision of wheel-transport had been abandoned on Long
Island, or captured by the British in New York; and
he could not avail himself of water-carriage because
Lord Howe's forty-four-gun ships had got past his batteries on the Hudson River, and had acquired an undis-
puted mastery of the upper, as well as the lower, reaches.
With the double object of delaying General Howe's

advance, and teaching his own troops to stand fire, Washington detached strong parties in a southernly direction with a commission to watch and, (wherever they saw an opportunity,) to harass the enemy. His people behaved well in several brisk encounters; and they were all the more pleased with themselves because their successes were won against a corps of Provincial loyalists, who, in their judgement, had no call to help the invaders, and against Hessians who had no business in the country at all. The activity of the American riflemen multiplied their apparent numbers to the imagination of their opponents, and provided Howe with a motive, or an excuse, for altogether superfluous prudence and deliberation. When he arrived near White Plains he found Washington's army already planted across his path. He again waited three days; and then, on Monday the twenty-eighth of October, orders were issued for a general engagement which, however ineffectually it terminated, at all events began in earnest.

Of that engagement there exist numerous narratives, as rich in similes drawn from the phenomena of nature as any battle of Homer. "We fired a volley at the Hessian Grenadiers at about twenty rods distance, and scattered them like leaves in a whirlwind. They ran away so far that some of our regiments ran out to the ground where they were, and brought off their arms and accoutrements, and rum, that the men who fell had with them; which we had time to drink round before they came on again."[1] So cheerful was the account subsequently transmitted to the newspapers by a Gentleman in General Washington's Army; but that army, to all appearance, cannot be said to have enjoyed itself greatly at the time. The Americans were ill posted; and their performance was what might be expected from raw troops who had some good stuff among them. A considerable body of Provincial infantry with which, (if only it had held its ground,) the advancing British would first have come in contact, re-

[1] *American Archives;* November 1776.

treated hastily and in confusion. Howe next assaulted a bold and rocky eminence, situated a mile to the west of the lines behind which the main force of the Americans lay. This isolated height, known as Chatterton's Hill, was occupied by a few slender battalions, numbering barely fourteen hundred men, who defended the position with coolness and tenacity. They were assailed by eight well-drilled regiments, supported by a powerful artillery to which they had very inadequate means of replying.[1] It was afterwards said by the Hessian Adjutant General that the German batteries made a thunderstorm, in which no man could either see or hear;[2] and the effect, as witnessed from across the valley, was still more impressive. The scene, (wrote an American officer,) was grand and solemn; the adjacent hills bellowed and trembled, and smoked like volcanoes; the air groaned with streams of shot, and echoed with the bursting of shells; and men's limbs and bodies strewed the ground, and the fences and walls were torn in pieces.

All the same, there was plenty of cover left; and the Marylanders and New Yorkers took steady aim from behind it. They and their comrades kept in play five regiments which attacked them in front, and retired only when three other regiments had turned their left flank. They got away safely "in a great body; neither running, nor observing the best order."[3] None of their wounded, who could stand upon their feet, remained behind to be taken. The Delaware regiment, which had learned at Long Island that prisoners are not easily

[1] Lieutenant Colonel Haslet, who commanded the Delaware battalion, wrote as follows: "The General ordered one field-piece forward, and that so poorly appointed that myself was forced to assist in dragging it along in rear of the regiment. While so employed a cannon-ball struck the carriage, and scattered the shot about ; a wad of tow blazing in the middle. The artillerymen fled. One alone was prevailed upon to tread out the blaze and collect the shot." There were three American cannon somewhere on the hill ; but that is the only gun of which the history is authentically known.

[2] *The Hessians, and the other German Auxiliaries of Great Britain in the Revolutionary War;* by Edward J. Lowell ; New York, 1884.

[3] *Memoirs of Major General Heath.*

made unless they make themselves, brought up the rear, and fought sullenly and composedly while any of the assailants followed them within shooting range. But the pursuit was neither long nor fierce. When the British and the Germans arrived on the summit of Chatterton's Hill, they formed and dressed their line. Their arms glittered in the bright sun; and to the view of Washington and the generals around him, who in their own camp saw little of war under its ornamental aspect, they made a most gallant show. That was the end of the battle. Neither on the same day, nor afterwards, did Howe thrust his whole army at, and across, the American lines with vigour and intention such as Frederic displayed against the Austrians at Prague, or Wellington against the French on the Nivelle and the Bidassoa. The position occupied by Washington on the twenty-eighth of October was not strong by nature; and the attempt to make it formidable by art had been baffled by the stony character of the soil, which did not admit of the ditches being deep or the parapets high.[1] Though there is, of course, no certainty in war, it is the first business of a general to discern, and to decide, what risks should be taken. Howe had travelled all the way from England in order to destroy the American army; and he now had such a chance at it as never occurred again. But in every heap of fresh-turned mould he seemed to see the blood-stained earthworks of Bunker's Hill; and he was appalled by the possibility, — the only thing in the world of which he was afraid, — that he might have to look on at a slaughter of his soldiers from that safe distance where, as Commander-in-Chief, he himself was in duty bound to remain.[2] At White Plains,

---

[1] *History of Westchester County;* Vol. I., page 449. The story of White Plains is there told with scrupulous care, and in vast detail.

[2] Howe's promotion was differently viewed by the ladies of a family which had already lost one beloved and revered member in the warfare of the American forests. "Mrs. Howe," said Lady Sarah Bunbury, "is vastly better since the General was made Commander-in-Chief; for he is at least safe for a time, and safe from bush-fighting, which seemed the most to be dreaded as more frequent than a regular action."

so far as the affair had gone, there was very little carnage. The Americans, who ran, had run so soon, —
and those who stood had fought so knowingly, — that
their loss, all told, did not exceed two hundred men.
Of English and Germans something more than that
number were killed or wounded; and particular sympathy was expressed in the British mess-tents for a
Colonel of the Thirty-fifth Foot, who was shot dead in
front of his regiment a short while after he had come
into a legacy of forty thousand pounds.[1]

Howe had the less reason for omitting to press his
advantage because he had quite recently obtained some
fresh troops, who for the most part were eager for battle. He was reinforced just before the engagement, in
the very presence of the enemy, by another division of
Hessians, four thousand strong; by the contingent from
the Principality of Waldeck; and by two English regiments of Light Dragoons. One of them was commanded
by the Honourable William Harcourt, an accomplished
leader of cavalry, and an officer whose curious fate destined him, at the most critical moment of the war, to perform an inestimable service to the American cause. It
is quite unnecessary to say that he was an honourable and
virtuous man; seeing that in after years he became, and
long remained, the intimate personal friend of George the
Third, who had a very different standard for the companions of his private life, and for the instruments of his
public policy. Colonel Harcourt now, at the age of three-
and-thirty, was going out to serve his King in buoyant
humour, and amply provided with all appliances which
could conduce to his dignity and comfort. He was the
younger son of the first Earl Harcourt, then Lord Lieutenant of Ireland, a nobleman of the good old school.
Rich and public-spirited, Lord Harcourt had raised a regiment for the defence of the country during the rebellion of
1745; and, when the son became a captain of cavalry, his
entire troop was enlisted and equipped at the father's
cost. Now that Colonel Harcourt was sailing for

[1] *Journal* kept during the campaign by Colonel Enoch Markham.

America in high command there was nothing which his family thought too good for him. They wanted to marry him to an heiress; a part of his outfit which he emphatically declined to accept.[1] His father pressed upon him a whole sideboard of plate, from which he selected a few useful and portable articles. He took in his train a Swiss servant, an old hussar who had smelt powder in the Seven Years' War; a cook who had served Lord Dunmore and General Gage; and a groom who had made a sea voyage with horses to the West Indies. "Your mind," (so the Colonel informed Lord Harcourt,) "will be perfectly at ease when I tell you that the transport in which I propose to embark is an extreme good sailer, remarkably strong, and very commodious; and, what is of still more consequence, that I am sure of having the Agent of Transports with me. In short, I shall have every advantage of a man-of-war, without any of its inconveniences."[2]

Harcourt, however, was no carpet soldier. He was always prepared to take the rough with the smooth; and on his way out to America he had it very rough indeed. He started from Portsmouth late in June; and the nineteenth of July found the convoy at Falmouth, replenishing water and forage, after two unsuccessful attempts to get clear of the Channel. His regiment reached New York on the seventh of October, having lost on the passage enough horses to have mounted half a troop. Harcourt's own chargers, however, bore the

[1] "I could not do more than catch a sight of the girl at Ranelagh. With respect to her person, I cannot say it is either disgusting or the contrary; but I find that the father is a vulgar fellow, and that he has already offered his daughter to half a dozen different people, — among whom are Charles Fox and Bolingbroke, — who have all of them broken off on the subject of Settlement. I am free to declare that I would rather marry an amiable woman, whom I liked, than this girl with all her pretensions, and what is worse, with all her family." Letter from Colonel Harcourt of May 23, 1776. Vol. XII. of the *Harcourt Papers;* Edited by Edward William Harcourt of Stanton Harcourt, and Nuneham Courtney, in the county of Oxfordshire.

[2] Colonel the Hon. W. Harcourt to his father, Earl Harcourt; Harcourt House, April 3, 1776.

journey well; and the army was soon talking both of them and of him. On a scouting expedition, (for he liked to see near-hand and with his own eyes,) he was once in imminent danger of being captured; whereupon he put his thorough-bred at a very high fence, knocked off the top rail, and rejoined his men in safety. But he could ride towards the enemy as well as away from them. Great things were expected of the British cavalry by the Government at home, and especially by Lord George Germaine, the Colonial Secretary;[1] and that expectation was not disappointed. At White Plains, their eagerness to advance within stroke of sabre was a main incentive to that premature retirement of the American advance-guard by which the engagement was prefaced. Indeed, the unexpected apparition of mounted warriors, among those armies of infantry, created an impression somewhat similar to that produced by the cavaliers of Pizarro and Cortés upon the primitive inhabitants of Peru and Mexico. Washington, in grave and measured phrases, confessed that his militiamen seemed unacquainted with the enemy's horse, and did not meet them with the same alacrity which they showed in other cases. Having no dragoons of his own, he did his best to combat the apprehensions of the soldiers by a General Order. Speaking from his long military experience, he assured them that, in a broken country full of stone walls, cavalry were the least formidable of all adversaries, because they could not leave the roads; and he promised them a hundred dollars for every trooper whom they could bring in prisoner with his horse and his accoutrements.

A very few days elapsed; and Howe's opportunity for forcing Washington to a battle on Westchester peninsula had finally departed. On the last night of Octo-

---

[1] "A great man in Administration," (so the *Public Advertiser* reported,) "whose military knowledge is unquestionable, is said to build his principal hopes as to a conquest of America upon the activity and resolution of the British Light Horse; who, (it is to be presumed,) are to gallop somewhat faster than the cavalry did at Minden."

ber, the Americans retired to a line of heights a short distance in rear of their former position. Felling the timber with the energy of a people who, during almost every year of their history, had cleared away as much forest as would cover half an English county, — and building the trunks into a wall, and interlacing the branches into an abattis, with practised dexterity, — in an incredibly short space of time they made their front as impenetrable as the curtain of a fortress. There they awaited the turn of events, in fairly good case, and with great and increasing complacency. A Massachusetts Brigadier told the authorities of his State that the Continental troops were stationed on a ridge of hills almost inaccessible on the side which faced the enemy, and finely covered with woods. Officers and soldiers, (so the despatch ran,) were in high spirits, and determined not to yield an inch to the invader. The British were labouring to out-flank them; but the General, divinely inspired, had been apprised of the design, and Howe would soon have to tread his surly steps back to the quarter whence he came.[1] The Americans, (this officer went on to say,) had not more sick than might be expected in so numerous an army; and there was good flour, beef, and pork in plenty, with grog to wash it down. "A lordly mansion," (a worthy New England Colonel wrote,) "never contained more health and contentment than the little cell, half underground, that I occupy here in the fields, dwelling with my own people."[2] The accounts from the front were so exhilarating that civilians at a distance were tempted to visit a scene where they might find the pleasure of intense excitement, combined with every circumstance of security.

[1] The same view had for some while been held by Captain Tilghman, who was already an acting aide-de-camp to Washington, and as good a judge as most. "I am really in hopes," (he wrote on the twenty-third of October,) "that we have fairly outflanked General Howe. We press him close to the ground, from which he has made no Westing, in the sea-phrase; and if he makes much more Easting, and endeavours to stretch across, he will need as large an army as Xerxes to form a line."

[2] Colonel Jedediah Huntingdon of Connecticut to Governor Trumbull.

"Mrs. Clinton," (her husband was informed,) "has a great desire to see the enemy routed. If there is any action while she is near camp, she wishes to go on a hill and see it, if you should not be engaged in it, which she would wish to know at the time." [1]

A most dangerous optimism, from which the Commander-in-Chief almost alone was free, reigned throughout the American army. As the actual experiences of Long Island, and Haerlem, and White Plains, receded in the distance, the distressful emotions of battle faded from the memory of the common men ; and only a sense of self-respect, and even self-admiration, remained. The militia began to regard themselves as invincible ; a persuasion which was accompanied by a strong, and to very many of them an uncontrollable, impulse to go back to their families, and tell them by word of mouth what heroes they had been. The satisfaction which very generally prevailed among the higher officers was expressed by Charles Lee, in unusually moderate and accurate language, when he congratulated Washington on the several advantages which their troops had lately gained, "though each small, yet in the whole considerable ; encouraging to the army and depressing to the enemy." [2] A sudden access of over-confidence, for the first and the last time in his military career, had affected the masculine intellect of Nathanael Greene. That was a very serious matter ; for Greene was no idle or timid

[1] Letter of Nov. 3, 1776, from John McKesson to General George Clinton, the Governor of New York State. The lady had over-rated her courage. A week afterwards the General heard from his niece, Miss Mary Tappen. "Mr. Addison," the girl said, "set out last Sunday with aunt Clinton for the Camp, but were terrified out of their wits at Fishkill. I think they are both cowards. O, Uncle, how much I am distressed when I think on the Situation of this country ! Do you think we are in great danger here this winter ? "

[2] Lee to Washington ; Oct. 27, 1776. Ten days afterwards Lee wrote to Benjamin Franklin. "We have," he said, "by proper measures brought Mr. Howe to his *ne plus ultra*. The spirit of our troops is on the whole good ; and, if America is lost, it is not, in my opinion, owing to want of courage in your soldiers ; but, (pardon me,) to want of prudence in Your High Mightinesses ! "

theorist, but a man instinctively impelled to translate his ideas, without delay, into vigorous and fearless action. Meanwhile General Howe's hesitating strategy, — resulting, as it had done, in a series of small reverses alternating with unremunerative successes, — had produced a sense of depression in the British ranks. For the first time since the campaign opened, our officers had become alive to the peculiar difficulties of the task upon which they were now engaged. Veterans, who had served with Prince Ferdinand in the plains of Western Germany, remembered the excellent roads along which Lord Granby's cavalry had made forced marches towards the sound of the cannon ; and the level forests of scientifically planted fir-trees, bare of underwood, which presented no unmanageable obstacle to an advancing infantry. They contrasted those halcyon days with the week which they had lately spent in traversing fifteen miles of marsh and thicket, swarming with backwoodsmen who seemed positively to enjoy the hazards of partisan warfare, and who spent hours in crawling about to get a shot "with their cursed twisted guns," which in their hands killed at three times the effective range of a regular musket.[1] A Colonel of the Guards, who had been invalided home within a few days after White Plains, told his friends in London that the country was so hilly, and the rebels such excellent marksmen, that it was almost impossible to catch them. Most of his comrades in the Guards, he said, had been very ill with the flux; and General Howe was urgent upon the Secretary at War to send him out one more officer for each company.[2]

If such was the feeling in a crack English regiment,

[1] An English officer who made a special study of the shooting in the American war, and who himself gained proficiency with the rifle, said that the best hunters of the Indian frontier, in a good light, when there was no wind to deflect the bullet, could hit a man's head at two hundred yards, or his body at three hundred, with great certainty.

[2] Letter, (hitherto unpublished,) from Captain the Hon. Richard Fitzpatrick, to his brother Lord Ossory, in the Russell collection of the Fox Correspondence.

it may well be believed that dejection and discontent prevailed among the less military-minded of the German conscripts. "Our scouting parties," wrote an officer on Washington's staff, "are very active and successful. Yesterday they brought in five British prisoners, and this morning twelve Waldeckers. The latter are amazed at the kind treatment they receive. They say they were torn away from their own country, and will willingly remain among us. They say that, if their fellow-soldiers knew how they would be treated, and how plentifully and happily they live, they would lay down their arms and come amongst us." These poor wretches did not claim to express the sentiments of Hessians or Brunswickers ; but the event proved that they had every title to speak for the Waldeck regiment. That regiment, during the next five years, neither did nor suffered much ; but at length its turn came. When hostilities commenced between England and Spain, the Waldeckers were stationed at points along the coast of Florida and Louisiana. In September 1781 a detachment of them capitulated on Lake Pontchartrain, and three entire companies at Baton Rouge. There is a letter, referring to these occurrences, from the head-quarters of the battalion at Pensacola, written by their chaplain. "Is not this a cursed country," the reverend gentleman asked, "in which to make war, where the greater part of a corps may be prisoners for five weeks, and the commanding general not know it with certainty ? " Certainty, however, soon arrived with the advent of a Spanish fleet, which took the town of Pensacola, and captured all that remained of the Waldeckers. Europe was ripe for the Revolution when a petty German prince could fill his purse by sending ship-loads of peasants to fight on the Gulf of Mexico, for a cause that was neither his nor theirs, against Spaniards who had never before even heard of Waldeck, any more than the rank and file of the Waldeckers had any intelligent notion about Spain.

The arrival of most re-assuring intelligence from another quarter enhanced the hopefulness which already permeated the American ranks. While Washington's army still lay in Westchester peninsula, it became known that, for many months to come, all danger from the North was past and over. On the fourth of October Sir Guy Carleton set in motion his military and naval forces, which were both of them excellent in quality and very formidable in numbers. Benedict Arnold was already at his post, on the flank of the route which the English commander was bound to follow. The American war-ships had started from Crown Point badly provided in most other respects, but with large and generous sailing orders. Arnold was instructed not to go beyond a certain distance down the lake; but everything else was left to his enterprise and discretion. He set out in a singular humour, and under very remarkable circumstances indeed. The main object of the campaign was already as good as accomplished, inasmuch as the fame of him, and of his squadron, had delayed Carleton's advance during ten precious weeks of summer; and, on the other hand, the impending battle might be reckoned by anticipation as a British victory. Compared with Carleton's vessels, the American sloops and galleys were mere cock-boats; carrying fewer cannon of smaller calibre, unhandy to steer and sail, and beyond any comparison less abundantly and effectively manned. On the eve of the encounter Arnold was expecting a large draft of New England seamen; but they never appeared. " I hope to be excused," (he wrote,) "if with five hundred men, half naked, I should not be able to beat the enemy." With ships which could not work to windward,[1] Arnold shunned the open water, and anchored his Armada, (as it was proudly called by Americans who were not going to fight on board of it,) in the channel between Valcour Island and the western shore. He had borrowed Dr. Price's pamphlet on

[1] Richard Varick to General Gates; Gates to Arnold. *American Archives* for October 1776.

Civil Liberty, from a friend who had borrowed it of Franklin, to read if ever he found time to repose on his cot and nurse his wounded leg; and on deck he enjoyed a view which lovers of the romantic now go many miles to contemplate. No less a judge than Nathaniel Hawthorne rated Lake Champlain as on a level of beauty with Windermere, and above Loch Lomond.[1]

At early morning on the eleventh of October the sails of the British fleet came into view, moving up the lake with a fair breeze behind them. Sir Guy Carleton himself was on one of their quarter-decks. As the leader of a conjoint expedition, he thought it right to share the dangers incurred by both the services for whose conduct he was responsible; but he did not interfere in matters which lay outside his own profession, and the manœuvres were directed by a post-captain of the Royal Navy. The whole squadron swept around the southeast point of Valcour Island, placed themselves in rear of the enemy, and tacked, or rowed, upwind towards the mouth of the channel where the Americans were stationed. Carleton's lighter craft, which were exceedingly numerous, soon drew ahead; and Arnold sallied forth in his flag-ship, (if such a name might be applied to a twelve-gun schooner,) in order to engage them before their more powerful consorts could beat up to their assistance. But his crew of landsmen ran their vessel aground; and, at the very outset of the affair, he lost the only one of his ships which could even by courtesy be termed a man-of-war.

Arnold transferred himself and his flag to the Congress, which was nothing more than a rowing galley with mast and sails. Half an hour after mid-day a score, and over, of Royal gun-boats attacked the American line at anchor in the narrow strait. It was Aboukir Bay, on a very small scale, and with a tough customer on either side. A horde of savages in British

---

[1] Hawthorne's *English Note-books*. Valcour Island and Crown Point as well as other places in the vicinity of Lake Champlain, are given in the map of the Northern Provinces at the end of this volume.

pay, who filled the woods both on the island and the main-shore, kept the air alive with a storm of bullets: but their shooting, as usual with the Indians, was detestably bad; and Arnold had protected his decks from rifle-fire by a barricade of faggots. The English cannon, plied carefully and at very close quarters, were a more weighty factor in the business of the afternoon. Junior officers, who are endowed with dash and emulation, generally contrive to be among the number of the selected whenever a naval brigade goes on special service; and the squadron on the Canadian station had contributed the pick of its ward-rooms and gun-rooms in order to increase the efficiency of Carleton's flotilla on the Lakes. American sailors, who survived that day's work, long talked about the skill with which the commander of a certain English boom-ketch chose a berth for his vessel, and the precision with which he pitched his shells into the hostile batteries. His name has not been recorded; but there was one young fellow there present who will be remembered as long as the history of the sea is read and written. The Carleton schooner, which was under the charge of a lieutenant and a pair of midshipmen, alone of the larger British ships succeeded in reaching the central spot of the action; and she was in a very hot place indeed. The two senior officers were severely wounded; and the burden of the fight devolved upon Edward Pellew, then a lad of nineteen. Forty years afterwards, as Lord Exmouth, he bombarded and took Algiers; and in the course of that long interval he established his reputation as the most brilliant known example of a frigate-captain.[1] Pellew's earliest feat in seamanship was to rescue the Carleton, on that October evening under Valcour Island, from a position of imminent peril; and he was rewarded by being forthwith confirmed in the command of the vessel which he had saved. The Americans held their own for five livelong hours. There were no trained artillerymen on board the Congress; and Arnold pointed

[1] That is Captain Mahan's expressed opinion.

every piece himself, stepping rapidly from gun to gun, and discharging them as fast as they could be loaded. The British retired at nightfall, having effected a greater ruin than they were aware of. The Congress had received seven shots between wind and water, and another vessel had been hulled so often that she sank at her moorings in the twilight. Most of Arnold's ships had nearly all their officers killed or disabled; he had expended three-fourths of his ammunition; and the next morning would bring down upon him the whole British fleet, and not the gun-boats only. When once the Inflexible, with her eighteen cannon and her thick bulwarks, got within point-blank range of the Americans, their doom was certain.

Arnold had no mind to rest passive until his fate overtook him so long as a single chance remained; and he still had two advantages left him, for the night was hazy, and the wind in his favour. He made his arrangements with speed, and issued to his subordinates minute and precise instructions. The tactics of the backwoods, — which he had long ago mastered, and often had practised, — were cleverly adapted by him to the requirements of naval warfare. Every light was extinguished, except a single lantern upon each poop, to guide the ship that followed; and then the squadron issued forth in a formation which might truly be described as Indian file. The Congress brought up the rear; and the entire column stole, unobserved and in breathless silence, through an interstice in the line of the British fleet. The Americans soon got beyond the immediate vicinity of their enemy; but the first stage of the retreat was a short one. They bore up at an island some twelve miles to the southward, in order to patch their rigging, and stop the leaks which would have sent most of them to the bottom before ever they reached a haven of refuge. The shrouds of the Congress were in tatters, and she was all but water-logged; the other large rowing-galley, the Washington, could with difficulty be kept afloat; and some of their companions were in even sor-

rier case. Two of the armed barges, classed as "gondolas" in the technical phraseology employed on those
inland lakes, had been injured beyond hope of mending,
and were accordingly scuttled and sunk. The rest of
the party, on the afternoon of the twelfth of October,
set forth once more upon their voyage. But it now blew
from the south; Arnold's vessels, at their very best,
had never sailed well except down-wind; and his
wearied decimated crews, labouring through the succeeding night, made little progress with their oars. In
the morning of the thirteenth the fog lifted, and dis-
closed the British fleet crowding down under full sail.
Sacrificing the half to save the remainder, Arnold sig-
nalled for the commanders of the sounder vessels in his
fleet to make good their escape; while he himself, with
the crippled portion of it, courted, and obtained, the
attention of the enemy. Three English ships, carrying
more than two score of cannon between them, were soon
within musket shot.[1] The Washington struck her
colours after a few broadsides; but the Congress, and
four of the gondolas, maintained a running fight during
several hours, and were then steered into a creek ten
miles to the north of Crown Point, driven to land, and
there set on fire. Arnold stayed on board until the
flames had fairly caught; and then, the last man to
leave, he clambered along the bowsprit, and dropped
on to the beach. He always was the last man on such
occasions. The long tale of his exploits is authentic
beyond dispute or suspicion; for it is preserved in the
public records, and in the national traditions, of a people
who execrated his memory.

Arnold did not affect to disguise the magnitude of the
destruction. "Of our whole fleet," (so he wrote in his
official account,) "we have saved only two galleys, two

---

[1] According to the despatch, brought home by Lieutenant Dacres to
the British Admiralty, the action of the thirteenth of October was decided
by the Inflexible, the Carleton, and the Maria; which last-named vessel
had Sir Guy on board. The Inflexible was armed with eighteen guns, and
each of the others with twelve.

small schooners, one gondola, and one sloop." **His** fellow countrymen repaid his frankness with almost universal approbation and gratitude. He had lost them a squadron which, but for his personal exertions, would never have been built; and he had lost it to some purpose. There were those who blamed him for not having withdrawn his ships betimes into the comparative safety of the upper waters, where the river was protected by a cross-fire from the strongholds of Ticonderoga on the one bank, and Mount Independence on the other;[1] but Arnold's resolution to face a battle had been determined by broad and far-seeing considerations. Carleton had unduly delayed his onward movement out of respect for the preparations which the Americans were making for his reception; and no English General after him would have consented to be hood-winked unless it was clearly shown that those preparations, which had been so widely and ably advertised, were a reality, and not a sham. Gun-boats and galleys, in Arnold's view, were made to be expended just as much as cartridges; and any fate would be better for his ships than to skulk away in front of the British advance until they were hunted up against the shore at the head of Lake George, and there trapped and taken like so many wild fowl in a decoy. For most assuredly, even at that late season of the year, Carleton would not have halted short of Albany, or of New York itself, if the Americans, whether on lake or land, had made the ignominious confession that they were afraid of fighting.

And again, in a war extending over an endless tract of country, — where the occasions for effective action were of a sudden and unexpected nature, and in infinite variety, — it was something to know that a leader existed who was eager to hurl himself at the enemy, and fight an almost desperate battle as vigorously and obstinately as if victory were not a bare chance, but a cheerful probability. The American troops were behindhand in drill and discipline; the American generals had no near

[1] Letter of General William Maxwell from Ticonderoga; Oct. 20, 1776.

prospect of a breathing-space during which they might improve their organisation, and train their regiments; and it behoved them to supplement the deficiencies of the means at their disposal by their own fiery courage and invincible pertinacity. Arnold's example aroused an outburst of enthusiasm and martial confidence throughout the States, and most of all among those of his countrymen who were nearest to the danger. On the afternoon of the thirteenth of October Colonel Hartley, who was in charge at Crown Point, heard the reports of heavy guns coming nearer and nearer from the north, across the surface of the water. He at once sent off his invalids and his baggage; and, later in the day, he fell back upon Ticonderoga. The outside of that fortress, — so he, and every one else who had a voice in the matter, were firmly determined, — should, for that year at least, be the southern limit of the invasion. "The English," (one officer of the garrison wrote,) "are in possession of Crown Point, and we expect they may fancy this ground in a day or two. They must pay a great price for it, however; as we value it highly." There was a sufficient force at Ticonderoga, and ample stores of food; and, above all, the Americans had got Arnold back among them, with no additional bullets in him.[1] The first use that he made of his shore-legs was to walk round the fortifications, which had been scientifically laid out by no less a personage than Thaddeus Kosciusko, the Polish patriot, who was serving Congress in the capacity of a military engineer. But the execution of the plan was not so forward as the security of the place demanded; and Arnold set all hands to work on the ramparts and ditches, and mounted, in carefully chosen positions, every cannon that could be brought to bear. He assured Schuyler by letter that General Gates and himself took a bright view of the situation. Their

[1] "It has pleased Providence to preserve General Arnold. Few men ever met with so many hair-breadth escapes in so short a space of time." Gates to Schuyler; Oct. 15, 1776.

people, (he said,) were daily growing more healthy; and if properly supported, they made no doubt of stopping the enemy.[1]

It was the opinion of General Phillips, who commanded the British artillery, that, if the proper measures had been adopted, Ticonderoga would have fallen without a blow. He spoke with every right to be heard. In the course of the next summer he himself had the satisfaction of proving that his judgement was correct; for in July 1777 he dragged his guns to the top of a steep and rugged hill overlooking the fortress, and Ticonderoga thereupon was unceremoniously abandoned by the American garrison. That was an occasion when Phillips, — a veteran who had served in Germany under the inspiration of the greatest of war-ministers, — exhibited to the younger generation a characteristic specimen of what might justly be styled the Chatham touch. Carleton, however, in October 1776, considered that he had effected, if not enough for one year, at any rate as much as the lateness of the season permitted him to attempt. Even if he could capture Ticonderoga, his serious difficulties would only then begin. Co-operation with Sir William Howe was the express object of the Northern campaign; and, to do any good, Carleton should have been at Albany at least six weeks anterior to the date when he actually reached Crown Point. It was no light matter, after November had set in, to undertake a winter expedition across a hundred miles of forest; beset on his march, in flank and rear, by gathering multitudes of frontiersmen, and with an army in front of him constantly strengthened by fresh contingents of militia pouring in from every province of New England. Nor would the powers of offence possessed by the Americans be frittered away, or left unused; because, (whoever might be their titular general between one engagement and another,) their fighting line in the hour of battle would infallibly be directed by Benedict Arnold, a leader equally at home on both elements,

[1] Arnold to Schuyler; Oct. 15, 1776.

wherever shot was flying. Carleton almost at once began to withdraw his army in the direction of Canada; and on the third of November his rear-guard evacuated Crown Point. One very large section of his followers accepted his decision with deep and placid resignation. The feelings of the Germans were expressed in a letter written by General Riedesel to his charming wife, who had already got as far as London on her way to join him. "Our campaign is at an end; and I shall go back to Three Rivers, where I am to be stationed, and await you with the greatest impatience. Oh how happy I should be if you came this winter, and I could enjoy your pleasant society! The winter-quarters will be very quiet, and I should be able to live entirely for you. General Carleton, like a hero, has routed the enemy's fleet, having left behind him his whole army. He has very properly spared those who are married; and, if this war is carried on in a similar manner next year, I shall be surer of my life in the midst of it than upon the parade grounds of Wolfenbüttel and Brunswick."

A cry of relief and delight went up from every town and village in America where adherents of the Revolution dwelt. Washington, indeed, was convinced that, although a part of the danger had been removed, the nation would have to fight for dear life before the winter was over; and he very soberly and briefly congratulated the President of Congress upon the important intelligence that General Carleton had been obliged to return to Canada empty-handed.[1] The popular sentiments and hopes were declared in much more exultant language by Robert Morris of Philadelphia, who had ordinarily as cool a head as any statesman of his time and party. "If you keep your ground," (so Morris wrote to General Gates,) "I think General Washington will keep his; and if both do this for the present Fall, and ensuing Winter, the good news I mean to tell you will be verified. It is that the French are undoubtedly disposed to assist us in this contest; and I have little doubt but

[1] Washington to the President of Congress; Peekskill, Nov. 11, 1776.

that they will take part in the war next summer." **The**
news of Carleton's retreat was received in England with
extreme disappointment and vexation.   Lord George
Germaine hated the Governor of Canada, who had declined to job for him, and whose contempt for his character most disagreeably flavoured the tone of the official
despatches which reached the Colonial Office from
Quebec.   It would have gone very hard with Carleton
if his Sovereign had thrown him over; but George the
Third, in words which became him, told Lord North
that in a certain breast there was a great prejudice, not
unaccompanied by rancour, against Sir Guy; but that
to recall him from his Government was a cruel suggestion, which the exigency did not authorise.[1]   The King
knew honest men when he found them, and cherished
them so long as they would consent to carry on his
policy.   Carleton's methods were not the Royal methods; but the master never forgot that his servant's
large-minded prudence had kept the province of Canada
inviolate and obedient, amid the crash and wreck of his
transatlantic dominions.   Burgoyne, on the other hand,
whom Lord George Germaine and his clique industriously put forward as a rival to Carleton, was not in high
favour at the Court of St. James's.[2]   The inevitable
sequel of a military disaster in America was the speedy
re-appearance in London of that very restless General,
who was so keen to give his own version, and to shift the
responsibility from his own shoulders.   Before the middle of December Burgoyne was already about town,
closeted with Secretaries of State, and insinuating in
club and drawing-room that a bold and skilful strategist,
with an eye for country, could easily cut the rebellion in
two by operating in the neighbourhood of Saratoga.

---

[1] George the Third to Lord North; Queen's House, December 13, 1776:
10 minutes past 9 A.M.

[2] "Lord George Germaine's people rail against Sir Guy most furiously,
and Lord North's friends seem most displeased that General Burgoyne's
reception at Court was not gracious.   There are certainly as great jealousies between the two ministers as between the two generals."   Fitzpatrick
to Ossory;   December 1776.

But he did not succeed, to any visible degree, in raising the spirits of fashionable and influential persons. "Candid people," (so Captain Fitzpatrick wrote to his brother Lord Ossory,) "will see the impracticability of the war more clearly than ever; for the Canada expedition has certainly proved ineffectual, although attended with all the success they could hope. Burgoyne is not very communicative; and it is easy to perceive that he and Carleton are not friends. I believe Ministry are not over and above satisfied with the conclusion of their successful campaign."

The belief that the campaign was already concluded, which was held both in London and in Philadelphia, accorded neither with the intentions of the British General, nor with the apprehensions of his adversary. Washington was seldom prone to entertain illusions; and he never had fewer of them than in the first week of November 1776. He made an official report to the effect that the situation was critical and alarming. The dissolution of his army, (so he foretold,) was fast approaching. Large numbers were on the eve of their departure, at a time when the enemy had a very numerous and formidable force, watching an opportunity to execute their plans for spreading ruin and devastation throughout the Confederacy.[1] Those were far-reaching words; but they fell short of the portentous reality. On the twenty-first of September the American returns showed sixteen thousand rank and file fit for duty; on the thirtieth of September there were fifteen thousand; and on the third of November under thirteen thousand five hundred. Only a few score soldiers had been killed or wounded; and a less creditable reason was required to account for the enormous waste of these six weeks, during which the men had never been under-fed, and so far from over-marched they had only travelled twenty miles since they first left their cantonments at Haerlem.

[1] Washington to the Assembly of Massachusetts; White Plains, Nov. 6, 1776.

The cause of the diminution of the American army was written in very legible characters over the face of the district in which it was stationed; for gentlemen, who went on a visit to their friends at White Plains, were encountered along every road by a stream of militiamen, setting steadily away from camp. Washington, when he took his rides abroad, was surprised and shocked at seeing officers and soldiers straggling all about the neighbourhood on one idle pretence and another; and most of them, so soon as they found themselves well beyond the American outposts, ceased to straggle, and plodded stubbornly homewards to their native villages in New Hampshire or Connecticut. This wholesale exodus soon attracted the attention of European military gossips, who had a great idea of Washington's genius, and a very superficial acquaintance with his difficulties. A London newspaper announced that General Washington had dismissed eleven thousand men to their respective farms, in order that agriculture might not suffer for want of labour. That sage commander, (so it was asserted,) had no fear that he could not hold his own against the invader; for he had retained with the colours two-and-twenty thousand troops, the flower of American chivalry. That estimate of Washington's numbers was ludicrously inaccurate: but it was literally true that the spontaneous chivalry of his troops would before very long be his only resource; for they were on the point of being released from all legal obligation to defend their country. Most of his battalions had been called out for six months; and the last of those months was November. Howe was poorly informed by his spies; but he knew the date at which the American militia had been embodied, the period for which they were bound to serve, and their very marked propensity to anticipate, rather than to postpone, the moment of liberty. It might be taken for granted that, with these facts before him, the British General would not prematurely retire into winter quarters. That was not all, nor the worst either. The regular Continental regiments, raised during the siege of Boston, had been enlisted for the year which expired on the thirty-first of December; and Washington thenceforward would have nothing on which to rely except the voluntary patriotic devotion of a handful of personal followers.[1]

While the Provincial troops dwindled hour by hour in quantity, their quality, in one serious respect, deteriorated rather than improved. Their equipment was deplorable; their preparatory training had stopped far below that line of perfection which befitted them to take the offensive against well-found regular soldiers; and men of experience and perception in both camps were well aware that an army, which is reduced to stand upon the defence, must sooner or later be discomfited. That view was clearly enforced in a letter addressed to the authorities of his State by a Maryland colonel, who, like a true-bred Southerner, attributed perils which arose from the cruelty of fate to the unwisdom of the Northern generals. "Instead of instructing their troops in military discipline, preparing and encouraging them to meet their enemies in the fields and woods, they train them to run away, and make them believe they never can be safe unless under cover of an intrenchment, which they would rather extend from the North to the South Pole than risk an engagement. Discipline is totally neglected; and yet, after all, it is the only bulwark in war. Had our troops been trained better, and worried less with the pickaxe and the spade, by this time our army would have been in a condition to have sought the enemy in turn. This cannot be the case under our present system."[2]

[1] Colonel Robert H. Harrison to the President of Congress; Washington's General Order; George Clinton to John McKesson, Esq. All these documents are dated on the same day of October 31, 1776.

"I do not understand," (General Clinton wrote,) "much of the refined art of war. This nevertheless is too obvious. The enemy are daily increasing their army by new recruits in those parts of the country which they have already acquired, whilst ours are daily decreasing by sickness, deaths, and desertion. Add to this, one month more disbands a considerable part of our army. How a new one will be recruited God only knows."

[2] Colonel Smallwood to the Maryland Council of Safety; October 1776.

The policy on which this gentleman animadverted was not a matter of system, but of imperative necessity. Northern, as well as Southern, generals understood the full advantages of drill and discipline. Lord Stirling was something too much of a martinet; Nathanael Greene had read his Manual of Exercises even more assiduously than his Plutarch; and Washington would gladly have given all he was worth in the world for a score of regiments which could march like the English Footguards. But time and place alike were wanting to convert his improvised levies into orderly and obedient veterans, wheeling like clock-work, and springing automatically to the word of command. The fields above Haerlem, and behind White Plains, did not afford as secure a parade-ground as Hyde Park or Hounslow Heath. If the Provincials had neglected to intrench their front while their companies were instructed in platoon-firing, and their battalions were being taught to counter-march, the first sham-fight in which they indulged themselves would have been quickly turned into a very real catastrophe by a forward movement of the British infantry. The American commander erelong gave striking evidence of the high value which he attached to the routine of military training. In 1778, during Howe's occupation of Philadelphia, — when the interposition of twenty miles of country, and the ascertained indolence of the British General, placed Washington in a position of comparative security, — the Continental soldiers had no sooner emerged from the worst hardships of that terrible winter than they were subjected to a strict course of exercises and manœuvres. It was in the stern and rude work-shop of Valley Forge that Washington fashioned his army into a weapon of rare temper and flexibility. But, during the operations on Manhattan Island and Westchester Peninsula, he was pressed by an enemy of overpowering strength, whose advanced parties were seldom many furlongs distant from his line of sentries; and his solitary resource was to stave off ruin from day to day by keeping his troops behind earthworks which, (although novices in war,) they were skilful to construct and competent to defend.

Howe, on his part, was firmly resolved to bring the Americans into the open, and try what they were worth, man to man. He went to work betimes. Before October ended he despatched General Knyphausen and two brigades of Hessians, with directions to cross King's Bridge, and establish themselves in the northern corner of Manhattan Island. In the night of the third of November the Provincial sentinels heard a rumbling of carriages within the British lines; and, on the morning of the fifth, Howe, who had already sent off his stores and train, broke up his encampment, and transferred the Royal army to Dobb's Ferry on the Hudson river. He there was in a position either to cover an attack upon Fort Washington; or to force his way up-country to Albany; or to pass to the opposite bank by aid of his brother's fleet, and march straight upon Philadelphia, where he might strike the rebellion in the heart. Washington, when the alarm reached him, called his generals into council, and arranged a provisional disposition of his army which was reasonably well calculated to meet each of those three contingencies. He threw one corps across the river to the westward, and stationed it at Hackensac in New Jersey under the command of Putnam. Heath and his division were sent north to Peekskill, with orders to fortify, and to hold, the pass where the stream of the Hudson penetrates the gorges of the Highlands in the neighbourhood of West Point. Charles Lee meanwhile remained near White Plains, with seven thousand men, under strict injunctions to keep himself in readiness for co-operating promptly in whatever direction Washington, when the future grew clearer to his mind, might subsequently determine.

The operations on Westchester Peninsula were signalised by no very dramatic or decisive military incidents; but events had there taken place, not greatly noticed at the time, which, in such a war as then was being waged, had more effect upon the ultimate result than half a dozen battles. A portion of both armies had seriously misbehaved themselves; and the gravest and most permanent consequences ensued from the very divergent spirit in which that misbehaviour was regarded by their respective generals. Westchester County everywhere presented an aspect of long-settled and well-ordered prosperity. The manor-houses, and the bettermost of the farmhouses, had nothing in and about them which was new, or cheap, or shabby. The carved wainscots; the old grates encased in tiles representing Scripture scenes, with fender and andirons of solid brass as brilliant as hands could make them; the heavy furniture of mahogany and stamped leather; the tall eight-day clocks of gilded ebony; the mirrors loaded with florid mouldings, which no one with a pure taste in art would have devised, but which, when they had hung on the wall for a century, no one who had the sense of association would ever part with; the perfection of needlework in the curtains, the screens, the cushions, and more especially in the bed-quilts; the glass cupboards with their display of antique plate, and high-coloured Lowestoft porcelain; the Delft-ware, the pewter, the copper vessels, the great wooden bowls for kitchen use, which the Indians fashioned from the knots of the maple tree; — everything was solid, everything was genuine, and, above all, everything was scrupulously and religiously clean. For the mansions of the country gentlemen, and the dwellings of their leading tenants, were maintained up to a standard of neatness surpassing the extreme point even of Anglo-Saxon respectability. There was a very large Dutch element in the population; and Dutch Christian names, and surnames, may still be read in large numbers at the foot of the Addresses and Resolutions which went across the Atlantic to assure King George of the affection with which he was regarded by his good people of Westchester. The fittings and utensils of these old-world habitations were daintily kept; but they were kept for use. There often was only too much mulled

wine in the silver tankards, and rack-punch in the china
bowls. At Christmas the stupendous brick ovens were
filled three times a day ; — first with generous loaves of
wheat and rye; then with chicken, and quail, and venison pasties; and lastly with long rows of fruit and mince-
pies. At the back of the furnace was a huge log, which
had been transported thither by the united efforts of
several serving men ; and the iron dogs were piled with
a blazing mass of hickory billets, in front of which turkeys, and geese, and large joints of meat, were turned
on the spits by one of the little negroes who peopled
the kitchen of every great homestead.[1]

Nowhere in Europe, nor in America, was there more
universal ease and plenty, or a larger infusion of that
natural and sincere conservatism which is based upon
content. Westchester County, and no wonder, was to
a marked degree a Loyalist district. The ablest of the
Tory controversialists, — who evoked in the greatest intensity the enthusiasm of his own party, and the anger
of the other, — had published a famous series of pamphlets under the title of a Westchester Farmer. That
was the appellation adopted by the Reverend Samuel Seabury, the Rector of St. Peter's Church in the town of
Westchester, who endured a very hot persecution at the
hands of his Whig adversaries with dignified fortitude.
His character and conduct won for him in many quarters
a tribute of sympathy and respect, which gradually deep-
ened into a sentiment little short of reverence. After
the Revolution he was chosen as the first Bishop of the
Protestant Episcopal Church in America; a function
which he long and worthily discharged.[2]

Seabury was a farmer only in the sense that he cultivated his glebe ; but he knew how farmers thought, and
he could write what they cared to read. Neither Cobbett

---

[1] The substance, and much of the language, in this paragraph are
taken from a chapter on the manners and customs of Westchester County,
by Mr. Thomas Scharf.

[2] Tyler's *Literary History;* Vol. I., chapter xv. *History of Westchester County ;* pages 600 and 601.

nor Cobden ever clothed an economical proposition in more pithy and homely words than Seabury's argument against the commercial policy of the Continental Congress in September 1774. Congress, by way of retaliation for the tea-duty, had recommended an agreement against exporting goods to Great Britain and Ireland. That agreement, (so the Westchester farmer truly asserted,) would ruin the market for American flax-seed, — a commodity for which the Ulster Irish had always been the best customers. That very year, according to his own account, he had threshed and cleaned up eleven bushels of the seed. " The common price now is at least ten shillings. My seed, then, will fetch me five pounds ten shillings. But I will throw in the ten shillings for expenses. There remain five pounds. In five pounds are four hundred three-pences. Four hundred three-pences, currency, will pay the duty upon two hundred pounds of tea, — even reckoning the exchange with London at two hundred per cent. I use in my family about six pounds of tea. Few farmers in my neighbourhood use so much ; but I hate to stint my wife and daughters, or my friendly neighbours when they come to see me. Besides, I like a dish of tea too, especially after a little more than ordinary fatigue in hot weather. Now two hundred pounds of tea, at six pounds a year, will just last thirty-three years and four months ; so that, in order to pay this monstrous duty on tea, which has raised all this confounded combustion in the country, I have only to sell the produce of a bushel of flax-seed once in thirty-three years." [1]

The political opinions, which Seabury humorously and fearlessly expressed in print, were held by a very large proportion of those agriculturists who tilled the soil of the peninsula on which, during the last fortnight of October and the first week of November, the Royal and the Republican armies were contending. Before the war broke out these Westchester copyholders enrolled themselves by their hundreds in Loyal Associations ;

[1] Tyler's *Literary History ;* Vol. I., chapter xv., section 3.

and they proclaimed their attachment to the Throne, and their detestation of revolutionary principles, in very spirited language, and at the inordinate length which was usual in all public documents issued on either side of the question in every colony.[1] When the poll for delegates to Congress was held at White Plains, a long procession marched from the Tory tavern to the Court-house, lodged a protest against the legality of the proceedings, and returned, "singing, as they went, the grand and animating Song of

God save great George our King !"

Armed parties scoured the country at night, throwing down Whig fences, and cropping the manes and tails of horses which grazed in Whig paddocks. And, — when the New York Committee of Safety had parked near King's Bridge all the artillery which could be collected in their city, — the custodians awoke one morning to find the guns spiked, and most of them with large stones rammed forcibly down their muzzles. Several hundred cannon had been thus treated ; and the number of persons concerned was notoriously very large. Many arbitrary arrests were made, and very harsh means were adopted in order to induce confession, or to extort testimony ; but the exploit was so much in unison with public opinion in Westchester County that the Revolutionary authorities were unable to bring the charge home to a single one of the perpetrators.

The welcome extended to the Royal army by the rural population of Westchester County did not outlast their first experience of the very peculiar conduct by which some of our soldiers, and notably our foreign

---

[1] The creed of Westchester Toryism is vigorously expounded in a couple of sentences extracted from one of these manifestoes. " Let us of Cortlandt's Manor clear ourselves of the general imputation. We never consented to Congresses or Committees ; we detest the destruction of private property ; we abhor the proceedings of riotous and disorderly people ; and, finally, we wish to live and die the same loyal subjects that we have ever been to his most Sacred Majesty George the Third."

auxiliaries, were accustomed to requite hospitality. "The enemy have treated all here without discrimination. The distinction of Whig and Tory has been lost in one general scene of ravage and desolation."[1] Those were Washington's words. They have obtained that corroboration, which a statement made by him never needs, from narratives written by prominent opponents of the American Revolution; for the story of the usage inflicted upon Loyalists in Westchester County by the Royal army is mainly derived from Loyalist sources. The work of devastation commenced with the smaller live-stock. Most Hessian regiments contained veterans of the Seven Years' War who long ago had learned how to find their way about the inside of a hen-roost; and the poultry yards were at once ransacked without any plea of military necessity, except the necessity which a grenadier felt to have a duck or a capon for his supper. The herds and flocks were next converted into beef and mutton, without a single halfpenny of payment to their owners; and the Germans especially luxuriated at free quarters in a country district which was noted for the curing of hams, and the manufacture of sausage-meat. Emboldened by impunity, the spoiler soon carried his operations into the inmost recesses of the home. The grand parlour of the Dutch household, — an apartment sacredly reserved for occasions of high ceremony, — was profaned and pillaged without any consideration for the political creed of the inmates. Those fine white tiles of the Van Cortlandt Manor-house, which are still prized as specimens of old colonial decoration, were torn from their sockets, and used as platters by the soldiery. Before three weeks had passed, the people of Westchester, though untouched in life and limb, were as utterly denuded and impoverished as if an incursion of Iroquois and Seneca warriors had swept the county. The Royal army was attended by a train of loose women, mostly brought from Europe, but in part

[1] Washington to Governor Livingston of New Jersey; White Plains, November 7, 1776.

recruited from the least reputable streets of certain American sea-ports. Their presence at Boston had, of recent years, contributed not a little to unite that sober and austere community in its aversion to a military occupation. When this flock of harpies descended upon the villages of a quiet country-side, — with their intimate knowledge of what was worth taking, and of the most likely places in which to find it, — the losses endured by a decent housewife were aggravated by a sense of altogether intolerable insult. These odious hussies have been described by indignant American Loyalists in the round and downright phrases which Smollett and Fielding so liberally employed, and which, when treating such a topic, might be permitted even to the delicacy of a modern author.[1]

Joseph Galloway, an eminent Tory lawyer and politician, was expelled by popular violence from his home in Pennsylvania, and forced to seek a refuge in England. He there faithfully and boldly served the Royal cause by his pen; and he was not sparing in his remonstrances against the excesses and errors by which that cause was disgraced and enfeebled on the further side of the Atlantic Ocean. He confessed with shame that, in the parts of America to which our armies had penetrated, friend and foe, ally and rebel, had met with the same fate;— "a series of continued plunder," (such was his actual language,) that could not fail to create dislike, even in the breast of fidelity, to a service which, under the pretence of giving the Loyalists protection, robbed them in many instances even of the necessaries of life.[2]

---

[1] Volume I. of the *History of New York during the Revolutionary War*, by Thomas Jones, Justice of the Supreme Court of the Province. The first paragraph of the seventh chapter contains some very outspoken remarks. The part played by "the wives and mistresses" of the soldiers in the spoliation of Westchester County is related by Mr. Henry Dawson, that fair-minded and painstaking writer of our own generation, whose sympathies are strongly with the rural Tories of 1776.

[2] Joseph Galloway's "Reply to the Observations of Lieutenant General Sir William Howe on a Pamphlet entitled *Letters to a Nobleman;* in which his Misrepresentations are detected, and those *Letters* are supported by a variety of new Matter and Argument."

The faults, at first, were not all on one side ; and it seemed probable that, unless speedy measures of repression were taken by the commanders of both armies, the unfortunate civil population would be ground to powder as between the upper and the nether mill-stone. A certain number of the Americans, both men and officers, had been guilty of grave irregularities. Their Adjutant General complained feelingly that those who enforced discipline upon new troops, among whom the principles of democracy so universally prevailed, must expect to be calumniated and detested.[1] But Congress had selected a general who was not afraid of his own men. Washington was sternly resolved that inhumanity and dishonesty should not go unchecked on the plea that they were sins to which the soldiers of democracy were especially prone. In September 1776, he cashiered an ensign "for the infamous crime of plundering the inhabitants of Haerlem;" on the last day of October he issued a fiery proclamation, threatening severe penalties against officers who had taken horses off the Westchester farms, and appropriated them to their own private use ;[2] and, a week later on, he seized his opportunity for making an example of some culprits high in rank, and thereby administered a death-blow to systematic brigandage in the armies which he personally commanded.

The watchers at Fishkill, on the Hudson river above West Point, reported that, from six in the evening of the fifth of November until very late, the glare of a great fire had been seen in the southeast quarter, and that fears were entertained for the safety of the town of Rye.[3] As a matter of fact, the light came from a nearer point on the horizon. No sooner was it rumoured in

---

[1] Colonel Reed to his wife; October 11, 1776.

[2] "Can it be possible that persons bearing Commissions, and fighting in such a cause, can degrade themselves into plunderers of horses? The General hopes every officer will set his face against it in future, and does insist that the Colonels, and commanding officers of Regiments, immediately inquire into the matter, and report to him who have been guilty of these practices."

[3] John McKesson to General George Clinton; Fishkill, November 5, 1776.

Washington's camp that Howe had evacuated his position at White Plains than a parcel of militiamen, — principally drawn, it is to be feared, from the State of
Massachusetts, — under the command of a certain
Major Austin, descended upon the village in order to
give their political opponents a lesson, and pay themselves very handsomely for the trouble of teaching it.
They began by plundering; and a curiously exact inven-
tory of their acquisitions is still in existence. One
woman lost two skips of bees, forty-three pounds of
butter, a lead glue-pot, and a tea canister, which in that
Loyalist region was probably well filled. Another was
robbed of ten yards of taffeta, a light blue silk quilt, a
satin cloak, a white satin hat, and all her father's title-
deeds and papers. When the larders and wardrobes
had been stripped bare, the inhabitants, young and old,
were turned out of doors, and fire was put to the eaves.
One lady, in her distress, hung on the Major's arm, and
appealed to his honour as a soldier; but he shook her
off, and cursed her for a Tory. The Court-house, the
Presbyterian Meeting House, and the greater part of
the private dwellings, were destroyed. Major Austin
afterwards admitted that he had received no orders to
burn houses from any superior authority; and General
Heath, at the time, noted in his journal that the outrage inspired great disgust in the whole of the American army.[1]

The very next morning Washington eagerly assured
that army that his sentiments on the matter were the
same as theirs. It was with the utmost astonishment
and abhorrence, (he announced,) that the General had

---

[1] Something has been made of a letter written on the seventh of
November by Colonel Huntingdon to Governor Trumbull of Connecticut,
in which the Colonel spoke with satisfaction of "the burning of a few
houses;" but the letter expressly relates to circumstances which accompanied the retirement of the Americans from White Plains on the thirty-
first of October. On that occasion General Heath, by orders from Washington, destroyed the barracks which the Continental troops had themselves
erected for their own accommodation; as well as some barns and a house,
containing forage and public stores, which there was no time to remove
before the enemy entered the place.

been informed how some base and cowardly wretches last night set fire to the Court-house, and other buildings, which the enemy had abandoned. Their comrades, however, might rely upon it that the criminals should be brought to justice, and meet with the punishment they deserved.[1] Those were no idle menaces. Amid all the reverses and anxieties which now came thick upon him, Washington never for a moment lost sight of Major Austin. A Court-martial sat; and, when a hitch in the proceedings occurred, another was convoked. Austin was dismissed from the service, and delivered over to the civil authorities of his native State, by whom he was committed to prison on a charge preferred under the ordinary law. Condign punishment was inflicted upon another officer, who appears to have been a favourite among the worst of the rank and file. When the marauders were dividing the booty, they were overheard to say that Captain Ford must have an equal share, although he had already secured for himself " quite a number of little notions." He was accordingly allotted a green silk gown, and other valuable articles; but he soon found his way into the common gaol of Dutchess County in the State of Pennsylvania, where history has left him to languish.[2]

Sir William Howe, speaking in Parliament after his return to England, claimed to have taken every means to prevent the devastation and destruction of the country, and reminded his hearers that he had been severely condemned by certain persons for the tenderness with which he had treated rebels.[3] Merciful and kindly by nature he undoubtedly was. The political party, to which he belonged, held that America could never be reclaimed by severity; and the men, and the women too, with whom he habitually lived when in London, did not conceal their disapprobation of harsh and violent measures.[4] But he was lazy and careless; and he

---

[1] General Order; Head-quarters, White Plains, November 6, 1776.

[2] *American Archives* for November 1776.

[3] Sir William Howe's speech of April 22, 1779.

[4] Lady Sarah Bunbury asked whether there ever was such a brute as General Burgoyne, who could find time to compose his bombast nonsense

shrank from the unpopularity which a strict disciplinarian must always be prepared to face. The allegation that Howe was very slow to reprove or punish even those excesses, which were committed within the range of his personal observation, rests upon the most unimpeachable authority. The Honourable Thomas Jones, one of the Royal Judges in the Supreme Court of New York Province, was an ardent and lifelong Loyalist. He did not love, and had no reason to love, the Revolutionary party in America; his relations with whom may properly, and literally, be described as internecine. When the war was over, his life was declared forfeit, and his estate was confiscated, by the New York Act of Attainder; and he, on the other hand, has left on record his opinion that the twenty-six hundred Provincial soldiers, who were taken prisoners at Fort Washington, should all have been put to the sword.[1] He consoled his exile, which only ended at his death, by compiling

about his rapid advance of eighteen miles in a fortnight, while he neglected to allay the anxieties of friends at home by sending to the War Office a return of the killed and wounded. "Only think too of the horrors of employing the Indians, and allowing them to fight their own way! I am not much pleased with my friend Sir William Howe neither; for, though a most humane man himself, he has not contrived to keep strict discipline in his army." That was what the mother of the Napiers wrote; and that was what her sons were brought up to think. They were not the worse soldiers on account of it.

Lady Sarah's detestation of cruelty was quite impartial. She had been taken in by the amazing legend which was circulated in London after the battle of Lexington. "I suppose," she wrote, "you are viollent for your American friends. I hope they are a good sort of people, but I don't love presbetiryans, and I love the English soldiers, so that I at present have a horror of those who use them ill beyond the laws of war, which *scalping* certainly is." Letter of July 6, 1775, in the *Correspondence of Lady Sarah Lennox*, published by the Countess of Ilchester and Lord Stavordale. The editors have placed before the reader full and well ordered materials for forming an opinion about a charming personality; and they then have courteously and wisely left him to form that opinion for himself.

[1] "The most rigid severity at the first would have been the greatest mercy and lenity in the end. How did Oliver Cromwell conquer Ireland? By the storm of Drogheda, and putting every soul to the sword. Had this precedent been followed at Fort Washington in November 1776, America would have been this day still a territory of Great Britain." Jones's *History of New York;* Volume II., chapter ii.

a vast history of his native province and city, from the commencement of the disturbances down to the Treaty of Peace in September 1783. Judge Jones was a landed proprietor in Long Island; and he has borne testimony to the surprise and disappointment of the residents in that well-affected district when it was brought home to their perceptions that plunder was rather encouraged than discouraged by some principal officers of the Royal army. He relates how a gentleman of fortune and character, as warm and faithful a subject of the Crown as ever had an existence, possessed a horse worth at least a hundred and fifty guineas, a descendant of the famous Wildair. An English cavalry colonel saw, and fancied, the animal; told the owner to dismount in the middle of the road, and hand the horse over to his own orderly; and bade him thank his stars that he was allowed to keep the saddle. All the fat cattle on the island, including those belonging to Judge Jones himself, were seized for the use of the troops. "The owners," (the Judge wrote,) "grumbled not. The chief of them were steady Loyalists, and were happy in having it in their power to assist the Royal army. Upon the close of the campaign applications were made for payment, agreeable to the General's promises. Notwithstanding which, in violation of his word, and of the public faith by him pledged, not a man ever received a farthing. Some of the applicants were damned for rebels, and ordered about their business. Others were threatened with the Provost Marshal for their impudence. Others were told their only remedy was against the original captors, and to them they might apply for redress." [1]

So it was on Long Island; so it had been during the still earlier occupation of Staten Island; and, by the time Howe entered New York city, violence and rapacity were ingrained habits among an ever-increasing proportion of his army. The troops broke open the City Hall, and carried away the books, and the mathe-

[1] Jones's *History of New York;* Volume I., chapter vi.

matical and philosophical apparatus, belonging to the College, which had been stored in that building for greater safety; and a collection of good pictures shared the same fate. They plundered likewise the Corporation library, and the subscription library of the town, containing between them no fewer than sixty thousand volumes, which were publicly hawked about for sale by private soldiers, and by their female companions. Judge Jones relates that he might have acquired a law library for next to nothing; and he saw in a drink-shop near forty books, — bound, lettered, and ornamented with a coat of arms, — which were on pawn for liquor, ticketed by the bar-keeper at the value of from one to three glasses of spirits apiece. "To do justice even to rebels," (so the Judge proceeded to say,) "let it here be mentioned that, though they were in full possession of New York for nearly seven months, and had in it at times above forty thousand men, neither of these libraries were ever meddled with; the telescopes, which General Washington took, excepted. Several rebel soldiers were indicted for some petty larcenies, tried, convicted, and punished by order of the Court, without any interference of the military. Their officers attended the trials, heard the evidence, and, upon their conviction, declared that ample justice was done them, and thanked the Judge for his candor and impartiality during the course of the trials." [1] That was the contrast, according to the close personal observation of an able magistrate and a staunch Tory, between the army of Washington and the army of Howe. If such things were done to the loyal population of the islands in New York Bay, and the streets of New York city, under the very eye of the British General, it was not difficult to foresee what would happen when, outside the purview of his own immediate supervision, his detached parties were ranging far and wide over the inland parishes of the rebellious colony of New Jersey.

[1] Jones's *History of New York;* Volume I., chapter vii.

APPENDICES

APPENDIX I

See page 126

WASHINGTON, during many years, suffered humbly and re-signedly at the hands of the Reverend William Gordon. He acceded to the historian's frequent demands for a sight of important documents, stipulating only that his own personal reputation should never be defended, or exalted, at the expense of his subordinates. He wrote, at some length, in reply to queries, which often were silly enough, at times when he himself was oppressed by a multitude of urgent and vexatious cares. In February 1778, amid the labours and distresses of Valley Forge, he was at the pains to assure Gordon that there was no truth in a report that he would shortly lay down his military command; although if ever the voice of his country, and not of a fraction, called him to resign, he would do it, (he said,) with as much pleasure as ever the weary traveller retired to rest. Three years later,—halfway between Benedict Arnold's treachery, and the expedition to Yorktown, — the generalissimo thought it necessary to apologise, on the score of pressing occupations, for not having written to the clergyman as often as the clergyman wrote to him. When the war was over, Gordon spent three weeks at Mount Vernon, rummaging among the heaps of boxes in which the whole Head-quarters correspondence of the Revolution was stored; and in 1788, when the History had not as yet been published in America, its author received a long and civil reply to a letter in which he enquired of Washington whether he had ever been invited by his admirers to make himself a king.

The American edition of Gordon's history appeared in 1789; and then Washington's eyes were opened, and his long-suffer-ance, but not his courtesy, came to an end. In October 1797, when he had laid down the Presidency of the United States, and had retired into private life, Gordon appears to have written him a letter reminding him that, during the eight years of his office, he had been a most neglectful correspondent, and urging him to atone for his remissness by transmitting a minute account of American politics, which then were in an exceedingly, (though not unusually,) inflamed condition. On this occasion Washington spoke out. The opening paragraph of his answer ran as follows : —

" Reverend Sir, your favor of the 20th of February has been received ; and I am indebted to you for many other unacknowledged letters. The truth is, I soon found, after entering upon the duties of my late public station, that private correspondence did not accord with official duties ; and, being determined to perform the latter to the best of my abilities, I early relinquished the former, when business was not the subject of them."

" For politics," (thus the letter ended,) " I shall refer you to the Gazettes of the country, with which I presume you are acquainted ; and with respect to other matters I have nothing which would be entertaining, or worth narrating."

Those are the last lines of the correspondence which remain on record ; and there is every reason to suppose that, on the part of Washington, the rest was silence.

APPENDIX II

See page 218

Extracts from Amos Farnsworth's diary for 1775–6[1]

Sunday May ye 14. Felt calm and serious. And I was filled with Anxious Desires after Holiness. And I Resolved Afresh to live and Devote myself more Strictly to Gods service than ever Yet I have Done. God Enabel me to keep this Resolution !

Sunday May 21. Attended Prayer on the Common in the morning. After that retired for Secret Prayer. About ten

[1] The spelling has been corrected, in a few instances, for the sake of intelligibility.

went to the Chapel, and herd the Reverend Doctor Langdon from the Hebrews 2, 10. He encorridged us to Enlist under the Great General of our Salvation.

Saturday May ye 27. About ten At night marched to Winnisimit ferry, whare thare was A Schooner and Sloop Afiring with grate fury on us thare. But thanks be unto God, that gave us the Victory at this time, for throu his Providence the Schooner ran Aground, and we sot fire to hur and consumed hur thare, and the Sloop receved much dammage. Thanks be unto God that so little hurt was Done us when the Balls Sang like Bees Round our heds !

Thursday June ye 1. Thare was Sheep, and Catel, and horses, to ye Amount of fore or five hundred sheep, twenty or thirty Cattel, and a number of horses brought along, that our Peopel took from the Regulors of Moddles island. Blessed be God in that he has Delivered into our hands So much of thare goods and Substance, And in saving of us in the late Battle ! Surely God fote the Battle, And not we !

Saturday June ye 3rd. Paraded with the battalion, and saw two men whipt for Stealing, and Another drommed out of ye Camps. O what a pernitious thing it is for A man to steal and cheat his feller nabors, and how Provocking it is to God !

Wednesday August 30th. The Enemy has Bin a Cannonading of us : But do little hurt. I found a young Gentleman that I Could Freely convers with on Speritual things. I find God has a Remnant in this Depraved, and Degenerated, and gloomy time.

Monday : Sept. 25th. One man was whipt and Drummed out for Stealing : he was a bold and unashamed wretch. O that men was wise that thay would consider on thare latter End !

Tuesday Oct. 17th. Our people went this evening with two floating Batteryes Down Cambridge River to fire on Boston : fired Sumtime, when one of thare Cannon split : wounded Eight Men, Whare of One Died. O the Sad Effect of war ! When will the time Com when we need larn war No more?

Thursday Oct. 19th. A Great talk of more troops being Sent to Boston, But our Men aint Scared at trifels. I would that our People had as good courage in the Speritual warfare as they have in the Temporal one.

Saturday Dec. 23rd. And now O Lord we are in troble. Boston is a seat whare our Unnatural Enemyes are in Possession. The people of Boston that are our friends have bin forced to leave the town, or be shut up thare amongst our foes. We have Sinned as a Continent ; we have sinned as a Province : we have Sinned as connected with a town, and as a Famerly, and Privates. But, O God, do not cast off this thy Land that thou hast Garded so long !

Monday 25 Dec. I fell dull in Duty, and yet I dont see my sin so as to follar it as I ought. I am a great sinner, yet I dont see my sin aright.

Lords-day Feby 25th. Went to Meeting, and heard Rev. Mr. Emerson of Concord. I pray God grant that by the Preaching of this worthy Man I may be stirred up to my duty, and to a holy walk with God.

March 20, 1778. I being prest with a sense of my duty in coming to the Lord's table, I went to our Pastor to offer myself to the Communion. I had thoughts of turning back ; but Considering how unsoldierlike it was to turn the back I went forward, and was in some Mesure enabled to lay open my Hart and desire to him, and he delt faithfully and kindly with me.

Those, to whom Ralph Waldo Emerson has been a guide in the conduct of life, may note with interest that the gift of imparting a healthy and cheerful view on Ethical questions was ancestral in his family.

LORD MACAULAY'S WORKS AND LIFE

THE COMPLETE WORKS OF LORD MACAULAY.
" Albany " Edition. 12 vols., with 12 portraits. Large cr. 8vo.

CRITICAL AND HISTORICAL ESSAYS, WITH LAYS OF ANCIENT ROME. Complete in one volume.
Popular Edition. Cr. 8vo.
" Silver Library " Edition. With Portrait and Illustrations to the "Lays" by J. R. WEGUELIN. Cr. 8vo.

HISTORY OF ENGLAND FROM THE ACCESSION OF JAMES THE SECOND.
Popular Edition. 2 vols., cr. 8vo.
Cabinet Edition. 8 vols., post 8vo.

LAYS OF ANCIENT ROME.
Popular Edition. Fcp. 4to. Sewed,   ; cloth,
Illustrated by J. R. Weguelin. Cr. 8vo, cloth extra, gilt edges.

MISCELLANEOUS WRITINGS AND SPEECHES.
Popular Edition. Cr. 8vo.

LONGMANS, GREEN, & CO.,
New York, London, Bombay, Calcutta, and Madras.

SELECTIONS FROM THE WRITINGS OF LORD MACAULAY.
Edited, with Occasional Notes by the Right Hon. Sir G. O. TREVELYAN, Bart. 8vo.

THE LIFE AND LETTERS OF LORD MACAULAY.
By the Right Hon. Sir G. O. TREVELYAN, Bart.
Library Edition. 2 vols., 8vo.
Popular Edition. 1 vol., 12mo.